Pioneer
Preacher

OPAL LEIGH BERRYMAN

Paap.

Pioneer Preacher

THOMAS Y. CROWELL COMPANY

NEW YORK

To my sister
MARJORIE FRENCH BERRYMAN
who in countless ways known to us both,
has contributed so much toward making
this book possible.

Foreword

It has long been a source of regret to me that fiction and history alike have emphasized the crime and lawlessness of the West and focused public attention upon its notorious bad men, while ignoring the good men who worked relentlessly to combat these prevailing evils. The fact that the West is evolving into the great, creative, constructive land that they envisioned is—though abstract and impersonal—the greatest tribute to their labors and their vision.

These good men were relatively few for so great an area. They came to a strange land, sparsely populated by strange people. They labored against the handicaps imposed by great distances, inclement weather, poverty, and discouragement. Their only weapons were their indomitable courage and the attributes of faith, hope, and brotherly love; and pitted against them were the seemingly immovable obstacles of greed, suspicion, intolerance, and hate. They worked with no thought of recognition nor hope of reward other than the satisfaction of fulfilling the driving urge within themselves, of bringing Christ's teachings to the people of these vast, neglected, and forgotten places.

So with the idea of belated recognition of such men, who have contributed so much to the proper development of the West, I have written this book primarily as a portrait of my father, Reverend George Carroll Berryman. I would not have you believe this a day-by-day diary of our life in La Mesa. No two years on the Llano Estacado in the early days of this century could contain all the incidents for an interesting narrative or the portrayal of a character. So I have taken the liberty of drawing from the ten years of Father's missionary pastorates in west Texas and in eastern New Mexico and telescoping these incidents into the two years of our residence there. I have connected and related them as best I could to secure dramatic unity and to make the reading of them interesting while presenting a more complete picture of the man my father was.

Likewise, a few of the characters may be termed composites—men or women who have had their counterparts in each field Father served. Most of the characters are people whom we knew, but none of them appears under his own name. I am quite sure that the majority of them would not mind my using their real names, but in forty years they have become too widely dispersed to obtain their permission. All members of our own family bear their true names.

In October of 1905, when this narrative begins, I was exactly eight years of age, and my memory of that time is exceedingly clear. Perhaps I was more precocious than the average eight-year-old child. More likely my remembrance stems from the fact that I was an only child at the time and was drawn into close contact with my father because in our moving from one outlying pastorate to another I made few of the usual childhood acquaintances. Father never talked down to me. Conversations with him were constant stimuli to learning and understanding. Consequently I made every effort to rise to his expectations.

Perhaps the West has been extremely fortunate in that "God sifted a whole nation that he might send choice grain over into this wilderness." Looking backward, I know that many of the missionary pastors were exceptional men. Throughout the years of association with my father, my realization of the special qualities that combined to make him an exceptional man was not completely dimmed by proximity. Yet it has taken the years without him to crystallize that knowledge and to bring it into sharp relief. By this biographical narrative I hope to share the privilege of those years with him, and to say, with Matthew Arnold,

"Be his
My special thanks, whose even-balanced soul,
From first youth tested up to extreme old age,
Business could not make dull, nor Passion wild;
Who saw life steadily and saw it whole."

OPAL LEIGH BERRYMAN

Pioneer
Preacher

Chapter One

THE day was mild for a west Texas October and we jogged along pleasantly through the breaks, rough and gulch-slashed, sloping ever upward toward the cap rock and the staked plains on top of it. At intervals for miles we had seen this long rim like an extended butte on the horizon, pastel-tinted by distance. Gradually its features emerged, the great upsweep of earth, crevassed by cloudbursts, lumpy with boulders; the massive rock ledge topping, jagged by fissures where only the hardiest of catclaws, prickly pears, and scarlet-berried algeritas could cling. In its shadow springs seeped out from the high bluff and pools of water bristling with reeds and coarse grasses lay half-sheltered by its formidable brow. Even in midday the great cap rock of the Llano Estacado was a wild and rugged area, lonely and austere.

Father drove off to the side of the two rocky creases serving as a road, halted the team, and got out of the buggy. He tested the water, located its source, and pronounced this a fit place for us to eat our lunch. Mother and I sat in the buggy while he unhitched the horses, led them down to water, then fastened on their noses the *morales* containing a ration of oats. By that time I had wriggled out and was poking about the edge of the pool with a dead mesquite branch.

"Come back here, Opal," Mother called. "You might stir up a water moccasin."

Unheeding, I dabbled my stick in the water, keeping a weather eye out for Mother lest she come and yank me back, although of late she had depended more on the urgency and threatening nature of her voice, or upon Father if he were handy.

"Opal, you hear me!" she spoke sharply, then called to Father. "Mr. Berryman, will you get that child away from there before she gets her feet soaking wet? There are no stockings in the satchel and we can't go into the valises."

The valises, two large telescope bags crisscrossed with ropes that bound them to the back of the buggy, contained our wardrobes. Not even the night before at the wagon yard in Colorado City had Father risked untying them, though Mother had forgotten to put his night shirt in the satchel. I remembered how funny Father had looked in his long underwear with the bulges at the knees and the baggy flap across his behind as he crossed the room to blow out the light. I had never seen Father without benefit of pants except when clothed in the all-encompassing night shirt.

Just then I started, blinked my eyes. A monster, flat of head and beady eyed, was skimming through a wake of ripples straight for me. I loosed a piercing scream and tore for the buggy. The mud sucked at my feet and each breath was a quavering howl. Mother grabbed me to her, examined my arms, peeled down my stockings. "Oh, good gracious—where did it bite you? Hold still, I tell you. Mr. Berryman come here—" Her voice was shrill and shaking.

On his way around the pool, Father stooped and retrieved something. He came up holding a wet green terrapin by the crust, its four feet sliding frantically back and forth.

"Calm yourself," he said. "Here's Opal's dinosaur."

Mother stared. "But they never turn loose until it thunders."

Father chuckled. "It didn't bite her. They rarely attack even small and succulent specimens of the genus homo."

Mother sighed, then I felt her stiffening with anger. She gave me a shake. "What were you screaming about?"

"I was scared," I whimpered. "It was coming straight at me."

"It's God's punishment for not minding me." She gave my rump a vigorous slap. "Get in that buggy."

There was a quirk in Father's voice. "Does providence no longer discriminate between the deserving and the undeserving? You too were frightened."

Mother sniffed. "Would you be happier if I switched her?"

"Slightly, perhaps. I don't subscribe to the idea of divine vengeance for trivialities. Why not say that the deed carries its own punishment?"

Mother laughed. "I'm still a bit too shaky to split theological hairs with you. Suppose we have some lunch."

"Fine," Father agreed. He took the canteen from under the buggy seat and went back to the spring. Mother opened and unpacked a shoe box of food—fried chicken and cold biscuits, cheese, crackers, and fried apple pies.

On the winding ascent to the top of the cap rock, horned toads with high heads and wild eyes scampered out of the ruts before the buggy wheels. Prince and Count, the team of matched bays Father had accepted as a part payment on his Coke County, Texas, homestead, buckled down to the pull and their backs stretched out level before me as I sat just back of the dash board at Father's and Mother's feet.

The wheels creaked and the tugs squeaked against their fastenings on the doubletrees as we tipped sideways in the washed-out road or turned sharply around great boulders embedded in the ground. The final pull came up the loose dirt of an eroded crevice in the limestone ledge, with the towering, jagged sides almost close enough to touch. And then we were out of the shadowed gorge and on the table land. Before us was a world straight and level as far as the eye could penetrate its haze.

"Good heavens!" mother exclaimed. "An ocean of land."

Father breathed deeply. "Its magnitude is inspiring."

"Also I imagine its monotony might prove very depressing."

"For me," Father said, "it has a fascination comparable to that of the sea for the sailor."

Father halted the horses to let them rest and blow. Mother nodded assent to my request to get out. By the look that passed between them I knew that they agreed that nature must be accommodated. I sidled around back of the buggy then made a dash for the ledge we had just surmounted. Cautiously I approached its abrupt ending and on the last yard of earth I stopped. There below me was that magnificent expanse of wild and broken country— the rocks, the small bright pools, the sprangling mesquites and gnarled hackberries, the winding white tracks of the road we had traveled. If only we could stay here in this endless variety of sun and shadow, pools and ravines, rocks and trees and cacti, where little wild things found shelter under the great frowning brow of the cap rock.

"God," I breathed, "let Prince get a rock under his shoe, or let the buggy break down—or anything so we can stay here. I don't like those ugly, bare plains. This is mine, God. I found it. Fix it so we can stay here and I won't ever ask for anything else."

3

The hand that closed about my arm was firm but not harsh. Only the strong pressure of Father's fingers betrayed his fear that I might jump. In his smile was a touch of sympathy, of wistfulness.

"We've forty miles yet to cover," he said.

There was nothing to do but to turn and go with him. Only once, like Lot's recalcitrant wife, did I turn and look back and breathe a frantic prayer to God to do something.

Mother's face, white and strained, peered out of the buggy.

"Opal, what in the world possessed you?"

Father's reproof was gentle. "When the heart must part from its treasures, do not make it the harder."

Father clucked to the horses and we started off over the bald prairie. One half of the road had been a cow trail and the other half was a bare impression in the buffalo grass. Father let the horses walk the rises flanking ravines. Coming up the first of these we rounded the top quietly. Below us a herd of cattle threw up their heads. One rangy fellow with enormous, spreading horns whirled and faced us, his front feet braced wide apart. Father slipped the whip from its socket.

"Will he fight?" I asked.

"A man on horseback or in a vehicle is usually safe." Father leaned out to better view the animal. "This must be a part of the Hamilton Ranch. Those cattle belong to T. P. Hamilton."

"How can you tell?" I wanted to know.

"By the brand—that triangle with the tuft at the top on the hips of those cows. That's a tepee—Hamilton's brand."

Mother spoke up. "Do the Hamiltons live out here?"

"Only in summers, I understand. Mr. Hamilton bought a bank in Fort Worth, and they stay there for the school term."

"Ever since I can remember I've heard of Teepee Hamilton and his fabulous ranch. I'd like to see it."

"You're probably looking at part of it right now."

"Don't be facetious," Mother snapped. "You know what I mean."

"Don't expect the West of fiction," Father advised. "Silver-inlaid saddles, goat-skin chaps, whirling lassos—"

"Father, look!" More interesting to me than a herd of cattle was the bare area warted with gravelly knobs. Over one swooped a bird. When it settled I saw it was a little owl that stared at us

4

blankly. On the next knoll stood a small animal on its haunches, barking frantically.

Father explained that we were driving through a prairie-dog town wherein lived prairie dogs, owls, and oftentimes snakes, apparently all in the same holes.

"Do they have prairie dogs at the cap rock?" I asked.

"They are native in most of the West," Father informed me.

If only some miracle would transpire, some vision appear directing us to turn back and seek our new home in the shadow of the rock. For all of an hour my ears were keyed to catch any unusual sound indicative of the buggy's sudden collapse. I watched Prince's sturdy feet with intense concentration, momentarily expecting him to jerk with a sharp pain of a rock wedged under a loose shoe. But he trotted along, sometimes synchronizing his gait with Count, sometimes jogging in the off-beat, but he was always steady and sure.

As hope for divine intervention dwindled, inertia took its place. What chance did Opal Berryman, a scrawny, spindle-legged, tow-headed girl of eight years, have against Father, who knew all the high-sounding words with which to engage God's attention? Possibly my inattentiveness during family devotion and my avoidance of memorizing a daily Bible verse weighed against me when I sought God's aid in a pinch. Whatever the reason, my appeal was unheeded, for Father with the unfaltering help of horses and buggy was taking us on to our destination on the plains.

Mile after mile we rolled along, sometimes down a gentle slope then up again, but with nothing by way of landmark, nothing to distinguish where dun grass merged with a hazy sky. Napping under my sunbonnet, I heard Father singing low but clearly in his rich baritone:

"*What wondrous love is this, oh my soul, oh my soul,*
  What wondrous love is this, oh my soul!
 What wondrous love is this, that fills my heart with bliss?
  What wondrous love is this, oh my soul!"

The mellow minor tones filtered into my mind like the haze and the warmth of the sun. It was consolation and acceptance, a paean of satisfaction and solitude. I was content, but after its third rendition Mother must have felt differently about it.

5

"Why not favor us with something bright and cheerful, such as *Hark from the Tombs a Doleful Sound?*"

"What's wrong with *What Wondrous Love Is This?*"

"Anyone who couldn't fashion at least four lines of rhyme out of eight shouldn't attempt poetry. The repetition is monotonous."

"I doubt if the writer was striving for entertainment value. He gives you a thought to contemplate until the rhythm and the melody and the harmony of God's love permeate your soul."

"The average person," Mother said, "hasn't that much imagination. He doesn't wish to retire into a dark corner and brood on his religion. He wants something he can carry with him about his daily tasks, freely and easily and joyously."

Father sighed. "Sometimes I regret the rollicking religion of Biederwulf and Rodeheaver. It's like sewing lace on a Chesterfield."

"Unless you make religion attractive, people won't accept it," Mother argued. "That's why ministers find an increasing number of empty pews—they forget that for five years now, we've been living in a new century and refuse to meet the demands of the times."

Father shook his head slowly. "Frequently during a minister's initial years his youthful zeal and constant prayer bring results. Unconsciously he begins to depend on his routine and permits it to displace the constant renewal of faith and strength through prayer. When a man's faith grows old and threadbare—"

"Faith without works is dead. He probably gets lazy or too egotistical to change. You can't live in the past and expect results in the present. Some new man will appear with fire and enthusiasm and the people will follow him."

"I have no desire," Father said, "that men should follow me."

He pushed back his wide hat. The dark hair lay in damp scallops against his high, white forehead. Surely some day I would learn the truth—that I was an adopted child. I could not be the natural daughter of a man so handsome, whose hair was black and wavy, whose eyes were the soft brown-black of a set of new harness, whose teeth were as matched as the grains in the center of an ear of corn.

Even Mother was pretty, with her long, taffy-tan hair coiled atop her head and her eyes the deep blue of a morning-glory. She was as round and compact as a Shetland pony, wore number three

6

shoes and number five gloves. It simply wasn't reasonable that I, scrawny and tow-headed, with two big rabbit teeth in the front of my mouth, could be the natural daughter of such handsome people. Yet why had Father not adopted a son instead?

"Pete," Father said, "suppose you select the song to sing."

That masculine nickname was a special bond between us. It was Father's only admission that he had hoped for a son, and an irritation to Mother for not having borne him one.

We sang as Prince and Count jogged toward the lowering sun. No tree, no house, no hill or lake appeared to vary the unending vista of rolling prairie. Once we came to a windmill with a round dirt tank of water, around which young cottonwoods thrived on the seepage. The brown grass was beaten out by the hooves of many cattle. Father watered the horses and we cleaned up the remainder of the lunch.

"This is Joyner's Well," Father told us, "the only water for twenty miles in any direction."

"Does Mr. Joyner own it?" I asked.

"That controversial question cost several men their lives in the days of free range. Mr. Joyner happened to be one of them."

So then Father told me the well's history. Situated at the junction of what was now T. P. Hamilton's ranch and the Falloon ranch, it was the only stock watering place for miles around. It had been put down by a man named Joyner on what was free land. A homesteader named Crossett had claimed it as within the bounds of his homestead and had fenced it in. Joyner objected by tearing down the fence to give his stock access to it. The feud waxed hotter and culminated when Joyner and Crossett met at the well and shot it out. Joyner had been killed and Crossett had fled the country, thus ending the controversy and returning the well to the use of the cattlemen.

The sun finally bedded down into the haze of the horizon and a few scattered wisps of clouds blushed rosily. Venus winked through while the sky was still light and the long diagonal shadow of the horses and the buggy stretched out behind us and melted with the dusk. Somewhere in the gloom a coyote barked harshly and Mother reached for the laprobe at our feet where I had sat at intervals throughout the day. Father tucked it about us and looked at Mother anxiously.

7

"I hope this journey doesn't prove too strenuous," he said.

"I'm quite all right," Mother assured him, "only tired."

I too was tired. I slept and woke with an aching neck, especially where my ears budded from my head. My garters cut my legs and my shoes had shrunk. My clothes felt twisted and when little specks of light flickered dimly I was sure of its being an illusion of sunburned eyes. But soon they grew brighter and steadier as though staked out on the rim of the darkened prairie.

"Look, Father," I said, "there must be a house over there."

Father leaned forward. He looked at the stars, then at the lights. "So it is. Several houses. That's Chicago."

Visions of a fabulous city of which I had heard flitted through my mind. "Have we traveled that far?"

"Chicago, Texas," Father said. "Your new home."

Chapter Two

O UR new home was even less prepossessing by day than by night. The road ran through what might have been its middle, had not all the inhabitants aligned themselves on one side, leaving only a lone store on the other side about the distance of three city blocks from the other houses. On the visit Father had made to prepare the way for us, he had found this vacant store the only available house, and with the cooperation of his congregation, furnished it with a stove, a bed, a cot, and a table which he had made with the help of Deacon Webb (who had a general store and was also postmaster of Chicago).

Deacon Webb had sold him a yardage of red calico with which to curtain the two front windows and had loaned him a wagon sheet which, attached to a wire, formed a partition between the living-bed-room front of the store and the kitchen-dining-room rear. Some empty dry-goods boxes served as cupboards and closets and in no time at all we were cooking, eating, and sleeping quite comfortably.

There was nothing snobbish about the population of Chicago. Within a week we knew all of the town's forty-nine inhabitants, including Deacon and Sister Webb and their three sons, Lincoln, Garfield, and McKinley; Brother Craddock, the blacksmith; Sister Craddock; their almost-grown son, Tom, and daughter, Mattie, a year my senior; Judge Pothast and his self-effacing wife; Sheriff Lubeck; and Mrs. Frisbie, the milliner-dressmaker, and her musician daughter, Bonnie Belle. I had entered the school improvised for the ten village children in the back of the two-room courthouse and land office.

If at first I envied the Webb boys their pony and Mattie her pet coon, Rastus, compensations soon came in the form of a mongrel dog, mainly shepherd. A mutual adoption took place and Shep became my dog. Father brought home a crate with a pair of bantam chickens that had been a week uncalled for at the post office. Mother allowed the cocky little rooster and prissy little hen to strut about the house at night only after Father assured her that one night's banishment would consign them to the coyotes.

Each afternoon after school, Father and I went out with our tow-sacks to gather fuel in the draw west of town. Cow chips that had not benefited by a whole summer's baking were deceptively dry of surface and green inside. Those from which grass sprouted were passed up, but the big gray pancakes with concentric ridges were tested and if suitably crumbly went into our sacks. After an unpleasant episode due to hasty judgment, I saw Father looking at me with a kind of pensive pity in his dark eyes. Before I could take thought the dam against such indignities as gathering cow chips had broken.

"Of all the nasty, stinky jobs," I exploded.

Father nodded. "I also was thinking that for a young lady of eight, life ought to be more than just a sack of cow chips."

"Oh, I don't mind," I protested, fearful now that he might get the notion such a job was not ladylike enough for me and refuse to let me assist him. Any task shared with Father was a privilege.

"We both mind." Father pulled a handkerchief from his hip pocket and wiped his hands. "Where wood is so scarce, we are fortunate in having at hand the means of cooking and keeping warm. But we don't have to pretend we enjoy tidying up after a herd of cattle."

9

"Honestly, I don't mind," I said airily. "I'd rather pick up cow chips any day than—than—" On the spur of the moment I could not recall a less appealing pastime.

"I know," Father said. "Suppose you round up Shep while I finish filling the sacks."

I cupped my hands over my mouth and sent out a shrill whistle, the result of Tom Craddock's coaching. Shep appeared at the top of the draw, his tongue lolling from the futile chase of a jackrabbit.

"Shep would never leave me," I bragged.

"Quite right," Father agreed. "I hope we don't have trouble relocating him when we move."

My heart jumped, crowding my tongue. "Are we going to move?" Already Chicago friends were precious.

Father explained to me then. Most of his congregation lived at La Mesa, a more recent settlement some five miles west of Chicago. He had bought a lot and would build us a two-room house there in the spring. They were building a schoolhouse in La Mesa and Father had been approached about teaching it, since our present teacher would be going back to college next fall. The La Mesa people were aggressively trying to improve their town in order to poll enough votes to get the county seat moved from Chicago to La Mesa. Undoubtedly there would be a stiff fight when it came to vote.

"But why don't the La Mesa people move to Chicago?" I asked. "It was built first. Why did they start another town anyway?"

"If and when the railroad is built, La Mesa is on the right-of-way. That is the most important thing in this sparsely settled land. In addition, they've good water at a shallower depth."

Father's sack was filled and shaken down. When mine was as full as I could drag, we started home amid a fanfare of cavorting and barking by Shep, who was aware that journey's end meant supper.

Mother was at the stove, frying a young cottontail. She looked grim and tight-lipped. I attributed it to the heat of the stove and that she was behind schedule for supper. But Father watched her gravely.

"Are you not feeling well?" he inquired gently.

"I'm perfectly well," Mother snapped, "but I'm fed up with

this wide spot in the road. Not a piece of lawn or dimity in the store. Not even muslin. Not a doctor, not a nurse—not even a midwife within fifty miles. Yet we have a milliner-dressmaker, scatterbrained as a kildee, and a music teacher less musical than a jaybird, to whom no decent woman would send her child for instruction."

I knew Mother's reference was to Mrs. Frisbie and her daughter, Bonnie Belle. Mrs. Frisbie was frivolous and flirtatious, professing that she and Bonnie Belle were always taken for sisters. Bonnie Belle's musical repertoire was completely contemporary, consisting of *Pony Boy, Cheyenne, Take Me Out to the Ball Game*, and as a concession to the sacred, *Sweet Bye and Bye, with Variations*.

To offset Mother's exasperation, Father spoke lightly.

"I grant that Sister Frisbie is not a profound thinker, and that Bonnie Belle's musical education is sketchy—or is 'blotchy' the word? But wouldn't you say that they add color to our somewhat stolid community?"

"I would not," Mother stated. "From what Sister Craddock tells me, they are nothing but light women. On Saturday nights the cowboys gather there, and that piano is blasting out dance tunes until all hours."

"It's possible," Father suggested, "we can in time turn their energies to worthier purposes."

"Let well enough alone," Mother warned. "Sister Craddock is taking care of the situation."

Father looked at her steadily. "In what manner?" His tone was dead serious.

"She's enlisted the aid of the women. They are boycotting Mrs. Frisbie. No one will have her make a dress or trim a hat." Mother sighed. "It works a hardship, since Mrs. Frisbie has the only sewing machine in town."

"What do you hope to accomplish by such an inquisition?" Father asked.

"What do you suppose?" Mother said. "To rid the town of such women. They'll move on."

"I deplore the thinking of people whose only solution of a moral obligation is to shove it off on someone else."

Mother's blue eyes were near black in her flushed face.

"Perhaps you forget that mothers have a moral obligation to their children, to keep the environment clean, to rear them free from contamination—"

"Free also," Father stated emphatically, "from prejudice and intolerance."

To me at that moment the delicious smell of fried rabbit was more important than environmental purity or prejudicial attitudes.

There were many strange people in town on the days the freighters brought the mail from Big Spring. Cowboys who rolled cigarettes from small, thin papers and little sacks with tags dangling from shirt pockets. Ranchers and homesteaders who came with their families, bought cheese and crackers and tins of sardines from Deacon Webb, and ate them in the shade of the wagon, while they watched their horses stamping and switching their tails against flies on legs and flanks. On such days I dashed from school hoping to reach the post office ahead of the freighters in order to stand with Father, mingle among the people, and listen to the fascinating talk of weather, crops, cattle, and election, while we waited for the window to open and Link, Deacon Webb's son, to hand out the mail.

"We're due a norther any day now," one weatherbitten rancher said to Father as he rubbed the knees of his bowed legs. "My j'ints tell me it ain't long off."

"I understand they're often very severe," Father said.

"Wust cat-astrophy ever befell this yere country was back in '88. We was a ridin' a herd up to Dodge City, me and Teepee Hamilton and Pat Falloon—" He suddenly grabbed his hat brim with both hands, lifted it straight up. "Speakin' of the devil—Pat, you dad-blasted old horned toad, how are ye?" He grabbed the hand of the big, red-faced, red-haired man and pumped it vigorously.

The man turned to Father, his blue eyes beaming. "Faith, and if it isn't Father Berryman. 'Tis foine seein' ye settled in your new parish and already knowin' my old friend Ira Severn."

Father's face lighted at the warmth of greeting. He acknowledged the introduction. "I'm indeed glad to be here. Brother Falloon and Brother Severn, this is my daughter, Opal."

Brother Severn tipped his hat. Lacking polite words, he caught the end of his drooping mustache between his teeth. Brother Falloon bowed and took my hand as though I were a big girl.

"Proud to know ye. 'Tis a blessing to have the children in this new and growin' land. They're the ones who'll make it great in times to come."

Adroitly as though cutting cattle, Brother Falloon edged us over to the corner, away from the crowd about the pickle and cracker barrels. "What do the people here think about the election?" he asked.

"It will work a hardship on some," Father answered. "Brother Webb, who owns his house and his store. Also Brother Craddock, who owns his blacksmith shop. But they'll create no trouble if La Mesa wins the county seat. They will move their buildings."

" 'Tis the ranchers from up north who'll be honery," Brother Falloon said, "not fancyin' goin' five miles further to do their trading and county business. Judge Pothast tells me he's handlin' their case."

"So I hear," Father agreed. "Whatever the majority of the people will should have amicable settlement."

" 'Tis not the way of the West as yet," Brother Falloon said. "Being from beyond La Mesa, I can take no part if trouble comes. I must vote and go home. 'Tis my hope you can kape peace."

"I've come too recently to have a vote," Father told him, "but what influence I have will be used in behalf of law and order."

" 'Tis that we are needing," Brother Falloon stated.

When Brother Falloon went to the window, I spoke to Father. "You're not his father. Why don't you tell him so?"

Father smiled. "Brother Falloon is a Roman Catholic. It is his form of address for a minister of his faith and denotes respect. I deem it an honor to be so designated."

Father came from the window with a month's accumulation of *Baptist Standards*, forwarded to him, a sample copy of the *Appeal to Reason*, and a letter from Aunt Tennie, Mother's younger sister who was married to Father's younger brother.

So delighted was Mother over the sight of the letter that she almost grabbed it from Father and read it while we ate supper.

Mother looked up, eyes shining. "She wants us to come up before winter sets in. She says I can bring back her sewing machine and she has some outing flannel and batiste for me. We could take

13

three days in the middle of the week and you could be back for the Sunday services."

"It's twenty-five miles, mostly sand and shinnery."

"What is shinnery?" I asked.

"A scrub oak that grows about shoulder high and so thick you cannot walk through it. It bears acorns as large as hen's eggs." Father saw my eyes widen and nodded affirmation. "The cup that holds the acorn is frequently two or three inches across. Shinnery grows in deep, loose sand that a team can scarcely pull a loaded buggy through."

"Why did Aunt Tennie want to move there?" I asked.

"I doubt if she did," Father said, "but your Uncle Johnnie bought a ranch in that region in order to conduct some kind of noble experiment. He believes he can raise so many and such fine hogs on those acorns that it will open up a whole new industry."

Mother snorted. "Johnnie is an impractical dreamer, full of theories and ideas calculated to save him work and make him rich quick. Only Tennie's common sense and level-headedness—"

"Tennie is an admirable woman," Father said with spirit, "but Johnnie has a logical mind and a fertile brain. His ideas are not whimsies. He works under handicaps, always with limited means. But who can say but that someday he may make a noted development?"

"I hope for Tennie's sake he does. What about the trip? We could make it this coming week."

"With less than a month to go, do you think it wise?"

"I stood the trip out here," Mother reminded him. "I'm sure Sister Craddock would keep Opal. The metal couch Mattie sleeps on opens out into a full bed."

Mother couldn't wait until the next day to see Sister Craddock, but went over while Father and I washed the dishes. This finished, I brought my books from their pillow-ticking bag. Father set the glass lamp in the center of the table and drew up two rope-bottomed chairs. Then began our tussle with the dates and names in *A History of Texas* by Mrs. Percy V. Pennybacker.

Mother came in and said Sister Craddock would be delighted to have me for a guest.

"So that's settled," she announced triumphantly.

"It is," Father agreed, "if it meets with Opal's approval. How about it, Petey?"

In the exquisite excitement creeping through me at the prospect of my first overnight visit, I still heard Mother's quick-drawn breath.

I bobbed my head. "It's all right with me." I dared not be more hearty, lest Father interpret such enthusiasm as permanent preference for the Craddocks.

"Then we'd better work ahead to compensate for the two nights I'll be away."

Father took my spelling book and pronounced the words. I spelled them, sounding each syllable and connecting it with the next. Mother was at the other side of the table cutting up a perfectly good petticoat, when suddenly there was a knock at the front door. It was hard and sharp and insistent. Automatically the three of us looked at each other, then Father pushed back his chair and went to answer it, taking the lamp with him while Mother lighted a lantern for us.

Mother and I sat very quietly, listening. At first I could hear nothing but Shep's bark, trending into a growling undertone. Then Father closed the door and I heard him say, "If you two will please be seated, there are a few questions I must ask you."

That was a familiar statement, one Father always made to couples intent on matrimony. I got up and Mother shook her head at me, warning me not to go in. But I knew of a three-cornered hole in the wagon-sheet partition that would accommodate my eye if I tiptoed. Mother laid her finger against her lips.

"We ain't come for to be quizzed about what's purely our own business. All we want is that you wed us," the man said. "Here's the license."

"Thank you," Father said. But for Shep's growling, everything was quiet while Father examined it. "This seems to be quite in order, but my status as a minister of the gospel imposes certain obligations. By this instrument I see that you are Mr. William Mc-Gurk of Fort Stockton, Pecos County, Texas. The license was issued there. May I ask why you were not married in Pecos County?"

"I toted it around quite a spell before she'd make up her mind,"

15

Mr. McGurk answered reluctantly. From my peephole I could see the back of a brawny man of medium height, dark pants stuffed into high-heeled boots, a dark coat with the collar of a checkered shirt showing. His arms were folded and his hat hung down beneath one arm. From the back, his dark hair looked closely cropped and his neck clean-shaven.

"I see," Father said. "And you are Miss Carrie Weatherhogg?"

"Y-yes." I saw her then, sitting on the edge of my cot, a small, flat-chested girl with enormous eyes that traveled from Father to McGurk as though in deathly fear of each of them. An ostrich tip on a black pancake hat bobbed when she spoke.

"Is this your first marriage?" Father asked Mr. McGurk.

McGurk's head bobbed. "Yup."

"Have you ever been married before, Miss Weatherhogg?"

"Just what business of yours is it?" McGurk demanded.

"Just this," Father said calmly. "My church does not sanction remarriage of divorced people unless such divorce was granted on scriptural grounds—namely, adultery."

Outside, Shep gave a series of short yelps, as though he heard the word. Miss Weatherhogg gasped. Her hands clenched and unclenched on top of her sharp knees. McGurk took two steps and grabbed her by the arm. He turned on Father, and I could see that his clean-shaven, heavy-jawed face was an angry brick red.

"There ain't no man, parson nor otherwise, that can use such talk before a lady friend of mine. Come on, Carrie. We're gettin' out."

There was the slam of the front door and Father was standing alone, the marriage license still in his hand, his face lax from bewilderment. Outside I heard Shep give a quick yelp, then a low, growling bark dogs use against enemy dogs. Mother had gone to the end of the wagon-sheet partition.

"What in the world happened?" she demanded.

"I don't quite know," Father replied, "but I suspect—"

"It was that word you used."

Father's eyes flashed.

Mother sighed. "If nothing else, a very expensive word. It cost us at least five dollars."

"I doubt it." Father was scrutinizing the paper in his hand.

16

"I don't know why you doubt it," Mother said.

"We may never know, of course. But it's my opinion that Miss Weatherhogg has had a previous marriage—might even have been attempting to contract a second one without benefit of divorce."

He laid the marriage license inside the cigar box on the shelf where all important papers and receipts were kept. Then he opened his Bible. That was our signal to get seated and ready for Evening Devotion.

Immediately after breakfast, as was our custom, I crumbled up some biscuits in the bacon grease for Shep's breakfast. Outside I called and whistled, blew shrilly through my thumbs, but no dog bounded up to the back steps. The house being perched upon posts made the area beneath it visible. I peered from all sides but Shep was not lying there injured or ill. Father came out and allayed my fears. He thought that a visiting lady dog might be proving an irresistible magnet. In that case Shep would show up later.

At noon I inquired at Deacon Webb's store, Brother Craddock's blacksmith shop, and various homes. But no one had seen him. By mid-afternoon when Father and I went for our usual supply of cow chips, I trudged along despondently, remembering how only a few days before I had bragged about Shep's devotion. Finally I mentioned it to Father.

"A dog's loyalty is the last thing one should doubt," he told me. "There are several logical explanations. Someone could have come through town and taken him along tied to the wagon. Or he and his former owner may have been reunited. In that case his first allegiance was there."

"If only," I gulped, "he isn't dead."

Father reached down and possessed my skinny hand.

"Believe me," his voice was low and earnest, "death is never terrifying or tragic. Only life contains pain, disappointment, bitterness, frustration. The erroneous conception of death as tragic comes from the fact that through life, with life's misfortunes, it must be approached. Death is the peace that comes as release from unsurvivable injuries inflicted by life. Do not mourn that death may have released Shep from some condition that made life untenable."

17

Through lack of understanding, my loss was still uncompensated, but Father's mellow voice and encompassing hand were comforting.

Early Tuesday morning Father and Mother drove away. It seemed to me Father almost stopped the horses as he looked back at me standing alone in the gray November dawn, in the bare back yard between the store and the privy. But the buggy bumped on across the brown-lumped prairie to the road. Inside, the house was cold and draughty because Father had extinguished the fire. I fed the bantams and turned them out. Walking to school without even a shaggy brown dog frisking beside me, I wondered why I had ever felt exuberance over the prospect of staying two nights with the Craddocks.

Mattie Craddock was a little older than I, somewhat taller and plumper, and considerably superior in attitude. I admired her dark hair, curling prettily about her face, and her bright black eyes. Tom, her brother, was tall for seventeen, brown-haired and blue-eyed, and spent all his free time reading a "doctor book" and the patent medicine almanacs. Toward all women, old or young, he had a deferential air amounting to almost an old-world elegance, accented by a delicately crooked little finger when he held his coffee cup.

Mattie must have seen me eying his hand while we ate our supper, for she gave me a stern look and afterward said, "Don't you dare plague Tom about his finger."

"But why? If he wants to crook his finger—"

"He'd be mortified. When he was little he got burned and it drew the skin inside his hand. He's afraid it'll keep him from doing operations if he ever gets to be a doctor. Ma'd tan my hide if I plagued him about it. He's her pet."

I was less interested in Tom than in Mattie's tame coon that dunked all his food in the water pan under the stove before eating it. Sister Craddock was setting a batch of light bread when Tom came in with a full pail from the evening milking. He was singing,

"Your wevilly wheat ain't fit to eat
Nor neither is your barley,
But I will take some of your flour
To make a cake for Charley.

18

Charley, he's a nice young man,
Charley, he's a dandy,
Every time he goes to town
He buys his gal some candy."

He set down the milk pail. "You fixin' to bake light bread, Ma? Would you make some of them cinnamon rolls?"

"Supposin' I did," she replied, "would you quit singing that song or find some other tune to sing it to?"

"What's the matter with the one it's got?"

"It's *Yankee Doodle*, that's what's the matter with it. A Dixon wouldn't be caught dead in the road singing a Yankee tune."

"Forget that stuff, Ma. There's no such things as Southerners and Yankees anymore. In west Texas I reckon we're just long-horns."

Brother Craddock laid down the copy of the *Appeal to Reason* he was reading. He was a brown, narrow-shouldered man with flecks of gray in his mahogany hair and the look of the forge on his face.

"You do as your Ma says," he told Tom. "If that song ain't fitten to be sung, then cut out singin' it. Mind what she says."

"O.K." Tom agreed. "But accordin' to my thinkin', it's all plumb foolishness to keep an old grudge goin'. Best forget it."

"The Dixons never forget," Sister Craddock snapped. "The world would come to a pretty pass if the fine old Southern families let down the bars."

"O.K., O.K.," Tom said, "I ain't argyfyin'." Indicative of ending the matter he hoisted Mattie's coon to his shoulder.

"That reminds me," Brother Craddock said, "there's a new dog in town. Slick and white and speckled as a guinea egg. You better see that Rastus don't get loose." He pulled a slab of Peachy Plug from his pocket, sank his teeth in, and twisted out a half-moon.

Suddenly I remembered Shep's growling bark. "Maybe he's the dog that killed Shep—if Shep was killed."

" 'Tain't likely this dog's kilt nothin' yet. Young feller came in to have his hoss shod and this yere dog never got a foot away from the hoss all the time he was there."

"What's the man's name?" Mattie wanted to know.

"Didn't say and I didn't ast him. Called the dog a 'damnation' and said they stick to hosses like flies to a molasses barrel."

"Dalmatian," Tom corrected. "I saw them leavin' town."

"Mebbe they did leave, but Mattie better look after her coon. Takes just one strange dog to shake the life out'n him."

Mattie tossed her head. "Don't get in such a swivet, Pa. I'll take care of Rastus. Ma, did you get my dress goods today?"

Sister Craddock scraped dough from her hands. "Simeon Webb ain't had a piece of dress goods in his store since he came here. I guess Yankee women don't care how they look, or else his wife—"

"Now, Millie," Brother Craddock said, "you got clothes."

"Just what I had when I come here, no more. And any day we may get word that Ma's took worse, and I'll have to pick up and go back to South Carolina wearin' the same old duds I left in. Your folks wouldn't think nothing of that, but mine's different."

"O.K.," Brother Craddock said hastily. "Tom can take you to Big Spring and get you and Mattie fixed up."

"Sure," Tom agreed, "there's a book I want—*Gray's Anatomy*."

Sister Craddock addressed me. "Your mother spoke about gettin' her sister's sewing machine. Perhaps she'd let me do the stitchin' on it. Mostly our dresses are handwork, but the long seams—"

Mattie interrupted. "Mrs. Frisbee would make the dresses."

Sister Craddock's lips set. "Mrs. Frisbee and her daughter left town today. And high time too. Unless I miss my guess, that girl's already in trouble. You, Mattie, pull out the cot and make it up for you and Opal. If you don't get to bed you'll be all tuckered out tomorrow."

After we were in bed my curiosity found voice.

"What kind of trouble is Bonnie Belle in?"

Mattie snickered. "Ma thinks she's in the family way."

Having heard this term whispered only in connection with married women, I felt Sister Craddock's judgment defective.

"But Bonnie Belle isn't married."

"Silly," Mattie hissed.

Her remark kept me pondering long after Mattie was gurgling into the quilts.

Each day after school I stopped by home to gather in the bantams for the night. On that second day the ominous chill of the dormant

20

house closed about my heart. Suppose Father and Mother should never return—supposing the horses ran away—Father and Mother, injured and lying somewhere in that impenetrable shinnery, might never be found. They would simply disappear like Shep. I couldn't live—I wouldn't even want to live if I never saw Father again. Panic gripped me. I slammed the door and ran all the way to Craddock's.

I never stopped until I was inside the kitchen, standing with eyes stretched to keep them from filling with tears. Sister Craddock took one look, drew me into the light.

"What's the matter, Opal? Looks like you're coming down with something. Probably bilious. Mattie, bring the sulphur and molasses."

"No," I protested, "it'll make me sick at my stomach."

"With your Ma gone, I can't take chances."

"Honest, I'm not sick," I quavered, but was near to it from looking at the nasty mustard-colored concoction in the fruit jar.

Brother Craddock spoke from the doorway. "I don't hold with that stuff, myself. There ain't nothin' wrong with her that a pepper-mint stick won't cure." He reached into his shirt pocket and pulled out two red-and-white striped sticks. "One for each of my favorite girls."

With that diplomatic and understanding act, Brother Craddock entrenched himself immoderately in my esteem. He assumed the status of a king who could do no wrong.

Returning from school on Thursday afternoon, I saw Father and Mother drive in. The joyous reunion that ensued made it seem as though we had been apart for a month. Mother hugged and kissed me. Father sat me on his shoulder for the trip to the house. Father built a fire in the stove, heated water, and dressed the prairie chicken he had shot. Mother fried it for supper, while Father and I got our tow-sacks and started on our routine fuel-gathering trip.

"By the way," Mother called gaily, "help Chicago manifest civic pride by depositing those empty cans on the dump in the ravine as you go by." Father dutifully dropped the cans into his tow-sack.

Like a peddler with pack on back, Father marched to the ravine, with me close beside him carrying my folded sack. At the top of the draw we both stopped. Father let his load slide to the ground. There before us on top of the rusting pile of cans lay a shaggy brown body. One side of the head was a mass of matted hair and dried blood. A swarm of green flies rose and buzzed and settled once more.

"It's Shep," I whispered. "Somebody—killed him."

Father nodded slowly. "Deliberately, it would seem." He went down a few steps, knelt, and examined the little dead dog. He lifted the stiff body, laid it over on the brown grass. Then he came back to me.

"I'm sorry, Petey. We'll go back and get the spade."

With my hand close in Father's, we trudged back to the house. We were almost there when my throat loosened enough for speech.

"Who do you suppose could have done it?"

"I don't know—yet." The words were pressed and tight.

Mother returned with us and stood on the bank with me while Father laid Shep's body in the newly-dug hole and covered it with clean prairie sod.

Chapter Three

Father and Mother had brought Aunt Tennie's sewing machine, wrapped in a comforter and bound to the back of the buggy. Friday and Saturday Mother was in an orgy of cutting, basting, and sewing. Much of the outing flannel she tore in squares and hemmed.

"Making dish towels?" I asked her.

She shrugged slightly. "Judge for yourself."

I looked at Father for confirmation and was surprised to see what appeared to be extreme disapproval on his face.

"Run outside now and play," Mother said impatiently. "Go over and see some of the other children for a while."

Being temporarily satiated with Mattie Craddock, I sought out the two younger Webb boys, Gar and Mac, knowing that their chronic awe of girls would bring out the reliable pony for rides.

On Saturday evening we Berrymans were enjoying our supper

—navy beans boiled with salt pork, hot biscuits, and tomato preserves (a gift from Aunt Tennie)—when there was a knock at the
door. Not harsh and insistent this time, but a timid series of light
knocks. Father picked up the lamp. Before Mother could remonstrate I slipped out behind him. Through the opened door I saw
two ranch hands. The one in front was young, wide-eyed, and a
little sheepish.

"Good evening," Father greeted them. "Won't you come in?"
One retreated into the shadows. The other cocked his head,
pushed back his white ten-gallon hat, and hooked his thumbs over
his belt. His mouth twisted into something that was not a smile.

"Them was our original intentions, but now I ain't sure."

"Just what may I do for you?" Father asked. "My name is
Berryman. I am the Baptist minister. May I ask your names?"

"You may. But I ain't a tellin' them."

"I'm sorry," Father said. "I intended no offense."

The young man shifted to his other foot and a spur clinked. He
hitched up his pants, that looked too snug to fall down.

"Listen, Reverend, do you actually live here?"

Father inclined his head. "I do—at least temporarily."

"Then take a tip from me. Get them red curtains out of your
front windows, or come Saturday nights, you're apt to have a lot
of callers. And some of them might not be so peaceable-inclined as
I am."

Father set the lamp on the table and stepped out of the door. The
windows must have gleamed scarlet, for Father stroked his chin
and smiled apologetically at the young man.

"I think I grasp your meaning. I'll replace them with ones more
appropriate for a parsonage. Thank you for the good advice."

"S'all right, Reverend." The young man moved off. "Adios."

"By the way, gentlemen," Father said, "I should be pleased to
have you attend church any Sunday. I wouldn't be able to recognize and greet you, since our meeting has been in the dark, but
I want you to know that you have a cordial invitation to our services."

"Thank you, Reverend," the fellow replied. "I've a right smart
idea I may take you up on that sometime."

I scooted for the back room. When Father came in he looked
from Mother to me. His eyes twinkled with amusement.

"Who was it?" Mother asked.

"I've not the slightest idea," Father replied.

"What did he want?" Mother prodded.

"He didn't say," Father countered.

Mother looked at him coldly, her lips set in a straight line.

"I do declare if sometimes you can't be the contrariest person I ever knew. Get ready for bed, Opal."

As I stood in the granite-ware wash pan while Mother washed my feet, Father remarked quite off-handedly, "The freighters brought Brother Webb some new yard goods today. I think we could now get curtains that would lend more decorum to our front windows."

Mother spoke complacently. "These are all right. I've been out and looked and you can't see a thing through them."

"That isn't the point. This house sits suspiciously alone. Red lights in the windows are misleading, to say the least. It is better that we avoid even the appearance of evil."

Mother straightened so quickly I almost toppled out of the wash pan. "So that was what those fellows were after. They thought this was a—a fancy house. I hope you told them plenty."

"What's a fancy house?" I asked.

"Shhh—" Mother hissed. "Don't even mention it."

"But you mentioned it and I want to know," I insisted.

"If you must know, it's a place where wicked people gather— like a saloon. Now be quiet." Then to Father, "What did you tell those horrible men?"

"I invited them to come to church."

Mother was aghast. "You—asked them to church? But why?"

"I thought they needed it even more than the average."

"And do you think that any respectable woman would sit in the same pew with such men?"

"I think so. No respectable woman believes that such a man ever attends church. Her respectability will keep her quite safe."

Mother's outraged dignity kept her shoulders rigidly upright all during Evening Devotion.

The Tuesday following the first Monday in November was a hazy, oppressive day, chill of a morning but warming as the sun climbed. Wagons, buggies, hacks, and horseback riders filtered in from both the east and the west on the road that ran through town. By noon all the hitching racks in front of Deacon Webb's store and the courthouse and land office were filled. Horses were tethered and staked out around homes and behind the store buildings and blacksmith shop.

Although only the men could vote, most families came to do trading or just for the outing. Mother and Sister Webb, Sister Craddock, and Mrs. Judge Pothast opened their homes to them for the day.

Brother Falloon and his wife, his daughter, Kate, and his son, Sam, drove up in front of our house. The women got out of the hack, drawn by spanking bays. Father met them and took the ladies in to Mother. Sister Falloon was genuinely happy to know Mother. She was small and compact, and her brown hair and eyes were duplicated in her tall son, Sam.

"It is so good to have a Baptist minister in our midst," she said. "It is the faith of my childhood. I still cling to it."

"It is our good fortune," Mother replied, "to find such wonderful people waiting to welcome us."

Buxom Kate, who sported her father's flaming hair, wore the loveliest clothes I had ever seen. A turquoise blue coat that matched her eyes had lustrous brown fur around the neck and the cuffs of the puff-shouldered sleeves. She carried a little brown barrel of a muff.

One moment of indecision tore me as Father got into the back of the Falloon hack. Then before Mother could protest, I was beside him.

We joined the crowds about the polling place. Brother Falloon and Sam left us, and when they came back, short, bow-legged Brother Severn was with them. Brother Falloon's attitude was one of long-standing affection.

"Father," he said. "Ira has need of your counsel. 'Tis a great problem he has. You can help him where we have failed."

At times such as this Father was very humble. "I can only try. But I shall be most happy to discuss it with him."

Brother Severn glanced at me, skipping no detail of my clean gingham dress and smooth braids.

"I got a gal," he blurted out, "that needs to be brung up as befits a lady."

25

"Indeed?" Father said. "How old is your daughter?"

"Nigh onto fifteen. She needs to wear women's clothes and learn women's ways. I got to do something pronto."

Father nodded. "She has no mother, I judge."

Brother Severn's pale eyes filled with tears. "Not since right after she was borned." He brushed his sleeve across his nose.

"The fact that she is now fifteen is a great tribute to your care. Mrs. Berryman and I know a number of good schools for girls."

Brother Severn shook his head. "Reckon no school would take her 'till she's more ladylike. Her ma would have brung her up right, had she o' lived. But now I got to do something," he finished vaguely.

I could see that Father lacked any specific suggestion. He resorted to the offer he made on many and diverse occasions.

"If Mrs. Berryman and I can be of any assistance, please feel free to call upon us."

"Thank you, Reverend." Brother Severn seemed somewhat relieved over this willingness to share his burden. "I'll figure out somethin'."

Brother Falloon gathered together his family and left for home. Father and I visited with other people who were in town for the day. Brother Slade from La Mesa (with whose daughters, Ora and Dora, I had had casual contact at church) had counted noses and felt sure La Mesa would win. Judge Pothast strutted about with a law tome under his arm, acknowledging the deferential hat-tippings of timid cowboys, responding to the respectful, "Howdy, Judge" of ranchers and homesteaders.

The atmosphere was still peaceful when Father and I returned home at evening. Only then did I view the havoc wrought by our guests and their progeny. The two bantams had fled to the open prairie for sanctuary from their rambunctious tormentors. Mother's protests that they would return when the company departed left me far from reassured. My small china-headed doll had been decapitated, my hoarded Easter-eggs were cracked, and much of my tea set broken.

After the polls closed and the votes were counted, the men came for their families. They brought the news that the county seat had been moved to La Mesa. Father made no comment, but helped Mother strip the bed and place the comforts about the stove to dry. One careless mother had let her husky brat wet the bed through to the shuck tick.

Deacon Webb called Father outside. In a minute Father came in and took his overcoat from the row of nails on the wall.

"Deacon Webb wants me down at the store. There may be trouble about moving the county records."

"Why should they move them tonight?" Mother asked.

"Because they might not be there tomorrow."

Mother cleared away the supper dishes. She washed them and I wiped them and set them in the goods-box cupboard.

"Do you suppose there'll be trouble?" I asked.

"I don't know." Mother's voice was tense. "Help me to get these comforts back on the bed." When the bed was remade, she motioned to me to get my coat. She threw her own over her shoulders, turned the light low, and held open the door.

From her silence I knew that this was to be a stealthy mission. We skirted the crowds, crossed the road, and stood in the shadow of the land office. There were knots of men on the porch of Deacon Webb's store and in front of the blacksmith shop. The big kerosene lamp swinging from the store ceiling shone through the windows and door and showed the men moving restlessly. Sometimes a voice rose loudly and profanely. Then the groups merged in front of the land office and courthouse. Mother and I slipped over to a parked wagon. By hugging its shadow we could see the front of the courthouse.

Sheriff Lubeck stood beside a stack of books. Men came and added to it from the files inside the building. Finally a desk was shoved out, then a tall cabinet. During all this time we saw no sign of Father.

Suddenly there were bright flashes and a popping like firecrackers. Mother and I huddled together. The porch was packed with men, the noise of voices punctuated with grunts and yelps. Through the pandemonium I heard Father's voice.

"Friends! Friends and fellow citizens!" he called. "Listen to me for a moment." Some of the men stepped back and a part of the noise died down. I looked, and there was Father standing in the middle of them, with Deacon Webb behind him.

"This is a democracy. You have just exercised one of its sacred privileges—that of the secret ballot. By decision of the majority, the county seat has been moved to La Mesa. Some of you are hurt by this move, but you are all pledged as American citizens to abide by the wishes of the majority. Only you can decide whether or not you behave as good sportsmen and gentlemen by offering your assistance to those delegated to make the transfer of the records."

An ominous, grumbling noise went through the crowd. Then we heard a high-pitched masculine voice: "The parson's meddlin' in something that ain't none of his put. I reckon it's high time he vamoosed."

At that moment a chap in a broad hat made a flying leap up onto the porch, collared the speaker, and gave him a heave. He sprawled off the porch.

"Listen, you hombres," the cowhand said, "the Reverend's right. You boys git your cayuses and line up out there. We're a-givin' the arm of the law a guard of honor clean into the new county seat."

I looked long and hard at the tall young wrangler with the voice that sounded familiar. It was the same young man who had knocked at our door in the shank of an evening only a few days back.

Mother was shaking when we reached home. We chucked cow chips in the stove until the lids turned pink, but still she shook. Her face was pale and drawn as she hustled me into my nightgown and tucked me into my cot bed. I was half asleep when Father returned, but I heard them whispering back of the wagon-sheet partition. The last I remembered was hearing spilled water hiss on the hot stove as Father emptied the pails into the dishpan.

Once or twice during the night some commotion half-woke me. Drowsily I wondered if Father had been followed home by vindictive members of the dispersed mob, or if I only dreamed a vague and troubled dream. Once it seemed to me the mob was in our house and that Mother was frightened and crying and Sister Webb was comforting her. But when I opened my eyes, there was a sheet draped across two chairs about my bed. There was but one explanation for this. We had had another bed-wetting visitor and I wanted no acquaintance with any more strange brats. I turned my face to the wall and went back to sleep.

When finally I woke, the sun was shining. There were no chairs and sheet around my bed. The room was warm. Father came over. His hair was tousled into a mass of curls and his eyes looked weary and dark-rimmed. I was about to ask if he had had more trouble

28

with the mob during the night, when I remembered that he did not know Mother and I had spied on the fight.

Father's cuffs were turned back to his elbows and the dark hair on his arms was glossy when the sun struck it. His collar band too was open at the throat and his cheeks looked blue from a shave past due. But when Father smiled with his lips and his eyes, I forgot the worn and neglected look of him and saw only his beauty.

"I've something to show you this morning." He sat me up on his strong arm and took me over to the bed where Mother lay. Mother turned back the covers, and beside her was a small red face topped by a mass of shaggy black hair. Of all the homely babies I had ever seen, this one struck me as being the most repulsive.

"Where did it come from?" I blurted out.

Father cleared his throat. "It's your new little sister."

"But where did it come from?" I persisted.

"Indirectly, from God," Father said.

"See," Mother held up her finger with the baby's tiny hand clasped about it like the bantam hen Henny-Penny's claws over a chair round, "how tiny and sweet she is. A beautiful baby. Her hair and eyes are like Father's."

I swallowed hard. I could have stood anything better than having this interloper look like Father. Never in my life had I felt so lonely and ugly and unwanted. I wriggled out of Father's arms and wandered across the room looking for my clothes.

Father put my long, ribbed stockings on me, folding the fleece-lined underwear smoothly beneath them. He laced and tied my shoes, and buttoned my dress down the back where I could not reach.

"Now for some breakfast," he said. "You wash your face while I fry pancakes. You and I must be cook and housekeeper for awhile."

It would have been fine, breakfasting alone with Father; but in the middle of it a funny grunting wail rose from the other room and Father left me. The pancakes with their ribbon-cane syrup became tasteless as I thought of the days to come. Father and Mother would no longer care for a tow-headed, rabbit-toothed child. They had a new love—one who had Father's wonderful hair and eyes.

I set my plate on the floor for Cocky-Doodle, the rooster, and

Henny-Penny. Father came back and saw the two bantams, feet braced, feathers ruffled, tugging on a pancake more than large enough to fill both their craws.

"Funny, aren't they?" he said. "Belligerent and distrustful, each afraid the other will get the lion's share. Yet there is more than plenty for both of them."

"They're greedy-guts," I said disdainfully.

"Yet they're a little like you," he reminded me. "You're unhappy for fear your baby sister will rob you of the love we have always given you. But when a new baby is born, new love is also born. We do not take from you to give to her. There is more than plenty for both of you."

Everything was all bottled up inside me. The tone I tried to make casual, even flippant, came out high and squeaky.

"If God was going to give us something, I'd rather have had a calf or a pony—like the Webb children."

Father looked a little perplexed. "Your mother and I discussed whether or not to tell you—"

My mouth flew open. "You mean you knew about it beforehand?"

Father nodded. "Your mother felt it more esthetic to let it come as a pleasant surprise—like a visit from Santa Claus."

I was really angry now. "You and God don't need to think you can dump her on me and make me like it."

"Sometimes," Father said wearily, "God expects us to adjust ourselves to His will instead of acquiescing in ours."

Silently and sulkily I dried the dishes. Had I deliberately been kept in ignorance of an event of such lasting consequences because I no longer counted? Or was there some suspicious circumstance surrounding the advent of new babies? I mulled over the hints I had heard regarding the origin of infants. Something Father had said might shed some light.

"Father," I asked. "What does esthetic mean?"

"Gracious, delicate—"

"I don't think you and Mother were very esthetic."

"I agree," Father said dryly. "And while we're on the subject of esthetics, we'd better go after our cow chips early today. From all indications we're due to get disagreeable weather any day now."

The auspiciously bright sunshine that had begun the day dimmed to a dove gray by noon. Chill flurries of wind whipped my skirts during the search for well-cured cow chips. Father worked with haste and concentration. When we were returning with our filled tow-sacks, I looked up at the sky. Although it was early afternoon, the sky was low as a corrugated steel roof.

"Look, Father." I pointed to the heavy wall of dull slate gray that blotted out the sky from north to west. "Is it a cloud, or is it a sand storm?"

Father paused and scanned the sky. "It's much more malicious than either. It is a genuine west Texas norther."

We hurried then, so that Sister Webb who was staying with Mother could get home before the norther struck. Father emptied the water from the two galvanized pails into the dishpan and went to the well for more. I was watching from the small back window. Suddenly the dark closed down, thick and grim. The wind hit. Father staggered to the house with his load and I flung open the door to him. In the suction the wagon-sheet swept out and back again.

Father closed and bolted the door. The walls of the store building creaked and its floor quivered. Father looked up at the rafters. In the lantern light their shadows wavered against the roof.

"Will it blow off?" I asked, my voice shaking with the walls.

"I think not," Father replied staunchly.

"How long does a norther last?"

"Perhaps a night, or a day and a night, or maybe two days. But with water and fuel in, we can be quite comfortable."

He had no more than uttered these reassuring words when that grunting wail came from the front part of the house. Father went quickly around the wagon-sheet, and I was alone by the window that rattled in its casing from the wind's fury. To my feel the pane was icy; the sand and pebbles beat against it like driven rain. It might be cozy inside for Father and Mother and the new little sister, but for me it looked like a long, cold winter ahead.

After my school work was done, I cast about for excuses to stay up. I was afraid to go to bed lest the house be demolished, and ashamed to let Father know I was scared. I professed to need additional tutoring on conjugations and declensions.

"Better go to bed," Father admonished. "In case the wind should abate during the night, you can go to school tomorrow as usual."

But still I sat, pretending to study, listening to the rattling windows, feeling the wind on my feet in spite of the tow-sack crammed under the back door. And then came a systematic knocking that was not the erratic manifestation of the wind. Father braced himself against the door, turned the key, and opened it slowly. The force of the wind flung him back, and the door flew open. A man stumbled in, and with him a crouching dog—a white dog overlaid with dime-sized black spots. The man stood there panting and blinking his eyes, with the dog pressed tightly against his legs.

"Sorry," the man gasped, "to come in on you like this, Reverend." He rubbed one beet-red hand against the other. "But I had to see you."

"Come warm yourself." Father lifted the stove cap and stuffed in more cow chips. He moved the teakettle to the front of the stove. "I'll have some hot coffee for you shortly."

The man removed his jammed-down hat and I saw that he was young, with tousled, straw-tan hair. His lower face was gray with the dirt of the norther, caught in a stubble-growth of beard; but his eyes were blue and trouble-sunken. I could give him but scant attention, for I was staring at the dog rubbing his sand-stung eyes with a foreleg—this startling black-and-white dog that was like nothing I had ever seen before.

Father too looked at the dog. "Is he friendly?"

"He'll bother no one who doesn't bother him or me—or the horse."

Father placed a chair in front of the opened oven and invited the man to be seated. The dog moved over beside him and laid his muzzle on the man's leg.

Father poured the steaming coffee into a cup. "Have you had supper?" As he spoke he set out the bowl of stewed dried apples and the biscuits left from our own supper.

"Not yet. But you musn't go to all this trouble. The coffee is plenty for me. If I could have a little food for the dog."

Father took the moistened cloth from the bowl of butter. As he placed the plate, a knife and fork, and the food on the table, he talked of the norther and the damage it might do. We learned that the man came from a goodly distance and that his horse was tied to the hitching rack along the side of the house. He ate as though famished, but carefully divided his food with the dog.

"Reverend," he said, "I came to ask you if you would keep my dog for me. He's all I've got in the world."

"But why," Father asked, "must you part with him?"

"I've got a job to do." Sitting across the table from him, I could see his gaze travel to the opposite wall. "Wherever I go, the dog is a dead give-away."

Father's voice was gentle. "Perhaps you had best abandon a cause that requires such stealth and secrecy."

"No!" The word was sharp and bitter. "I've sworn to go through with it if it's the last thing I ever do. Will you keep him? He's a fine dog—" He looked down, put his hand on the dog's neck, and ran a finger under his collar.

"May I ask, why did you come to me?" Father asked.

"I want him to have a good home. So many people think that dogs are just dogs. But he isn't. He's—" He looked down at his empty plate and caught his lip between his teeth. "He's almost like a person. He'll grow to love you all. He'll stand by you through thick and thin." The man's eyes were on Father, tense as his voice, pleading.

"Will you come for him later?" Father asked.

"That all depends. But I won't take him away unless you're willing. If you'll just give him a good home."

Father smiled. "We'll do our best. Opal loves dogs."

"Oh, Father," I breathed, "may I just pet him?"

"Wait until I am gone," his owner told me. "Keep him in the house or tie him up for a week. Otherwise he will be able to follow me. Then when he knows that I have—deserted him, he will turn to you." He rose and took his hat from the floor. The dog was immediately on his feet, his slick white tail wagging, his eyes focused on his master's face.

Father too had risen. "I regret we haven't a spare room, or even an extra bed to offer. But we've ample comforts for a pallet here on the floor. Won't you remain with us for the night?"

"I've imposed enough already," our visitor replied. "I'll be on my way." He squatted and put his arm about the speckled dog. I had to turn away. There was something about the young man's face I couldn't bear to see.

33

Chapter Four

Next morning Father rose later than was his custom. When he went into the kitchen, the black-and-white dog stood with his nose at the lock of the back door.

In successive crescendos and diminuendos, the norther persisted throughout the day and the following night. On the second morning the sun came out to sparkle the salting of snow in the prairie grass. Ranchers found their cattle drifted against far fences and into the meager shelter of draws, and many of them were dead. The townspeople were out repairing damaged roofs, replacing broken stove pipes, searching for lost articles and tools left about their places when the storm broke. Father and I were again faced with a problem in esthetics, for during the violence of the wind our privy had completely vanished. Again Deacon Webb came to our assistance with odds and ends from the store's construction, and some large dry-goods boxes. Father first demolished then refashioned them into a structure which, if not a thing of beauty, was at least a joy forever, after the days we had been without.

At first the Dalmatian would neither eat nor sleep, but traveled from window to window awaiting the return of his master. He tolerated us, being only passively aware of our existence. The owner had told Father that the dog's name was Lord Nelson of Wyverncliffe—shortened to Nelson. After a week Father made a bed for him in the shed with the horses, because he seemed happier there.

Little by little he lost his attitude of constant listening and watchful waiting and showed more interest in us. He was not exuberant like Shep, and it took us a while to recognize that he had a great capacity for affection back of his reticent and dignified demeanor. Only when Father hitched up the horses for his trips to Seminole, (almost fifty miles distant, where he preached on alternate Sundays), or to make pastoral calls on country members, did Nelson become excited and effervescent.

Whereas before the new baby's advent Mother accompanied Father on pastoral calls, now he went alone. Saturdays, when previously I could go, had devolved into the week's second day of steaming wash boilers, streaming windowpanes, and lines of baby diapers whipping in the wind.

On one such Saturday afternoon Father came into the overheated kitchen, that smelled of yellow soap and freshly ironed clothes. I was folding diapers, pressing them dry with the heavy, solid sad irons and a sadder contemplation of my lot.

"I called on Brother and Sister Kelso," Father said.

Mother covered her bared breast, from which the baby nursed with muffled grunts of satisfaction.

"How are Sister Kelso, and Henry and Harry?" she asked. "A dugout on a homestead must be pretty grim in winter."

"On the contrary," Father replied, "a dugout is warmer in winter and cooler in summer than a house. Theirs is spacious, clean, and attractive. Brother Kelso has great ingenuity in making furniture. The boys' trundle bed fits deftly beneath the big bed. His tables, chairs, and cabinets are the work of a skilled artisan."

"Sister Kelso and the boys always look nice," Mother admitted.

"Her home also is quite charming due to her own handiwork. I hope you can go, on our next visit. I did not know until today that Sister Kelso was T. P. Hamilton's niece and a college graduate."

"Incredible," Mother said, "and living in a dugout."

Father was irritated at such a criterion. "Not so incredible when you know the circumstances. Some ten years ago she came out to visit the Hamiltons, met Emmett Kelso, who was a hand on her uncle's ranch—"

"Foolishly fell in love and made a hasty marriage," Mother interpolated.

"Not exactly. She returned and finished college, then came back the next summer. By that time she was certain. She seems never to have regretted her bargain."

"Surely if they were provident, in eight or nine years they could have built a home," Mother said.

"Their first child, Henry, was very delicate. She went back to Fort Worth before he was born, and it was a year before she could risk bringing him out. Brother Kelso continued working for T. P. Hamilton, but it took all they made. They had to try to equip the homestead practically without funds. Henry's health is still precarious, though improving. Fortunately Harry is husky and strong."

"He's a beautiful child," Mother said, "a veritable cherub with golden curls and violet eyes." Mother looked down at the baby, now fast asleep. "He reminds me of Opal when she was a baby."

I stood at the ironing pad, fairly entranced with the vision of my infantile charm, until an acrid smell startled me. Hastily I folded the diaper to hide the yellow wedge and hoped Mother had not caught the tell-tale odor. I began to sympathize with the women who moaned over the depredations of time. The years had certainly played havoc with Opal Berryman.

The baby asleep, Mother took over that I might go with Father to gather our week-end supply of cow chips. More like an excursion was this chore now, with Nelson trotting about, worrying horned toads and chasing jackrabbits.

As we were trudging home with our loaded tow-sacks and dead mesquite branches, Sheriff Lubeck came riding over the prairie toward us. His verbal approach was just as direct.

"Reverend," he said, "where did you get that dog?"

"He was given to me," Father told him.

"Y'don't say. Mind tellin' me who gave him to you?"

"Not at all. A young man who visited us the night the norther struck."

"Wes Enright?" Sheriff Lubeck's eyes were like gimlets under bushy brows. "Was that his name?"

"I believe it was," Father answered.

"Where was he headin'?"

"He didn't say."

"Just what kind of a story did he put up anyway?" There was more than a trace of sarcasm in the sheriff's tone.

"No story at all. He was cold and hungry. I insisted that he eat and tried to get him to spend the night in the hope that the storm would abate."

Sheriff Lubeck swung out of the saddle. "Unless you tell me all you know about this hombre, I'll have to subpoena you and have you testify under oath. Now just what do you know about Wes Enright?"

Father laid down the mesquite boughs. His voice was patient.

"Very little. I never saw him before that night. I have not seen him since. He mentioned that he formerly worked in a bank in Fort Worth. His health became impaired and his employer, Mr. Hamilton, sent him out to his ranch to do light work and recuperate."

"Is that all?"

Father nodded. "The storm was raging. We talked very little."

There was a suspicious look on the sheriff's browned face.

"He didn't tell you that he brought his young wife with him and that they were living in a small house on a far corner of the ranch—a lonesome spot used before that for shelter for range riders? He didn't tell you that he'd murdered his wife and was shakin' the dust of Texas off his feet, hoping to get away before anyone found her body?"

"No," Father said gravely, "he didn't tell me that."

"Nor that he wanted to get rid of the dog so the law couldn't trace him so easy? The dog was a dead give-away."

Father looked the sheriff straight in the eye. "If such a thing were true, is it logical that he would have confided in me?"

The sheriff looked abashed. "I reckon not," he admitted. "Do you have any idea which direction he went?"

"Not the slightest." Father picked up the wood once more. Sheriff Lubeck swung into his saddle.

"Sometimes men are funny about dogs. If this feller writes you or if he sends you any word, lose no time in gettin' hold of me."

"Of course," Father agreed. "It is not my desire to obstruct justice."

Mother was waiting for us at the window. She was holding open the door before we had our fuel stacked and the wood chopped stove-length.

"Did Sheriff Lubeck find you?" she asked.

"Of course," Father replied. "We hadn't even a barbed-wire fence to hide behind."

"Don't try to be funny," Mother snapped. "The sheriff was looking for the owner of Nelson. He murdered his wife."

"Aren't you jumping at conclusions?" Father suggested. He calmly poured water in the wash pan and motioned me to wash my hands. "As yet he has not been convicted of murder, only suspected."

Mother snorted. "What will you do with that dog you let him leave here?"

"Keep him. The dog isn't under suspicion."

"And let people think you're in cahoots with a murderer?"

"Are you suggesting that I take the dog out and shoot him?"

"Don't talk foolishness. He's a valuable dog. Give him to some rancher on your next trip to Seminole."

"No," I shouted, "he's my dog. You can't give him away."

"The dog was entrusted to us and we will keep him until his owner claims him. That is the only honorable way. If some wish to censure us, they are at liberty to do so."

Mother sat down at the table, dropped her face into her hands, and burst into tears. Father went over and laid his hand on her shoulder.

"There now," he said, "calm yourself. I was as shocked over this as you, but I couldn't weep on Sheriff Lubeck's bosom."

A strange thing happened then. Nelson, who seemed perpetually cold, got himself unwound from the round ball he made back of the stove, went over to Mother, and nudged his nose against her arm. Mother looked down at him in surprise, put her hand on his neck, and drew him close.

"I am being silly," she said shakily. "He's part of our family, and we wouldn't think of deserting our own."

Thanksgiving Day was raw and blustery, but Deacon Webb's two-room house was warm and cozy and redolent with the odors of sage dressing in fat roasting hens and spicy pumpkin pies. Father complimented the Webbs on the fine food and ate with a hearty appetite.

"Pumpkin pies were our winter stand-bys back in Ohio," Sister Webb told us. "They're easier to make than mince meat or fruit cake."

"Someday," Mother sighed, "I hope to be a good cook. There are so few things I can cook expertly."

"There are so few things to cook," Sister Webb said. "Back in Ohio we raised everything—butchered hogs, had our orchards full of fruit, and gardens of all kinds of vegetables. At first I thought we'd starve slap-to-death in this barren country."

"Don't you get homesick for it?" Mother asked.

"Only at times," Sister Webb admitted, "when people look down on us because we are from the North."

"But Ohio isn't really so far north," Mother protested.

"Some folks consider it so," Sister Webb said sadly.

On the way home we dropped in at Brother Craddock's and asked him and Tom and Mattie to spend the evening with us. Sister Craddock had been called back to South Carolina by the illness of her mother. To top off the evening, mother made a fluffy, melt-in-your-mouth rice pudding—one dish at which no one could surpass her—and a pot of gunpowder tea. It was a personal satisfaction to me to treat Brother Craddock to this exquisite dessert without having to include Sister Craddock. It constituted a fitting reward for my rescue from the sulphur and molasses ordeal.

December brought tarnished pewter skies, an epidemic of grippe (which depleted the school to three or four pupils), and tumbleweeds. They banked up solid against the north and west sides of the houses, and any machinery or vehicles left standing outside. The fence surrounding the little cemetery between Chicago and La Mesa was a solid, bristling hedge, completely concealing the dozen bare mounds with their leaning weathered pine markers.

Talk of Christmas brought worried frowns to Mother's brow. Stores in barren little towns on the staked plains were concerned only with necessities, and precious freight space could not be allotted to toys and trinkets.

How Father ever managed to find a silver thimble to go in the toe of my stocking, I never knew. Brother Craddock had carved my initial on the scroll imbedded in the blossom border. A mystery too, how Mother had acquired a china doll head, had made a body of muslin, stuffed it to lifelike proportions, and dressed it in long, lace-trimmed clothes, without my ever suspecting such activities were in progress. But there it stood on top of the apple and stick-candy in my black, ribbed stocking on Christmas morning. After those magnificent gifts I could scarcely doubt that my father and mother still loved me.

It was unfortunate that Sheriff Lubeck had to pick Christmas night to remind us once more of the murder. Father was popping a pan of popcorn in the big iron skillet while Mother pulled two handfuls of sorghum taffy, fast turning to pale gold. I was permitted to answer the knock of (we thought) a neighbor come to share our cheer.

Sheriff Lubeck stepped in, while I stood tongue-tied with astonishment. Father invited him to sit down. The sheriff perched on a chair, held his hat between his knees, and came immediately to the nature of his business.

" 'Pears to me now like Enright got clean over the border into New Mexico. We notified the officers over there, but so far they ain't seen hide nor hair of him."

"I see," Father said. "Have you found additional evidence that he actually murdered his wife?"

"Don't need none," the sheriff said confidently. "The woman was brutally murdered. One side of her head was bashed in. Her husband skipped the country. What more could you want?"

"It seems conclusive," Father said.

"You ain't by chance had no word from him?" Lubeck asked. Father shook his head. "None whatever."

The sheriff's eyes sought the floor. "I had the sad duty of takin' her body back to her folks in Fort Worth. They're pore folks, but they raised a hundred dollars reward. The state's offerin' another hundred. If you could help us, it'd pay you plenty."

"If I could help you, I'd be glad to do so without remuneration," Father told him, "but I've received no information whatever."

"Her folks done all they could to help us." The sheriff pulled a fat leather case from an inside pocket of his vest. "They gave me all the pictures they had." He handed them to Father one by one. I leaned over Father's arm to view them as he took them.

There were several of Wes Enright, and in all of them he was clean-shaven, neatly dressed, and looked very much as one might imagine a city bank clerk to look.

"That's the boy we're after." The sheriff spoke a bit pompously. "The same hombre that gave you the dog, isn't it?"

"I would say that it was the same man," Father replied.

"From what Miz Enright's ma and pa told me, there wasn't no trouble between Wes and his wife when they come out here. Then seems like he was gone a lot, riding for T. P. Hamilton, and their

40

girl got powerful lonesome sittin' all day waitin' for her man to come home. She wasn't used to that kind of life."

"I can understand that," Father commented.

"She made a few friends. We been tryin' to trace them, but ain't had no luck. She sent her folks one picture, and in the letter that went with it she was a lot more cheerful. All she said about the picture was 'This is me and a friend of mine.' " He passed a camera snapshot to Father.

Even before I saw the photo, it seemed to me Father stiffened. It took me a moment to recognize the smiling girl and her chesty, pompous friend. But all at once I knew that I was seeing Miss Carrie Weatherhogg and Mr. William McGurk. Father scrutinized the print.

Finally he spoke. "Sheriff Lubeck, I don't know what this may mean to you. But early in October, shortly after we came here, this couple came to me and requested that I marry them."

"Are you kiddin'?" The voice was incredulous.

"I'm serious," Father said. "As I remember, I still have the marriage license to prove it." He took the cigar box off the shelf and removed a paper from it. He handed the folded document to the sheriff.

Sheriff Lubeck's lips moved as he read the words contained in it. He looked up at Father. "Tell me just what happened."

Father recounted in detail what had transpired on the night that Mr. McGurk and Miss Weatherhogg had requested him to marry them.

"And would you swear under oath that these folks in the picture were the ones that asked you to marry them that night?"

"I would," Father said.

The sheriff was quiet for a time. "Then I reckon Enright must have found out what was goin' on and knocked her off for it."

"It's possible," Father said.

"We were short on motive before. But now it looks like this McGurk come and tolled her off. When you wouldn't perform no ceremony, he takes her back home. Enright finds out about it and kills her. This here shore cinches the case agin him."

"As I understand the unwritten law of the West, it also constitutes some justification," Father mentioned.

41

"There ain't no kind of justification for a guy's bashin' his wife's head in. If he'd a shot her, it'd be different."

Even to me there seemed to be some peculiarity in this logic, but I couldn't analyze it. The sheriff got up, informed Father that he was taking the marriage license with him for evidence, and left.

Our family, now four, gathered about the kitchen table for Evening Devotion. Father must have felt the significance of this Christmas night—the stars of a clear, cold December sky shining down on an old store building sheltering a family where a young baby lay sleeping on a new straw tick in a cradle fashioned from a dry-goods box, with rockers Father himself had made. We had come to this town to render both unto Caesar and unto God. In less than three months we had already found in this new land many vices—bigotry, intolerance, lawlessness; also great virtues— kindness, the endurance of hardships, brotherly love. We had experienced the wonder of a life's beginning, had touched the tragedy of its ending. This composite knowledge and the depths of its meaning glowed in Father's face as his eyes rested upon first Mother, then me.

Mother's hands lay on the table before her—smooth, young hands, tapering beautifully to the first pink of the nails. Her gaze lifted from them and met Father's.

"Before you read," she said softly, "shall we bestow a name upon our baby so that she may be properly introduced to God?"

Father's smile was of tender amusement.

"It's a propitious time. The decision is yours."

"It belongs to us both," Mother said. "I favor Marjorie. It seems fitting for the vivid brunette she'll be—just as Opal's name denotes her more subdued coloring and concealed sparkle. If you agree, then you confer the middle name."

"French," Father said, "in honor of my dear friend, Dr. French, pastor of the First Baptist Church in Austin."

"Marjorie French Berryman," I said, savoring each word. The old envy possessed me briefly that she should have such an elegant name while my own was so poor and common.

Chapter Five

Spring on the Llano Estacado was the most paradoxical season of the year. The sun shone and the buffalo grass greened under the pressure of the rains. The mesquites put out dainty leaves like ferns. The bear grass and prickly pears heightened their color and sharpened their spines for the protection of bloomstems and buds. And in the midst of all this freshening, the sand storms rolled over the horizon and tried to beat the life from every living thing.

In whatever time he could spare during midweeks, Father helped Brother Slade, the carpenter in La Mesa, who was building our new home. It was March when the two-room house, together with a shed for the horses and a lean-to for chickens, was complete. With the coming of spring, one by one the houses and stores that had made up old Chicago came creeping down the road on great rollers, behind four or six horses, and were shifted into place on La Mesa home sites and business lots.

Our satisfaction in our clean new home was short-lived when we found that the yellow pine from the forests of southeast Texas was rampant with bedbugs. Thereafter it was our weekly duty to fill syrup cans with kerosene, dismantle the beds, douse the wooden steads (every hole and groove), and examine and depopulate pillows and feather beds. This was usually scheduled for Saturday morning, for Father was now teaching the La Mesa school and could not help on other weekdays.

We were thus engaged when we saw two horseback riders making a beeline across the prairie to our house. Father put down the can of kerosene, in which floated several defunct chinches.

"Why, I do believe it's Brother Severn," he exclaimed.

"And who, pray tell, is Brother Severn?" Mother asked.

"A rancher from between Pride and Seagraves. But who comes with him?"

Young eyes are sharp. "A girl—with pants on," I said.

Mother gasped. "I do declare!" For one who subscribed only to a neatly tailored riding habit and a sidesaddle for women riders, the sight of a girl with wild red hair under a wide Stetson, wearing a checked shirt stuffed into form-fitting jeans, was a decided shock.

Father steadied the headboard of the bed against the shed wall and went out to meet our guests. Brother Severn rolled from the saddle, grasped Father's hand, and gave it a vigorous pump.

"Howdy, Reverend." He nodded to the girl sitting with lowered head, her mouth in a pout, her eyes peering sidewise under the hat brim. "This here is Sammy. Sammy, meet the Reverend."

Sammy accorded Father a sulky, "Howdy."

"How do you do, Sammy," Father replied pleasantly. "That's an odd name for a young lady. But I think it's rather nice."

"Her name's Samanthy, same as her ma's was."

"This is my wife, and my daughter Opal." Father included us both in a nod and smile. "We are all happy to know you."

"Howdy," Sammy said and looked down at the saddle horn.

Brother Severn braced his convex legs. "You might as well git off. This is where you're goin' to stay, whether you like it or not."

Sammy gave her parent a sultry look and swung out of the saddle.

Brother Severn chewed a corner of his drooping mustache. "You recollect, Reverend, I told you I had a girl I wanted to be a lady?"

Father nodded. "I remember."

"Well, here she is," Brother Severn stated flatly, "spoilt rotten by the men folks. Her two brothers and all the wranglers think her devilishness is cute, and she's growin' up wild as a bobcat. Time she learnt something besides how to bust a bronc and punch cows."

I caught a glimpse of Mother's snapping eyes and straight mouth. It was fortunate Father didn't look at her, or he might have tempered his hospitality. "We haven't the best of accommodations," he said, "but if Sammy will take what we have—"

Brother Severn shrugged it off. "Sammy can sleep on the floor, rolled up in a blanket. She's peart enough. The boys been a-teachin' her readin', writin', and 'rithmetic for years. And they've brung her jography and history books, along with some she maybe shouldn't have had. She'll do all right in school. But she's got to learn how to act like a lady and dress in women's clothes."

Father's voice was optimistic. "I'm sure my wife can do much by precept and example. If you will come in the house—"

"I got to be gittin' back. I ain't aimin' you should do this for nothin'." He gouged a roll from his hip pocket, wet his thumb, and slid off two twenty-dollar bills. "This here'll be a starter."

"My wife will keep strict account," Father assured him as he handed the money to Mother. "We'll spend it judiciously—"

"I don't mean you should be stingy. I got plenty to pay you for doin' a good job on her. I ain't scared but what you'll do right."

From Mother's horrified expression, I feared that she was going to return the money. But Brother Severn was untying a large bundle from behind Sammy's saddle. He handed the bundle to Father, threw his leg over his saddle, and settled himself in the shiny leather seat.

"Now you behave yourself," he warned Sammy and tossed the reins forward over her horse's head. For a moment he looked at his daughter; then he blinked his eyes rapidly, pressed his heels against his horse's flank, and lit out over the prairie, leading Sammy's sorrel.

Apparently Sammy had never quite believed he meant to leave her there. Her eyes and mouth flew open, but for a minute no sound came. Then she let out a howl like a timber wolf and a string of words that backed Mother against the shed wall. Father reached a hand to her, but she flailed out a fist. She stamped the dirt into a cloud and kicked Father's kerosene can across the yard and into the side of the house, where it splashed a great blob on the new pine siding.

When Brother Severn was only a puff of dust far out on the road, Sammy put her hard fists into her eyes and stood there shaking and bawling. After some persuasion she permitted Mother to herd her into the house and finally yielded to the suggestion that she wash her face and have a cup of tea. Mother sent me out to help Father finish debugging the beds. Shortly thereafter Mother came out and spoke to Father.

"Why didn't you tell me of your arrangements with Brother Severn? You know we haven't an inch of extra room."

"I had no arrangements with him," Father said. "He spoke to me of his daughter. I offered our assistance. That I did not foresee such a literal application of the word does not relieve us of the obligation I incurred."

"What are we going to do with her?" Mother asked.

"I may be able to find a bed to replace Opal's cot. We'll need one later anyway, when Marjorie outgrows her cradle."

Mother was aghast. "You mean for Opal to sleep with that— that vixen? Have you no regard for your own family?"

"It seems the only logical thing to do. I doubt if Sammy will harm Opal, either awake or asleep."

"I declare," Mother said vehemently, "sometimes I fail completely to understand you." She turned shortly and went to the house.

Sammy's saddlebags revealed a weird assortment of items: a dress, doubtless her mother's, of watered gray silk, braid-trimmed, with black jet buttons down its boned basque top and a gored and bustled skirt; low-necked, ruffled dress of Turkey-red mull which was Sammy's idea of an evening gown; some long, fleece-lined underwear; two shirts and a pair of jeans; a divided skirt of khaki, whose panel crossed and buttoned into a solid front; some stockings; and a box of trinkets.

Mother went to the store and purchased two five-yard pieces of chambray, one blue and one pink, and some white rep for collars and cuffs. She sat up half the night making up the blue one, so that Sammy could appear appropriately dressed for church on Sunday and school on Monday.

Just before we left for church next day, Sammy opened the box of trinkets and took out a bow-knot pin with a pendant filigree heart. Inside the heart was a rose-colored, rose-scented cake of perfume. She held it up.

"My feller give it to me." She pinned it on her bosom.

Mother eyed it dubiously. "Wouldn't it be nicer inside, pinned to your corset-cover, like a little bag of sachet?"

"No'm," Sammy replied promptly. "Pretty as it is, I reckon it was meant to hang outside and not be hid like a bag of assfittity."

At the schoolhouse where church services were held, Sammy looked longingly at the back seats but dutifully followed Mother to the front. She and I scooted into a seat back of a double desk. Sammy fidgeted at incarceration and turned to look at each new arrival. Though Mother had threatened to punish me for so doing, the half-pleased, half-sheepish look which soon appeared on Sammy's face was more than I could bear. I too looked back, and there in the last seat was a newcomer who was not exactly a stranger. I remembered him even though this morning he was dressed up: his blonde head bare, his hair pasted and dried in the grooves of the comb, his blue suit neat, his white hat on the desk before him. It was the man who had objected to our red window curtains and who had later supported Father in his appeal for peace on election night.

Excitement boiled within me. Maybe this was Sammy's feller. But if so, Mother had said that no decent woman would sit by him even in church. Should I tell Sammy, or should I tell Mother? The remainder of the service was one vast blur. When we emerged from the schoolhouse after shaking hands with all the congregation, the young wrangler was far out on the road, a plume of dust spreading out in the wind from the heels of his galloping horse.

During Sammy's first week with us, Mother was harassed almost beyond endurance. Marjorie developed a cold and an attendant diarrhea that did not respond to a sizable dose of castor oil. Sammy talked little, was awkward about bed-making, and broke many of Mother's treasured dishes. She made a bolt for the door to help Father whenever it came time to feed or curry the horses. She carried water from the pump to wash their manure-plastered rumps whenever they had rolled on a green cow-chip, combed their manes, tails, and fetlocks, and had them looking like show horses.

"Are they broke to ride?" she asked Father one day.

"Yes, they've both been ridden. Count is a good saddle horse. He can fox trot all day. Prince is slower and quieter."

Sammy turned to me. "Can you ride?"

I hung my head. "Mother won't let me."

"Why the hell not?" Sammy demanded.

Father rescued me from my embarrassment. "Opal's mother fears for her safety on horses only occasionally ridden."

"I've ridden Webb's pony," I reminded him. "I got along all right, even when he did a single-foot."

"A girl ain't no damn good in this country if she can't ride," Sammy stated. "If 'twas me, I'd learn or else."

I went immediately inside the house and found Sister Slade there, brewing watermelon-seed tea as a remedy for Marjorie's diarrhea.

"If this doesn't work," she said, "we'll try sheep-pill tea—if we can get the sheep pills. Sheep are scarce in west Texas."

"We will not," Mother said under her breath as Sister Slade left.

"Mother," I asked as she rocked Marjorie in the low sewing rocker, "may I ride Prince? Father thinks he's safe."

"That being the case," Mother's voice was thin from worry and lack of sleep, "we'll rely on your father's judgment. If he is wrong, I suppose burying two children is not much more of a problem than burying one."

I dashed out to the shed.

"Mother says if you think it's all right, I can ride Prince."

Father's brow puckered. "Are you sure she said exactly that?"

"Cross my heart" (I demonstrated) "and hope to die."

Father put the bridle on Prince and led him out of the stall. "We'll have to use this blanket. Perhaps I can borrow a saddle later."

Father lifted me up on Prince. Sammy came up to us.

"Reverend Berryman," she said. "Did you see my pa or either one of my brothers in town today?"

"No, Sammy, I didn't," Father replied.

"Those dirty sons-of-guns." Sammy ground out the words. "They knew I was a countin' on goin' home over Sunday. And not a one of them shows his dad-blasted hide. Them low-down, stinkin' turkey buzzards."

"Now Sammy," Father soothed, "the spring work is on. The cattle have weathered a hard winter, and every hand is working long hours, riding the ranges, hunting for cows that are down or have new calves—"

"I don't give a good damn," Sammy stormed. "One of 'em could have brought in my horse."

"Perhaps even yet one may come in," Father suggested.

"Not now no more." She choked back a sob. "They can't treat me like this. I'll learn 'em to quit suckin' eggs." She fled to the house.

"Poor Sammy," Father said. "I sometimes wonder if this business of refinement isn't gilding the tiger lily."

I straddled Prince's broad back while Father led him out on the open prairie. Obviously Prince had no enthusiasm for this sort of thing. He moseyed along with his head down, grabbing now and then for a sprig of green in a tuft of grass, determined to ignore the ignominy of this menial job. When we were well away from vehicles or bits of stray paper, Father gave the reins to me.

"Now walk him away, then turn him with the pressure of the rein against his neck, by bringing your hand over in the direction you wish him to take." Father spoke to Prince and he started off, ambling along from sheer duty and completely without zest for the task. I slapped his shoulder with an ineffectual hand to keep him in motion.

Then suddenly, without warning, Prince threw up his head and gave a little snort. His nostrils were distended in half-circles. He made a short whirl. There, sweeping past not a hundred yards from us, cutting through to the road, was Sammy bareback on Count, her wild red hair flying. Her heels hugged Count's sides and she lay low on his back as they sped like a streak across the prairie. Prince gave one lunge and took out after Count.

Only faintly did I hear Father's frantic shout. The blanket skidded from beneath me, and with every bounce after Prince's front feet hit the ground I came down on the ridge of his spine. I clung to his mane in a frenzy of blind fear. My feet went into the air and I flew at a tangent through space. I lit in a bed of prickly pears. My memory of Father's arrival and of his carrying me home, a sorry and moaning specimen, was never very clear.

Other events in the following days were also indistinct. But I was aware of a strange chill whenever Father and Mother were together. One thing I did remember was Mother's insisting that Father deliver a stern reprimand to Sammy about her language, and Father's refusal.

"At present," Father explained, "Sammy feels she has been sold into bondage. Any prohibitions would only stir up antagonism and resentment. We must depend upon influencing her in the manner to which she has been accustomed—by example rather than by precept."

Mother was dubious. "Sammy's impervious to subtlety. You'll never change her that way."

"Sammy will change," Father said confidently, "but not by our edict. When it becomes desirable to her to be a lady—which it will

—she'll throw herself into it wholeheartedly, and the metamorphosis will be complete and permanent."

Mother sighed. "And in the meantime our children acquire a slave-driver's vocabulary."

"I don't think so," Father said. "Only Opal is old enough to be impressed by the words, and she'd scarcely have the fortitude to use them." On that I could agree with Father, for had I had the courage I would have used them when Mother was removing prickly pear thorns from my back and bottom.

Father hired a livery team to make the drive to Seminole, and Marjorie recovered from her diarrhea without the aid of more nostrums of doubtful efficacy.

When Sammy returned, it was quite evident by her chastened air that Brother Severn had already administered punishment. She came and stood by my bed.

"Gee, kid," she said. "I'm sorry as hell about this. Believe me, I'm goin' to find some way to make it up to you." She reached down and pressed my hand. "That's an honest-to-God promise."

After that I made such rapid improvement that Mother let me resume school Monday morning.

Father always went to school early; for in addition to teaching he was also janitor and had to make the fire in the big pot-bellied stove, sweep and dust the desks, and bring in fresh water. Sammy and I waited for the shoebox lunch Mother put up for the three of us. This morning Sammy wore the pink dress and had a white bow in her red hair. Because it was late in the season, Mother had stretched a point and let Sammy get slippers for school instead of high-topped shoes. We walked along the trail with due care for Sammy's slippers.

"What was the name of that young man who came to church last Sunday?" I asked.

"What young man?" Sammy countered.

"The one with the yellow hair and the blue suit."

"You mean Ford Hamilton? He was there."

"Is—is he your feller?" I ventured.

Sammy shook her head. "I ain't in his class."

"You mean he's ahead of you in school?"

"Hell no," Sammy said. "I mean I'm pore and he's rich."

"Your father's not poor," I told her. "He has a ranch."

50

"Compared to the Hamiltons, Pa's as pore as a shitepoke."

Obviously Sammy wanted to change the subject, for she started singing lustily in a voice a bit twangy but melodious,

"What did the shitepoke say to the crane,
I hope and I pray that we'll have a little rain,
Creeks all muddy and the ponds all dry,
If it wasn't for the tadpoles, we'd all die."

I wasn't of a mind to be thus easily disposed of. "Just how rich are the Hamiltons?" I asked.

Sammy turned around. "Ain't you never heard of the Hamilton Ranch? More'n a million acres, maybe two—three million, I dunno."

"That Hamilton?" I gasped. "Is Ford T. P. Hamilton's son?"

Sammy nodded and her crisp white ribbon bobbed.

"What's he doing around here?"

"A long time ago my pa and Teepee used to ride trail together. Last fall when Ford got a hackin' cough, Teepee sent him out to Pa. He said, that way Ford would learn more about ranchin' than he would on the Hamilton Ranch, where the wranglers might make it tough on him. Wranglers don't knuckle to nobody, specially a feller that coughs."

"His being rich doesn't keep him from being sweet on you," I said.

Sammy laughed. "He thinks I'm some kind of a freak—like a two-headed calf. He ain't never seen a girl like me and can't make me out."

I mulled this over, but still hadn't learned what I wanted to know about the "feller" she had spoken of.

"The one that gave you the perfume heart, is he sweet on you?"

"Oh, you mean Slim Breedlove. Yeah, I reckon so."

"Who is he?" I questioned.

Sammy stepped out of the path, hauled back, and with the toe of her new slipper sent a sardine can sailing into the air. Then she grabbed her foot, polished off the dust, spit on the scuff, and pasted it down. She shook her head.

"It's shore hard rememberin' to be a lady. I reckon I'd best a-gone barefoot and put my shoes on at school."

"Slim Breedlove," I reminded her. "Does he live here?"

"Gol dang it, you got the cure-osity of a cat. I don't know nothin' about him. He's been head man for Pa a long time. But lately him and Pa don't hit it off."

Here seemed an opportunity to scatter a bit of sunshine.

"But if you are sweet on him, you could help to make things up between him and your father," I suggested nobly.

Sammy looked around at me as though I were an oddity, like the chaparral bird with its long eyelashes. "Maybe you got a pitcher of me flittin' from Slim to Pa and back again, billin' and cooin', tollin' 'em towards one another." Her laugh rang out on the morning air.

"But if you married Slim, you'd want them to be friends."

Sammy tossed her head. "I ain't sure that I got my mind set for bein' an old man's darlin'. Maybe I druther be a young man's slave. I'm aimin' on lookin' 'em all over and pickin' the best in the herd."

Sammy's words disarmed me and for the remainder of the week I thought no more about her potential suitors. But on Friday afternoon as we returned from school, Ford Hamilton rode in, leading Sammy's sorrel. Sammy let out a "Yippee," threw her books in the air, grabbed Ford about the waist as he dismounted, smacked him on the cheek, and then ran in the house to change clothes. I watched them ride away, the tall blond Hamilton boy and flame-haired Sammy Severn, side by side in the two tracks of the road that led straight toward the lowering sun in the western sky.

Chapter Six

THINGS progressed well that spring. In spite of the lack of spring rains, that caused the lagoons to dry early and frequent severe sand storms, our population increased. Brother Hinkins, the banker, moved his family into a luxurious four-room bungalow that Brother Slade built for him. Georgia

Hinkins, a coy, fluttery blonde, and Brother Slade's oldest daughter, Vela, eyed each other with the mutual affection of two strange dogs.

Straight from Dallas came Ruby Tuttle, Mrs. Judge Pothast's ten-year-old niece, to live with them. Her citified clothes were a source of envy to Ora, Dora, Mattie, and me, and our constant plaguing for identical apparel exasperated Mother and Sister Slade almost to tears. On the other hand, Sister Craddock seemed delighted to produce replicas for Mattie regardless of trouble and expense. It tended to substantiate the rumors that after Sister Craddock's return from her mother's funeral in South Carolina she had come into money. The proof came when Brother Craddock bought the lumber yard.

Things were looking up for others in the town. Sister Mahoney, who with her daughter, Rosemary, and son, Jim, ran the boarding house and wagon yard, had long struggled to eke out a living. Now each freighter brought them a drummer or two as guests.

Frequently new arrivals left their families for a week while they fashioned a dugout or a one-room house on a recently acquired homestead.

Each day brought new faces. Just before noon one Saturday we received our first visit from Brother Dissey. Brother Dissey was an itinerant minister who earned a precarious livelihood going from town to town and ranch to ranch, collecting meals and gifts to maintain the Lord's work and planning revival meetings for the summer months. He was neither licensed nor ordained, and while Father deplored this lack of credentials he did not hold that it necessarily prevented Brother Dissey from being a man of God.

This visitor was a large, untidy man whose sagging cheeks seemed always to have at least one day's growth of beard. Now he stopped at the pump. Father went out, greeted him, and pumped water for his horses. He took oats from our own bin in the shed, filled the *morales*, and hung them over the horses' noses. Then they came to the house, Brother Dissey hugging a middling large, limp, Morocco-bound Bible to his bosom. From the back door I could see muddy spots on the front of his black-figured white vest, which fit his upper chest loosely and would barely button over his paunch. Its points stood apart like tent flaps.

Mother turned another plate face down on the table, gathered up the black-handled knives and forks, and reset the table with the bone-handled ones. Brother Dissey stepped into the door as though he were mounting a rostrum. He anchored both hat and Bible under his left arm.

Father was speaking. "—my wife, Mrs. Berryman. This is a co-laborer of ours, Reverend P. Sylvester Dissey."

Brushing her hands quickly down her apron, Mother came forward. Brother Dissey grasped her hand between pudgy fingers and bowed low.

"It is indeed an honor and a pleasure to find such a charming accomplice in our crusade for Christ," Brother Dissey said.

This sounded a bit peculiar to me and I glanced at Father. His eyes twinkled but his face was gravely impassive.

"My wife is an accomplished assistant," he said.

"I can discern that." Brother Dissey sighed voluminously. "How very fortunate are you John the Baptists crying in this wilderness, who have a wife to hold up your hands."

Even Father gasped a little at this jumbled eloquence; but Brother Dissey had plunked himself into his chair at the table, and Mother and I fairly scampered to our seats. According to his custom with visiting preachers, Father asked Brother Dissey to return thanks. We bowed our heads and kept our hands sedately in our laps. But Brother Dissey clasped his above his plate and lifted his face to the ceiling.

"Kind and indulgent Heavenly Father," he began, and from there on he gained momentum and fluency so rapidly that the next understandable word was, "Amen." Mother managed to keep a calm countenance as she passed the frijoles and the hot potato salad. Brother Dissey wasted no time in getting to his business.

"I tell you, Brother Berryman, what this town needs is a good, old-fashioned revival. It'll start things off with a bang."

"As yet," Father demurred, "we haven't the facilities."

"That's just it," Brother Dissey nodded vigorously. "You never will have at this rate. The Lord helps those who help themselves. There's no time like the present. Procrastination is the thief of time."

Father seemed unimpressed by this barrage of platitudes.

"We've no meeting house," he pointed out. "The school board

wouldn't let us use the schoolhouse for a protracted meeting. I had difficulty even getting it for Sunday services."

"Build a brush arbor," Brother Dissey suggested glibly. "There's plenty of brush down the draws toward the cap rock. I tell you, Brother Berryman, the field is white unto the harvest. The summer is almost here. The time is ripe. Unless you get these people filled with the Holy Ghost, the whole thing will peter out when winter comes."

"Perhaps you're right," Father admitted. "I'll consider it and we'll discuss it further on your next visit."

"Cast your burdens upon the Lord," Brother Dissey advised, "and pray without ceasing. But," he winked at father coyly, "one mustn't forget he must work out his own salvation with fear and trembling."

By this time Father was annoyed. "I'm quite aware of the individual's own responsibility."

"Of course, of course," Brother Dissey agreed. "Sister Berryman, I hope you won't consider me officious if I ask for another helping of that potato salad. It's like manna from Heaven."

After dinner, Father and Brother Dissey repaired to the front room for further talk. Mother washed the dishes. I dried them and set them in the "safe," a tall cupboard with metal-paneled doors punched with nail holes in a rose design. I could never see the sense to it, for a fly could and often did squeeze himself in but could never get out, since the nail holes were as rough inside as a nutmeg grater. But Mother valued it because Sister Falloon had given it to her when our new house was completed.

This task finished, I grabbed my sunbonnet and took the short cut to Brother Slade's. The Slade girls were on the back porch shelling black-eyed peas. Ora, a year older than I, was dark and gangling. Dora, who was some months younger, was plump and blonde. Inside the house Vela, their older sister, was playing *In the Shade of the Old Apple Tree* on the gramophone. Ora piped up in explanation of Vela's gay mood.

"Vela's going to a play-party next Friday night."

"What's a play-party?" I inquired.

"A party where they play 'Skip-to-My-Lou' and 'The Farmer Choose His Wife'—I mean 'The Farmer's in the Dell'—play-party games."

I made a mental note to ask Mother who the farmer's "infidel" was and why he should see fit to chew his wife.

Ora cocked her head sagely. "All the big kids are invited except Link Webb. He's not, because the Webbs are Black Republicans."

"They are not," I spoke out. "They're not black anything."

"They are so," Dora put in. "Papa says so. Brother Webb wouldn't be postmaster if he wasn't a Black Republican. It's only Black Republicans that get 'pointed to those jobs."

Considering this, my gaze wandered across to the vacant Ewing house. Brother Ewing, I had heard it whispered, was a Republican. I wondered if that had had anything to do with his T.B. getting worse. It had forced him to sell his interest in the barber shop to his partner, Brother Hepplehite, and take himself off to a sanitarium. I wondered—but just then noticed that peculiar things were going on at the vacant Ewing house.

"Looky," I pointed. "Somebody's moving in."

The half-shelled peas were forgotten as the three of us lit out to see these new neighbors. A big chap in a checkered suit was directing the unloading of the wagon backed up to the door.

"Mighty lucky," we heard him say to the freighter. "Hadn't been in town thirty minutes when they told me at the Betz House about this place."

The freighter grimaced. "Stinks like the pest house."

The big man laughed. "Couldn't find anything but creosote to fumigate with. It'll air out." He turned and saw the three of us staring at the strange articles coming out of the freight wagons.

"Good afternoon, young ladies," he bowed. "I'm Dr. Bachellor, your new dentist."

Though undoubtedly heading for obesity, Dr. Bachellor was a friendly soul with carroty hair and eyes, a porous-looking nose, and soft white hands, one of which he offered to each of us in turn. Bashfully we told him our names, while straining to see what looked like a barber chair and a long jointed pole-and-line contraption with a foot pedal being carried into the front room. Along with it there was a beautiful square piano. At that juncture a thin, tired-looking young woman dressed in a lace-trimmed black taffeta suit came out of the house.

"My wife," Dr. Bachellor said. "The Misses Ora and Dora

Slade and Miss Opal Berryman." He winked at us. "If you tried hard, you might persuade Mrs. Bachellor to give you piano lessons."

"Now, Oliver." Mrs. Bachellor looked down at her long hands, half-hidden under lace wrist ruffles. "The girls will have to take it up with their parents."

It sounded as if Dr. Bachellor accidentally made a queer noise through his tongue and teeth, but his head was turned toward his wife. Then he smiled at us.

"It isn't often children in small western towns have a fine musician to teach them. You girls are very fortunate."

I could scarcely wait to get home and give the news to Father and Mother. Perhaps also we would now have an organist for church. Sister Falloon had presented a small organ to the church at the time she got for herself a fine new parlor organ with a high carved top, fluted lampstands, and a beveled mirror. Up to now Father had had both to play the organ and lead the singing.

On Sunday afternoon, Father asked Mother to go with him to call on Brother and Sister Kelso, who, strangely for them, had not been to church for two Sundays. Mother pled that she needed rest, but I suspected that she might wish to use the time to whip the val lace edging on the corset-cover and petticoat she had made for Sammy during the previous week.

"Then I'll take Petey," Father said.

"Make sure before you go in that they've no contagious disease," Mother admonished.

Father hitched up the team and we started east across Lobo Creek. At this season Lobo Creek seemed grossly misnamed. It was a wide draw with a deposit of stones and pebbles in its bed. But when the rains came, if they came at all, it was a raging torrent. A wall of water twenty feet high had been known to come down from the higher reaches of the Llano Estacado and expand Lobo Creek into a roaring river.

The road to Big Spring then became impassable. Citizens told of how the mail carrier had had to wait sometimes a whole day on the other side until the flood receded. And only last spring three wagons freighting lumber were forced to camp the night there before delivering their loads to the lumber yard.

There had been much discussion about moving the town across the creek. Some far-sighted citizens felt it would be better to do so before more dwellings and businesses were built. But others, those who had moved from old Chicago and already had homes and stores built for permanence, violently disagreed. All the buildings, they contended, were safe. But that was before Adolph Betz came out from St. Louis. Unfamiliar with the ways of west Texas creeks, he had built his saloon on the side where the creek cut in toward the town. Already, in but a few weeks, there was a landslide of debris, bottles, cans, and broken boxes down the bank of the creek where it sloped off sharply behind the saloon.

"Whose house is that," I asked, "with all that trash?"

"Adolph Betz," Father replied shortly. "And there's more trash than meets the eye. It's a saloon—the Betz House."

I was shocked. Saloons were dens of iniquity. Decent women passed them on the far side of the street, holding their skirts up and keeping their eyes averted, as though by ignoring them they made them nonexistent. When alone with Father I could risk being boldly curious.

"What do they do in saloons?"

"Drink. And gamble. If there are two rooms, the front is usually a bar and the back has tables for cards, dice, or dominoes."

"Did Ford Hamilton think our house was a saloon the night he came to see us in Chicago?" I inquired.

"How did you know that was Ford Hamilton?" Father demanded.

"I saw him good in the light. And when Mother and I went down to see the fight on election night, I recognized him."

"You mean that you and your mother were in that crowd?"

"We stood back of somebody's wagon and watched," I admitted.

"I see," Father said. "That was the night Marjorie was born."

"Then when I saw him in church, I asked Sammy who he was. You remember you asked him to come to church," I reminded him.

"Does your mother know all this?"

"I don't know. I haven't told her."

"Then don't," Father said. "Women frequently take a circumscribed view of a young man's foolishness—or curiosity."

"Do you think Ford is sweet on Sammy?" I asked.

"I don't know. But I plan to have a talk with him one of these days. In the meantime, don't inform anyone of your precocious deductions. It is better to leave some things in the lap of the gods."

Several miles out, Father turned off the Big Spring road into two faint ruts through the carpet of buffalo grass. The mesquites showed signs of leafing, though many old beans still clung to their twisted branches. In sections of gravel the greasewood shone with an oily gleam and gave off its pungent aroma.

We turned toward a windmill and a shed, and soon we came in view of a roof some four feet off the ground. Steps cut into the dirt led down to the door. Father tied his team to the windmill tower and met Brother Kelso coming from the house.

"We've missed you at church these past two Sundays," Father said. "Have you illness in your family?"

"We're none of us sick, as yet." Brother Kelso made a sign to Father and they moved back of the buggy, out of my sight but not quite out of hearing (due to the brisk wind that blew his words straight in my direction). "We're living under the shadow of death," he said in a low, tight voice.

Father said simply, "Can I be of any help?"

"Nobody can help us. It's far worse for Kathie than for me. Our three-year-old, Harry—" Brother Kelso blew his nose. "It happened two weeks ago last night. The lumber yard's been promising me screen wire, but so far it ain't come. It ain't fly time yet. But we'd a had it on if we could of."

"I know," Father commented. "We too are waiting for screens."

"Henry, our seven-year-old, and Harry, our three-year-old, sleep in the trundle bed. In the middle of the night Harry screamed out. I hit the floor and lit the lantern. He'd been bit on the arm. I looked all over for a vinegarroon or a centipede, but there wasn't none. The bite looked more like a weasel bite. I shone the light back under the bed and seen eyes a-glowin'. Then all of a sudden the place was full of stink, and I knowed it was a pole cat."

"Came in through those ground-height windows," Father said.

"I hauled my .22 off the wall and let him have it right between the eyes. He ran out in the room, frothin' and fightin', and fell over dead. He was plumb full of hydrophobia."

59

"Did you get Harry to a doctor? The Pasteur treatment for rabies is very effective."

"I tied off his arm, het the ramrod, and seared the place. I put Harry on the horse with me and we went hell-bent for Big Spring. But when we got there, the Doc had took his wife to Fort Worth for an operation. The drug-store man telephoned to Dallas. They said they'd get the serum on the train and told the drug-store man how to give it. Well, Harry and me waited for a solid week before it came. We just got home yesterday."

When Father said nothing, I knew this had hit him hard.

There was a choked sound to Brother Kelso's voice. "If we could only have had it sooner! But this god-forsaken jumpin'-off place—there ain't no homestead in the world worth the life of a rosy-cheeked—"

"I know," Father said softly. "You've done everything possible. We can only pray, and if it is God's will that his life be spared—"

"I wish I'd never seen this darned worthless land, creepin' and crawlin' with snakes and scorpions. Where even wild things go mad—"

"Brother Kelso," Father said, "not one of us could have done more than you have done. For Sister Kelso's sake, gather yourself together. Could we go in and visit with her, or had you rather we didn't?"

The high note of hysteria was gone from Brother Kelso's voice. "Of course, Reverend, you-all come in." Now he came around the buggy and held out his hand to me. "I think I got a stick of peppermint candy in the house for you, if them boys of mine ain't et it all up."

The smell of creosote greeted us when the door was opened. It had erased the skunk smell. Sister Kelso came forward, a small, bright woman who smiled at us exactly as though nothing had happened.

"Reverend Berryman—and Opal. I'm so glad to see you. Have chairs and make yourselves at home. Henry has gone to the pasture to fetch home the milk cow, and Harry and I are baking cookies."

Father took his cue from her bright and cheerful manner. He

shook hands with her and with little Harry, a sturdy chap with fine, fair ringlets over his head, whose smile sparkled in his blue eyes and showed a mouthful of little white teeth. He looked like the pictures of cherubim and seraphim on our Sunday school cards.

"Those cookies certainly smell good," Father said. "I venture they have ginger in them. Maybe they look like mens' faces with raisins for eyes. How about it, Harry? Did I guess right?"

Harry smiled and hugged his mother's skirts. She picked him up and pressed him to her, closed her eyes for a second, touched his cheek with her lips.

"Tell Reverend Berryman" (she spoke with amazing lightness) "what we did. We put red cinnamon candies on them for mouths."

Harry nodded his head vigorously and buried his face on his mother's neck. She loosed his chubby arms and set him on a chair.

"They're ready to take from the oven." She spread a white tea towel on the table. "Go out to the water box, Emmett, and get a pan of milk. We'll have milk and cookies. Harry, you go with papa and bring back a pat of butter for Mama."

I couldn't take my eyes off little Harry, stretching his fat legs up the hard clay steps. But when they had gone Sister Kelso spoke.

"Emmett has told you?"

Father nodded. "Yes, he has told me. Would it help if you came in town and stayed with us? I can arrange for a part of my family to stay with neighbors for a while."

"No, Brother Berryman. If Harry should leave us, we want all the time we have here at home—just the four of us."

"I understand. You shall be in our prayers night and day."

"Oh," her hands gripped each other so the knuckles were white, "do pray for us. Pray for Emmett—it is so much harder on him than on me. Pray that we may have strength to meet whatever comes—" She looked up as the light faded in the room.

Harry was coming down the steps in front of his father, water dripping from his fingers and the white, wet cloth that enclosed the pat of butter. "Put it right on this little plate," said his mother. "You and Opal can have first choice of all the gingerbread men."

Somehow I could never remember much about the lovely cookies or the cold, sweet milk from the shining tin pan. Constantly before me was Harry Kelso's angelic face, and continuously in my mind—sometimes even moving my lips—was the prayer, "God, don't let little Harry die."

And on the way home, Father and I were silent.

Soon after the juncture of the side road with the main road, a rider coming from the direction of Big Spring overtook us. It was Sheriff Lubeck. He came up beside us and Father stopped the team. The sheriff drew a card from his pocket and handed it to Father.

"Did you ever see that hombre?" he asked.

I looked across Father's arm at the photograph, a full-face view of a grim-looking young man who was totally unfamiliar to me.

"Not that I remember," Father said.

"That there," the sheriff spoke emphatically, "is Mr. William McGurk, of Fort Stockton, Pecos County, Texas."

Father shook his head. "Not the William McGurk that came to me with his marriage license."

There was an acid tinge to Sheriff Lubeck's tone. "That there's the only William McGurk I was able to scare up in all of Pecos County. Folks say he's the only one there."

"You've been down to Pecos County?" Father asked.

The sheriff nodded while he rolled a cigarette on his saddle horn. "Been scourin' the country for weeks. This here McGurk says he don't even know any Miss Carrie Weatherhogg. The county clerk don't remember what the guy looked like that bought that marriage license. There don't seem to be anybody in Pecos County that knows nothin' about nothin'."

"That's too bad," Father sympathized. "Then your trip was completely fruitless." He handed the photograph back to the sheriff.

"Well, mebbe—mebbe not." The sheriff cupped his hands over a lighted match and drew on his cigarette. "I found out that this McGurk is a friend of the Slothower boys."

"And who are the Slothower boys?" Father asked.

"Horse traders from up around Tahoka. They go through the country buyin' and sellin' and tradin'. They been down around Pyote and Pecos and Fort Stockton not so long ago. Nobody down there seems to know where they are now and I ain't seen them around here lately."

"You think the Slothowers might know something?"

"Well, the way I figure it, if this feller that bought the marriage license wasn't William McGurk he must a knowed McGurk and used his name. I reckon I can't chase down everybody that knows William McGurk, but I can catch the Slothower boys when they come through this part of the country and ask them some questions. You're sure this ain't the guy that asked you to marry him that night?"

"Positive," Father said. "I've never seen this man before."

"You ain't heard nothin' from Wes Enright yet?" the sheriff asked. "I see you still got his dog." He motioned toward Nelson, who lay in the road just in front of the horses, ready to leap the minute they started.

"Not a word," Father said.

"Well, adios." The sheriff pressed his heels into his horse's flanks. The horse broke into a short lope on the road ahead of us.

Father laid his palm hard against his cheek. His gaze took in the prairie, wind-swept and sun-glossed, vibrant with the pains of its seasonal rebirth. The brown crust of winter was yielding grudgingly to the stirring of life beneath it. The green touch of spring barely spotted the country. Down the road ahead of us was Sheriff Lubeck on his mount, shrinking before our eyes as though his importance was vaporizing into the dusty fuzz beside him and drifting away in the wind. One man—what chance had he in this vast and stubborn land?

I turned to Father. "Why doesn't he just give up?"

"Probably because his conscience would rise up and smite him. A man's contract with the people is often only a token of the pledge he has made to himself."

"But he's been all over and nobody can give him any help. He doesn't get anywhere."

"Sometimes," Father said, "obstacles wear spurs."

When we reached home we found that Sammy had ridden in ahead of us and had put up her horse at the livery stable. Mother took a look at me and at Sammy and said, "You girls look so tired, you'd better not go to church tonight. I'll get Marjorie to bed. You can all three stay—and that way I'll share in the rest."

I looked about, and there, tucked down at the foot of the bed, was the corset-cover with its frilly edging of val lace.

After Sammy and I were in bed, Sammy said, "I got an invite to a play-party Friday night. I'm a-goin' to wear my red evening dress and knock their eyes out."

"But you always go home on Friday night," I said.

"Not this time. I'll go on Saturday morning."

"Won't Ford Hamilton be here to ride home with you?"

"Nope. Me and him had a ruckus. He thinks I'm getting too thick with the town boys."

"You haven't gone anywhere with any of them."

"I guess maybe I talk too much," Sammy admitted humbly, then flared up, "but I don't care. Him nor nobody else ain't goin' to tell me where to get off. I'll do as I gol-danged please."

With this subject closed, I told Sammy about little Harry.

"He'll die," Sammy said flatly.

"Maybe if we prayed real hard," I suggested.

"It won't do no good," Sammy said, and in her voice was a sympathetic hopelessness. "Not after they get bit by a mad pole cat."

From the back side of the bed where I lay I could look out the window and see the stars closer together even than Nelson's spots. God was omnipotent. God could move mountains. He could work miracles like bringing Lazarus to life.

"God, don't let little Harry die," I breathed. "If you'll just do that, I won't ask for anything ever again—"

Sammy was propped up on her elbow looking at me.

"Has Tommy Craddock got a case on Vela Slade?"

With difficulty I brought myself back to mundane things.

"I don't know. Why?"

"I just wondered," Sammy tossed her head. "I don't know what he can see in her. She ain't so very pretty, do you think?"

"Not as pretty as you are," I answered after a moment.

That pleased Sammy and she rested her head back on the pillow. Before long we were both sound asleep.

Chapter Seven

FATHER received a letter from a church in Georgia, stating that we had been chosen by the good ladies of the church to be the recipients of a mission box. They requested that Father send his measurements and a suit would be made for him. Father had always fancied himself as a large man and optimistically insisted that Mother add a little to each dimension lest the suit be too small in case he gained some weight.

For weeks we had speculated on the contents of the box. Mother hoped for blankets, bed and table linens, and heavy coats for all. Father, who had the advantage of knowing at least one item, maintained that anything would be quite acceptable. I longed for a French doll with long golden curls, ruffled, lace-trimmed skirts, and bows on her little kid slippers—a doll I could name Marie; also a watch like Mother's, that hung from a long chain with a slide upon it set with two fire opals.

We had long since quit discussing the mission box, tacitly deciding that the Georgia ladies had wearied and abandoned the task, when Brother Webb sent Link over after school to tell Father that an enormous box had come for him with the Big Spring freight. Father got a team and wagon from the livery stable to haul it home.

Mother and I held our breath while Sammy and Father wielded a chisel and claw-headed hammer to pry loose the boards. With the top off, Father took out the items one by one; and at once we gave thanks to the thoughtfulness of the congregation of that Georgia church. We unwrapped hand-quilted quilts, one with the names of the ladies embroidered on the silk and velvet pieces. This represented community effort, but the individual donations were most interesting. Mother received long, drop-seat underwear, black stockings, petticoats, corset-covers, a knitted shoulderette, a pink fascinator with a top-knot of bugle beads, a plum-colored redingote of uncertain size, a pair of black lace mitts, and a little barrel muff.

I received a shopworn edition of the big doll I craved. The yellow hair was a bit matted, but she was intact, with a beautiful bisque head with sleepy eyes and parted lips, and a rock-hard body with hinged hips. She *was* Marie, and the fact that she was not immaculate made her more companionable. The suit Father had planned on wearing day in and day out was an elegant Prince Albert of lustrous black broadcloth, undoubtedly a duplicate of the one the Georgia minister wore before his fashionable congregation. At sight of it Mother gave a little wail of disappointment.

"When ever will you wear it?"

Father examined the fine buttons covered in corded silk, the exquisite lap of its ample front, and the delicate tailoring of the pleating at the split tail.

"It's quite appropriate for weddings and funerals. And when we have a church building, I can wear it on Sunday morning. With care, it should last my life through and serve as my burial shroud."

"That's the most suitable use you've mentioned," Mother replied tartly. "Go in yonder and try it on. I want to know how it fits."

A few moments later Father emerged from the front room. The suit enveloped him, only his fingers showing from the sleeves, the back of the pants under his heels. Mother simply stared at it, then sighed.

"Put it in the box couch with our winter clothes. I'll get it out and shorten the sleeves and pants if you ever happen to need it."

The winter overcoat was of fine black melton, and over Father's suit the slack was less noticeable.

"Wonderful," Mother said, "for those long, cold trips to Seminole and back."

In addition there were hard-boiled shirts with tucked bosoms, long red wool underwear, and a derby hat carefully packed in a three-legged kettle. Hiding in the bottom of the box was a velvet toque with a moth-eaten plume, a white net dress of many ruffles, and a red-and-green homespun rug large enough for our front room. As though in compensation for any inadvertant slight to an individual was a ten-pound fruit cake wrapped in spiced cloth, packed in a wooden box.

All this excitement called for a pot of coffee for Mother and Sammy and a pot of tea for Father and me, and the evening ended like a party. Amid the chaos on beds and floor, we sat at the table and discussed the gifts.

Suddenly Sammy snickered behind her hand. "I was just a-thinkin' that if some Saturday night the Reverend put on that suit of long red flannels and a red stocking cap and took his pitchfork and walked into the Betz House, them fellers would vacate so fast there wouldn't be no use in a local option election."

"It might increase church attendance," Mother suggested.

Father sighed. "Not for long, I fear. I've always heard that if a man is determined to drink, he'll do it in spite of the devil."

It was the only time I ever heard Father speak lightly of the thorn in his flesh, the licensed saloon.

Sammy clasped her hands in front of her. "Honest, Sister Berryman, I'm crazy about that little muff. Could I please wear it to the play-party on Friday night? I'll be mighty careful with it."

Mother looked up. "A party? Where is it to be?"

"At Mahoney's. Rose asked the girls and Jim asked the boys. I guess everybody in town is asked to it."

"Would your father approve?" Mother inquired.

Sammy nodded. "Pa lets me go to dances and play-parties."

Mother turned to Father. "What do you think about it?"

"If Sammy's father approves, it is scarcely within our province to deny her the privilege. But I'll escort her to the party and call for her by eleven."

"Gee, that's swell," Sammy exclaimed. "Thanks a heap."

Mother went to the bed and picked up the white net dress with its tiers of ruffles. "We can cut off these long sleeves and make a round neck; and ruffles off the bottom of the skirt can go at the neck and sleeves. It will make a lovely party dress—"

"Oh, no'm, I got an evenin' dress—a bright red one."

"Young girls don't wear low-cut, scarlet gowns—"

"But I've seen pitchers," Sammy contended. "We got a calendar at home with a girl in a skin-tight red dress cut down to here—" she laid a hand half way down her chest. "She's awful pretty—"

Astutely Mother changed tactics. "What color is her hair?"

"It's black—shiny coal-black. But that don't matter—"

"Of course it does," Mother said gently. "Your red hair is beautiful. But you must never wear colors that make it look drab by comparison. Green, blue, black, white, pale yellow, gray— even pink—all of them will compliment your gorgeous hair. Brown, like the little muff, is splendid. But bright red is for the black-haired girls."

Sammy's forehead wrinkled and her lips pouted a little.

"All right," she conceded, then bounded up from the table and flipped the white net dress over her head, drew it down over her slim hips. "Gee, this is really scrumptious. Reckon I'll be the belle of the ball."

The box couch and all the chairs were still piled with clothing when we went to bed. I was so excited I could not sleep for thinking of the sleepy eyes and little teeth in my new doll. I lay there staring into the dark when I heard Father's voice from the other room.

"I'm going to dismiss school early tomorrow. You'd better ask Sister Slade to keep Marjorie and go out to Kelso's with me."

"Of course," Mother told him. "I'll have the team harnessed and ready when you get here."

But Mother reckoned without Marjorie. Mother had placed her on a pallet on the kitchen floor with a pie tin and a spoon for entertainment while she went to harness the horses. An errant frijole caught Marjorie's eye. She worked herself to the edge of the pallet, and when Mother came in the frijole was wedged tightly in Marjorie's nose. Father found Mother working frantically with a button hook to dislodge it. Marjorie finally solved the problem herself by sneezing.

Too late then for the trip by buggy, Sammy insisted that Father go to the livery stable and get *her* horse. His return late that night woke us. Mother got up and lighted the lamp. Though none of us asked, we all looked the question.

"The child is ill." That was all Father had to tell us.

Sister Slade took Marjorie for the day and Mother drove to Kelso's, taking with her part of the fruit cake, bags of corn meal and navy beans that Sister Slade brought, a side of bacon, and a bag of dried apples that Sister Webb sent from the store. Mother must have cried the whole trip home, for when she came in her eyes were bloodshot and swollen. She went to bed with a violent headache. I heard her say to Sister Slade, who put cold compresses on her forehead, "It's the most terrible thing I've ever seen."

Once more Father took Sammy's horse when he came from school, and this time he stayed the night through. He returned only for breakfast and was to go immediately to the school. With his breakfast untasted, his tea cooling in the cup, he rested his face in his hands.

"I've seen children die," he said to Mother, "but never like this. He cannot even swallow the morphine tablets."

On my way to school I saw Brother Slade riding out the Big Spring road and knew he had gone to look after the stock and carry on the ranch duties for Brother Kelso. All that day I could not study, for the sweet face of little Harry Kelso lay on the page before me, no matter how many I turned. I could not have recited had Father called upon me. But I do not think Father would have known if he had.

I had forgotten the play-party at Mahoney's until I saw the white net dress, crisp as a cabbage leaf, lying on the bed. Sammy stood and stared at it, as though also just remembering.

"I ain't a-goin'," she said, "not with that little tyke a-lyin' out yonder and a-dyin'. No siree, I ain't a-goin' no place."

Mother put her arm around Sammy's shoulders. "Of course you are going, Sammy dear. A minister's family lives vicariously all the joys and sorrows of the community. While living the sorrow of one, we must also share the joy of another. We want you to go."

"It don't seem right," Sammy objected, but her eyes were on the fluff of net and lace lying on the bed.

"Let's try it on," Mother said. "Mr. Berryman has gone back to the Kelso's, but I've asked Vela and Tommy to stop for you."

"You have?" Sammy grabbed the dress. It was apparent that she had made up her mind to go.

Mother undid Sammy's short braids, dipped the comb in warm water, and let the curls form around her finger. Deftly she tied the cluster of curls with a white bow at the back of Sammy's neck. Then she dusted Sammy's neck and arms with talcum and put the white net on over a lace-trimmed petticoat. Sammy was beautiful!

Mother laid her tan cape about Sammy's shoulders and gave her the little muff. Sammy agreed to have the perfume heart pinned *beneath* her dress.

At a last-minute inspection, I heard Mother's admonition.

"Lovely ladies are soft-spoken and gracious. Profanity or even slang would destroy the illusion. Don't step out of character."

"No'm," Sammy said humbly. "I'll be plumb proper."

While Mother and I sat reading, there was a knock at the front door. I left *Little Women* lying open on the table, but Mother still had *St. Elmo* in her hand as she went to the door. A young man yanked off his hat and I saw that it was Ford Hamilton.

"Won't you come in?" Mother said politely, then thoughtfully: "I'm sure I should know you."

"He came for Sammy one week-end," I prompted.

"I remember now. It was in Chicago—on election night. You helped Mr. Berryman control the crowd."

Ford looked a bit embarrassed. "Yes'm, I reckon I helped a little. My name is Ford Hamilton, and I would like to—"

"Of course." Mother drew out a chair. "You did come for Sammy, but I only saw you from a distance. But you were splendid that election night. I wish Mr. Berryman were here to meet you."

"Oh, we've met," Ford said. "Didn't he ever tell you about the night I called at your house in Chicago? You had some gaudy red window curtains." Ford grinned broadly and his blue eyes twinkled.

St. Elmo plopped on the floor. I could see Mother stiffen and a frozen look come over her face. Ford saw it too and the crinkly look of amusement fell apart.

"Yes, he told me." Mother's words were square and hard as ice cubes. "But I didn't know that you were that—person."

"Yes, ma'am." Ford turned his hat in his hands. "I'm that person. But I never intended to make you-all mad. I came here today to find out what happened to Sammy. I rode out to meet her but she never showed up. I thought maybe she was sick."

"No, she isn't ill. She has gone to a party. She'll be back by eleven. If you care to wait—"

"Thank you, ma'am." Ford moved to the door. "But I reckon I'll mosey down to the Betz House. If you don't mind tellin' me where the party is, I might drop by and see her before I light out for home."

"Mahoney's boarding house," Mother said.

"Thank you, ma'am. Goodnight, you-all."

Mother stared at the closed door as though she could not quite believe we had had such a visitor and that he was really gone.

"He's Teepee Hamilton's son," I said reproachfully.

Mother whirled about. "I don't care if he's Theodore Roosevelt's son. He has a lot of gall coming into the house of decent people. And it's time someone told Brother Severn what kind of trash he is."

"He came to church one Sunday," I reminded Mother.

"He did? Some people either have no sense of propriety or become so depraved they lose it."

It seemed to me that while the bag lay in the lap of the gods, as Father had suggested, the cat had certainly wiggled out of it.

Mother even forgot to send me to bed. I became more and more fidgety, and when finally we heard voices outside Mother dropped another stick of mesquite wood in the stove and set the teakettle on the front. I could hear Vela's giggle, then Tommy Craddock's "Adios."

The teakettle was singing and I was biting my nails when the door opened softly and Sammy came in. Her hair was wind-blown, her face radiant. She laid the little muff on the table.

"I'm sorry I was late. We were here by eleven, but we stood and talked."

Mother smiled. "Did you have a nice time?"

"Oh, scrumptious. We played 'Skip-to-My-Lou, and 'Two in the Boat.' And then charades. There's one I never could figger out. Tommy gets a Bible and puts a spud on it. Nobody could guess it. Then he says, 'A common tater on the Bible.' But that don't mean nothin'."

Mother got out a big volume that Father used when preparing his sermons. "See the title? That's a commentator on the Bible."

Sammy's face lighted. "That Tommy is awfully smart. And you'd ought to see how elegant he holds his coffee cup." She raised her hand with the little finger curved. "He's goin' to collitch and learn to be a doctor. He's a-tryin' to get Vela to go too, but she says she'd get too homesick."

"Vela's a timid girl," Mother said, "not very self-reliant."

"She's a sissy." Sammy kicked off her slippers and sat with her feet extended, wiggling her toes. "Tied to her ma's apron strings. If I had a wishy-washy like that, I'd give her a swift kick in the pants."

Mother poured each of us a cup of tea. "Ford Hamilton called. I asked him to wait until you came in, but he preferred to spend his time at the Betz House."

"Yeah," Sammy said nonchalantly. "There's usually a bunch of hands from Hamilton Ranch there on Friday and Saturday nights. Ford came as the party was breakin' up and walked home with us. Mrs. Mahoney will put him up for the night and he'll ride out with me tomorrow."

I could see that Mother was in a quandary, debating whether to tell Sammy about Ford or leave this to Father. Sammy poured her tea into her saucer and blew on it.

"I betcha I could go to collitch without the heebie-jeebies."

"Of course you could," Mother agreed.

Ford came the next morning, leading Sammy's sorrel, Alazan; and they took out over the prairie, their horses' hoofs kicking up little spurts of dust. We were standing in the doorway watching them when Mother said, "There comes your father."

We went out to meet him as he drove up to the shed.

Mother's voice was low and hoarse. "How is Harry?"

"It's all over. Brother Kelso is at the lumber yard having a coffin made. The funeral is set for tomorrow afternoon."

Father's eyes had great smudges beneath them and he moved like an old man, with drooping shoulders and unsure hands. After he had eaten he went into the front room and lay down.

"Wake me at noon," he said. "I've three sermons to prepare."

While he slept Mother tip-toed in and took the Prince Albert from the box couch. She measured the sleeves and pants legs by Father's old suit, then carefully whipped in new hems and pressed them.

Heretofore my experience at funerals had been limited to old people in whom I had small interest. But the funeral at the school-house that Sunday afternoon was different.

I sat beside Mother, resentful and rebellious, as people filled every seat and the spaces beside the walls. Others stood outside by the windows, holding their hats in their hands. Brother and Sister Kelso and Henry sat on folding chairs at the front, where they could almost reach out and touch the little coffin covered in black cloth. Upon it lay precious Boston and asparagus ferns, clipped from carefully tended pots on pedestals over town, and Chinese lilies and narcissus, cut from bowls filled with stones and water in which these flowers were grown.

Father stood at the head of the coffin and talked more to Brother and Sister Kelso than to the audience.

I could not listen well because I was occupied in looking at Father in the lustrous broadcloth Prince Albert. This week Father had been too busy to go to Brother Hipplehite, the barber, so Mother had clipped his hair. The top was longer and wavier than usual. His glasses pinched the bridge of his nose and were anchored to his coat by a tiny hook at the end of a fine gold chain. Father was handsome, and more, he was wise and smart. I couldn't figure how it was that God had him so fooled. It seemed to me Father was being deliberately blind to the dirty trick God had pulled on the Kelsos.

When Father had finished speaking, Brother Slade opened the lid of the casket and Brother and Sister Kelso and Henry stood beside it. Then Brother Kelso led his wife away. After that, we all went past the coffin. Little Harry lay in a plain box lined with white muslin, tacked into tucks at the corners. His fair hair made gold circles on the little pillow beneath his head. He wore black velvet pants and a short black velvet jacket over a white blouse with a ruffled collar. His dark lashes lay in small violet pools beneath his eyes, and his lids looked thin and stretched. Instead of lips bow-shaped and smiling around square new teeth, they now were straight and had a bruised look.

Back of the improvised hearse from Brother Craddock's lumber yard, the Kelsos rode in a livery stable rig, and Father drove behind them. There were seventeen hacks, surreys, buggies, and wagons, and many on horseback in the funeral cortege that traveled out the road toward old Chicago. There on a slope of higher ground was the cemetery, square and bare in its four-strand binding of barbed wire.

We stood about the heap of clay-colored dirt, and Father led the crowd in singing *In the Sweet Bye and Bye.*

There was a softness to the air and the sun seemed to float in it. Our shadows stretched out, long and grotesque, between the dozen graves scattered about with their weathered markers. I glanced at Brother Kelso. He wasn't listening to Father. He was looking across the bare cemetery, where no tree or shrub softened the bleak humps of earth, where only rusty strands of wire kept them from being trampled by the vandal feet of a thousand cattle in round-up season. There were lumps at the hinges of his jaws. His nostrils were stretched like a blowing horse.

Once more Brother Slade laid open the coffin. This time only Sister Kelso stepped forward. She stood with her hands clasped before her, looking at her baby for the last time. Swiftly she dropped to her knees.

"Baby," she said almost in a whisper, "we'll never leave you."

Brother Kelso reached down to lift her, but she rose without his assistance and motioned with her hand. Brother Slade closed the lid, and four men lowered the box with two ropes beneath it.

When the first spadeful of clods thudded on the box, Brother Kelso winced. But Sister Kelso gazed far to the west, where the purple edge of the horizon fused into the glow of a waning sun. She appeared not to hear the sound of the spades, and almost in a trance she let Brother Kelso lead her back to the buggy.

Mother went up to her and spoke. "Won't you-all come and have a little supper with us before you start home?"

"Oh!" For an instant she seemed to hang between her detached state and reality. "You've been so very kind—both of you. But we must go home—we've so much to do and so little time."

On the way home Mother said to Father, "Sister Kelso is a very exceptional woman."

"She is indeed."

"And now they'll probably need money more than ever."

"I think we have that figured out," Father said. "Brother Craddock heads the school board. I've talked to him and the board has agreed to give the school to Sister Kelso next year. She holds a first-grade certificate."

"That will leave us pretty short," Mother told him.

"I know. But now that Marjorie's arrival is paid for, we shouldn't require so much. The mission box has helped too. If I am to do the Lord's work, I owe it a full measure of devotion. Because of school duties, I've not visited some of our members since we came."

"I suppose your plan is for the best," Mother conceded. "Yet I don't see how Sister Kelso will manage about her home if she takes the school."

"She and Henry will ride back and forth morning and evening. During the worst weather, they can get a room at Mahoney's."

Mother nodded her head. "And on such a grueling schedule one can sublimate grief. But what of this summer?"

"There is the planting and tending of crops. All their farm work has been neglected these past weeks. Then Sister Kelso plans a refresher course of six weeks at the State Normal, which her uncle, T. P. Hamilton, has insisted on paying for."

Mother's head went back with a jerk. "So that's the kind of Scrooge T. P. Hamilton is. With all his money he pays for a measly summer school, so his niece can work herself into exhaustion for their necessities this winter."

"In addition," Father spoke quietly, "Mr. Hamilton has offered Brother Kelso a job for the winter when work is slack."

Mother's eyes flashed ultra-violet fire. "Profiting on their misfortunes. I loathe the whole tribe."

Father gave her a puzzled glance but said nothing.

Chapter Eight

I T seemed to me eminently unfair that both T. P. Hamilton and God should combine against the Kelsos. Life was so wrong that when we reached home I was tempted to leave Henny-Penny and Cocky-Doodle to the penalty of their own foolishness (which consisted of their daily escape from the pen which adequately held the larger chickens). If during the night the coyotes found them huddling under a clump of loco and made short work of them, it would serve them right.

But force of habit carried me out past Dr. Bachellor's house, with its shades drawn even before sundown, and on to the open prairie. The bantams, coming home of their own accord, looked at me smugly, as though I were the silly one, and made a beeline for home.

Suddenly the back door of the Bachellor house flew open and Sister Bachellor came tearing out with Dr. Bachellor but a few steps behind her. She turned and ducked and twisted, for all the world like Henny-Penny did when Cocky-Doodle chased her. But suddenly Dr. Bachellor made a quick leap, caught her to him, and held her for a long moment.

"Oh, Oliver," she gasped. "You're so strong."

He lifted her bodily and carried her into the house. Demure Sister Bachellor giggled and snuggled her face against his neck.

I had a squeamish feeling that I had witnessed something not intended for an audience, and the meaning of which escaped me. It added to the feeling of frustration and depression. Life was full of complexities and injustices that an eight-year-old could not understand.

Rather than go in the house and face Mother and Father, I sought the dim seclusion of the shed. Acting on the instinct to right a topsy-turvy world by inverting oneself, I crawled up into the buggy, lay down, and hoisted my feet up on the back of the seat.

It was here that Father found me. Hastily I assumed a more normal position as Father sat down beside me. For once I wasn't happy for companionship, preferring to nurse my misery alone.

"I'm tired too," Father said. "I'd like to run away and hide and just let everything go."

I was alarmed. "But you can't. You've got to preach tonight."

"There's no one to force me to," Father said.

"But what will people think?"

"I could pretend I was ill. If I pretended well enough, your mother would believe it and carry word to the people."

Something must be wrong for Father to suggest such a thing.

"But—that wouldn't be honest."

Father looked at me. "I guess I was mistaken. I thought you felt the same way."

I shook my head. "I'm just mad at God. He did the Kelsos a dirty trick, letting Harry die."

"It would seem so on the face of it," Father agreed, "but it is God's prerogative to give and to take away."

"Then He's an Indian giver," I said with conviction.

"Look at it this way. God gave Harry to the Kelsos. Inadvertently, they failed to protect him against all hazards. When a terrible accident befell him and life became untenable, God in His infinite mercy gathered Harry home to Him."

This sounded reasonable but did not exonerate God from ignoring my prayer.

"But God could have saved him," I mumbled.

"God is quite capable of producing miracles. We may not see why he did not choose to perform one in this case. But we can have faith that He knew best."

Faith did not prove the great shock-absorber for me that it seemed to be for Father. But there was nothing more to be done for Harry and there was still Father's unusual attitude to deal with. It was up to me to see that he did not renege on his evening service.

"I'm hungry," I said, and knew it for gospel truth. "If we get some hot victuals we'll feel better." I had Mother's oft-repeated advice as authority for this statement.

Father's tone was dubious. "It's barely possible—"

"Sure." I was crawling out of the buggy. "I'm starved. You probably are too and just don't know it."

"I believe you're right," Father agreed. He came around the buggy tongue, and this time I grabbed Father's hand and hurried him along with me.

Mother was setting supper on the table. Sammy was washing her face, and when she came to the table I saw that her eyes were red and swollen. During the meal she picked at her food in stony silence.

"Sammy," Mother said sharply, "if it's Ford Hamilton you've been crying over, you'd as well spare your tears. He's not worth them."

Father looked surprised. Sammy also was startled.

"Knowing the truth about him may save you a lot of pining. He spends his spare time at the Betz House—drinking and worse—"

Sammy stared. "But all the ranch hands get together in the

77

saloons on Saturday nights. There ain't no other place to go."

"The only people who frequent saloons are those who like them. But that might be condoned. The fact that he visits places where women are kept is a good bit less innocent, even if one is liberal on vice."

Sammy's chin dropped. "You mean that Ford goes to—"

"I'm sure you know what I mean." Mother clipped her words, "Quit moping over a man who's not fit to touch your finger."

"Your judgment may be a bit premature," Father suggested.

"It's neither premature nor erroneous. He told me himself that he was the man who visited us in Chicago and advised you to change the color of our curtains."

"But why shouldn't he do that?"

"You mean to tell me you knew it was he?" Mother demanded.

"Of course. But that doesn't explain—"

"It doesn't explain why you didn't advise Brother Severn what kind of man Ford Hamilton is. Or why you didn't apprize Sammy of his character. Sometimes"—Mother threw her hands outward—"I simply can't understand you."

"Then don't try. At least," Father added, "until you have calmed yourself enough to consider this dispassionately."

"Had Sammy known sooner, it might have saved heartache—"

"I ain't worryin' about Ford," Sammy said complacently.

Mother dropped into a chair. "Then for pity's sake, just what is ailing you?"

"I ain't been aimin' to tell nobody. I been lettin' myself go on plumb foolishness, but I just can't hep myself—"

"If it's important enough to cry over, it's important enough to try to settle in some becoming manner," Mother told her.

"It's Tommy Craddock," Sammy sniffled. "I'm sweet on him."

"Tommy Craddock!" Mother exclaimed. "But he's Vela's beau."

Sammy nodded vigorously. "That's the trouble. If I was a mind, I reckon I could take him away from her. But Tommy ought to have a lady, somebody educated and refined, and so—" Sammy's voice gave out, then she broke into a loud wail. "I reckon I just got to let her have him—" She shoved her chair back so violently it toppled over and crashed on the floor. Sammy flung herself on the bed, and sobs beat up and down inside her like a dasher in a churn.

Mother and Father looked at each other. Then Mother got up and sat on the bed beside Sammy. She began in a calm and soothing way to talk to her.

She didn't think Sammy foolish, she told her. In fact, Sammy had the solution to her problem within her grasp. It would take Tommy six or seven years to become a doctor and establish a practice. In that time Sammy could become exactly the kind of girl he needed.

She explained then how Father would give extra instruction so that Sammy could enter the academy in the fall. If she worked hard she could finish college by the time Tommy got his M.D. Mother painted a fine picture of an ambitious young man and the lady of his choice working side by side in a place like La Mesa, where doctors were so vitally needed. Sammy listened as one entranced.

Father broke the spell by snapping open the lid on his gold watch and announcing that it was time we went to church.

As we picked our way along the path to the schoolhouse, Sammy pointed to Deacon Webb's team, hobbled and now a goodly distance out on the darkening prairie.

"If I was Brother Webb, I'd be a-keepin' them horses close to home. Chances are the Slothower boys'll get 'em."

"The Slothower boys?" Father said sharply.

"Sure. I saw 'em on my way in from the ranch. They got a string of first-rate horses, and 'tain't likely they bought 'em all."

"Suppose we go out and look over their stock after school to-morrow," Father suggested.

"But you've got a good team," Mother protested.

"I know," Father said, "but the kind of driving I do, I need younger, tougher horses."

"Them Slothower boys will skin you out of your eye teeth if they get half a chance," Sammy told him.

"Not with you to advise me," Father replied.

After school on Monday I watched longingly while Father saddled Count, and he and Sammy and Nelson went off to see the Slothower boys. It was dark when they returned. At supper

Father informed us that the Slothower boys had an exceptionally good young team for sale. Sammy substantiated him.

"And those high-strung horses will probably run away and tear the buggy all to pieces every time a paper blows by," Mother commented.

"They're young," Sammy said, "and I reckon they ain't too gentle. But that long trip to Seminole and back will do a lot toward steadyin' them if they're driven right. They ain't heavy, ain't got no spavins nor fistulas; they ain't got no galled shoulders nor sore withers, and they ain't too tough-mouthed."

"How do you know they aren't balky, or won't stand up in the harness and fall over backward, or run under tree limbs?" Mother asked.

"We don't know," Father told her. "But should I get them, we'll likely find out very shortly."

Sammy had a faraway look in her eyes. "They're shore pretty. Matched light bays—mighty near sorrel; Spanish and steel-dust. And I ain't dumb enough to believe that tale Lem Slothower told about findin' them half-starved in a pocket of Palo Dura Canyon and gettin' them out."

"You don't think they might be stolen?" Mother asked.

"I don't think anybody is goin' to find out anything but what the Slothowers want 'em to. That's their story and they'll stick to it."

Mother turned to Father. "But would you want them?"

"Indeed I do." Father's tone was more than positive. "And I'm going to find some way to get them, other than trading them my team."

I saw Mother's face take on that resigned look.

When left to their own devices, the ladies of the church sometimes showed strange ingenuity for arrangements. On Wednesday afternoon the Ladies Aid was to meet with one of the farmers several miles from town. Mother hitched up Prince and Count and took them over to Sister Craddock's, where a new phaeton sat in the shed.

Father and Sammy and I had supper ready when Mother came in. She looked all tuckered out and sank on the bed beside Marjorie.

"You must have been one of the casualties of the feline foray today," Father chided.

"I'm exhausted listening to Sister Craddock prate about illustrious ancestors and fine family. You'd think nothing a man said or did or was mattered one whit. Only the stock from which he sprang. She wants to establish a chapter of the United Daughters of the Confederacy now."

"What's stopping her? There ought to be plenty of 'jiners.'"

"She can't establish their eligibility. She's flabbergasted that women don't carry their genealogies in their diaper satchels."

"Don't they?" Father inquired. "Sandwiched in between the teething rings and tea cakes?"

Mother ignored this. "Are you still determined to buy that pair of wild horses from the Slothowers?"

"I'm going back to see them tomorrow."

Mother sighed. "I have a buyer for Prince and Count." She was looking at Father with the shy and expectant expression she sometimes had.

Father's eyes became big and black. "You have? But who—I've scoured the town. How in the world did you find one?"

Mother shrugged a trifle. "I just picked a logical prospect and worked on her. I gave her an excellent demonstration."

"You mean—" There was more than admiration in Father's eyes.

Mother nodded. "Sister Craddock. She had about settled on a team in Big Spring. But I convinced her that Prince and Count were much better. She's coming over in the morning to buy them from you. I asked a good stiff price—more than enough to buy those Slothower horses."

"How much?" Father asked.

"One hundred and fifty dollars," Mother stated flatly. "And don't you cut it a penny. They are worth fifty dollars more than that pair of wild ponies you are so set on getting."

"Splendid." Father rubbed his hands together. "I was confident that some way or another it could be done—but just how escaped me."

Mother got up and shook her skirts. "For the life of me I don't see why you want to change horses."

I looked to Father for some adequate explanation, but on his face was an enigmatic expression that I knew never evolved into words.

Sister Craddock was there bright and early the next morning and persuaded Father to take one hundred and fifty dollars for his team and make delivery immediately. Father rented a horse from the livery stable, and that afternoon after school he and Sammy made another trip out to see the horse-swappers. They came back just before dark leading the two young horses, and stabled them in the shed.

"What are their names?" I asked Father.

"Flush and Straight—not exactly appropriate names for a preacher's nags. Suppose you and Sammy rename them."

Sammy and I undertook this assignment with all the seriousness of a young couple naming their first baby. We finally settled on two short names, suggesting high-born Spanish ancestry: Duke and Don.

The possession of a nice driving team proved another step upward in Sister Craddock's social climb. Day after day she could be seen driving the spanking team and shiny phaeton about the town and over the surrounding country on various errands. Father finally mentioned it.

"I assume we'll soon have a flourishing U.D.C. in La Mesa."

"I think not," Mother replied. "I understand Sister Craddock had to abandon that. Too few had proper credentials."

"It's probably just as well not to divide the community into pedigreed and non-pedigreed camps."

Mother nodded. "From what I hear, Sister Craddock only transferred her recruiting talents to some other organization not requiring genealogies. I've not yet learned the name of it."

At that moment Sammy burst into the room and tossed off her sunbonnet and jacket. "You know what? Me and Tommy Craddock's a-goin' for a ride. I been a-tellin' him what I was goin' to do and he's strong for it. I got to get in a lot of good licks 'fore I go 'way."

"Wouldn't it be better to let Tommy do the courting?" asked Mother. "Men like to make the advances—or so I've been told."

"I ain't got time." Sammy grabbed up her jeans and shirt. "I got to cinch him while that there weak-kneed Vela's still staggerin' around like a locoed calf, tryin' to make up her little mind."

Sammy ducked into the other room and we heard her stamping into her boots. Then she was through the room like a whirlwind, waving to us from the back door. "Adios. See you at chuck."

I dashed out after Sammy. Tommy was waiting on Prince, holding Alazan's reins. Sammy swung into the saddle and I watched them riding along slowly, talking together, laughing, until a curve in the trail brought the pest house between them and me.

Suddenly, with no specific reason except perhaps one of the unaccountable moods of childhood, I felt lonely. Very, very lonely. I could not ride. Since Prince had dumped me into the prickly pears, not one of us had suggested another trial. And now we no longer had him. That he was amenable to being ridden was being demonstrated by Tommy. And I had lost my chance.

All the bitter dislike that had assailed me the day we ascended the cap rock and caught our first staggering view of this great sweep of borderless land, came back to me now. Six months we had been on the Llano Estacado and the country was no different. Not a tree worthy of the name graced the knotty fabric of the ground. Never a brook or a pool of clear blue water, or a shady spot where grass grew green and soft. Every indigenous plant of any size bore spines and thorns. In order to exist, small animals must take refuge underground. A child dared not wander more than a few yards from home lest he become hopelessly lost. To drop exhausted made one a living sacrifice to the fierce red ants, whose gravelly mounds were never more than a few yards apart. In this harsh land what chance did an ugly, awkward child have ever to be anything but ugly and awkward?

I looked down at Nelson, sitting gingerly on his tail, intently watching the riders that had reappeared beyond the pest house. His body quivered, his nose twitched, his ears moved in response to scents and sounds I could not detect. I put my hand on his head.

One gesture of companionship and all the whispers on the breath of the wind, all the clues to the secret life of the Great Plains were forgotten. Nelson bounded to his feet, his tail beat the breeze, and his tongue lolled as his eyes begged for the intimate little journey we often took about town just before supper.

I moved to the corner of the house to gauge the height of the sun. There was still an hour before its fire would go below the rim of the prairie, and for another half hour its glow would paint the wisps of clouds across the sky.

"Come on, Nelson," I said.

"May I join you?"

It was Father speaking. I was so pleased I could only stammer my answer.

"I think it would be nice—I mean—"

"Thank you," Father said. "Which way shall we go?"

"Could we—kind of go close to the pest house?"

Only with Father would I dare go near the square little structure of cheap box-siding resembling an overgrown outhouse. Ghoulish tales of lonely and horrible deaths there, intimations that the tormented victims still haunted the tiny house with its one window and closed door, had scared me away up to now.

"Of course," Father said. "I doubt if we can enter, as the town health officer has the key."

"I don't want to go in," I hastened to say. "Is it true that when anyone gets smallpox or bubonic plague they lock him in and leave him until he dies?"

"Of course not," Father said impatiently. "Whoever told you such things?"

"All the children say so," I affirmed. "Ora and Dora say they've heard them screaming."

"I doubt that," Father said.

With Father I was not afraid to go to the window and look through the pane. Inside there was an iron bed, a table, a stove, and shelves upon one wall. Everything was immaculately clean. Father explained that when a case of contagious disease—more virulent than the ordinary childhood variety—appeared, the victim was removed to the pest house. The family furnished bedding, which after death or recovery was burned and the place completely fumigated. In a shed lean-to at the back the patient's nurse or attendant changed clothes before entering or upon leaving, and disinfected himself with carbolic acid and water.

"These wild tales you've heard," Father said, "are completely false. I assume that parents have used drastic measures to keep the children away. But patients get the best care available—and often the town is spared an epidemic."

"Do people often get smallpox, and do they always die?" I asked tremulously.

"It is rare in communities like this. And more recover than die." Father looked down at me, smiling from one side of his mouth. "Unfortunately the world is full of distorted information. Sometimes it is difficult to sift out the truth from exaggerations or distinguish it from pure fabrication."

"But how can you tell?" I wanted to know.

"You can't, but you can reserve judgment until you have more information, or await developments."

Knowing Father, I thought perhaps he had in mind Ford Hamilton. Father seemed to like Ford in spite of his going to a saloon and mistaking our home for a fancy house. Or perhaps he referred to Wes Enright, for I was sure Father had not yet reached the conclusion that he murdered his wife. Or it could be that he was waiting to learn who was making it unpleasant for Deacon Webb's family—even going so far as not to invite Link to a party—because Deacon Webb was a Republican.

I didn't ask him, because it might have spoiled the pleasure of the walk we had together.

Chapter Nine

DINNER was over and Father and Brother Dissey had moved into the front room. Since this was only the second of Brother Dissey's visits, we were yet to learn that with the regularity of moon changes and tides, each month would bring us Brother Dissey.

The day was pleasant for May and the dinner with a young cottontail as *pièce de résistance* was excellent. As Mother and I did the dishes, I began singing in an exuberant soprano:

"Jesus wants me for a sunbeam,
To shine for Him each day—"

Mother took her hand from the dishpan and tweaked my sleeve. "Shine silently and listen."

Brother Dissey was speaking. "What this town needs is a good, old-fashioned revival. Saturday night the saloon is filled and Sunday morning the church is empty."

"I realize that," Father agreed. "Since Adolph Betz put in free lunches, the saloon has done a land-office business."

"Then go him one better. Have all-day services and picnic dinners, Bible stories for the children, and song services for the young folks. The whole countryside will attend."

"We couldn't accommodate the whole countryside."

"With a brush arbor you could. The field is white unto the harvest. Unless you strike while the iron is hot, you haven't a leg to stand on. Unless this wave of ungodliness is stamped out, your church will fall by the wayside." Brother Dissey's metaphors may have been mixed, but his stand was firm, with a fist on the table for emphasis.

Father spoke. "A revival loses much of its value unless the converts are baptized into the church. All the lakes and tanks are dry. There's been practically no rain this spring."

Brother Dissey had an answer for everything. "Where is your faith, Brother? What human hands cannot accomplish, the Lord will provide. We must trust him to fill the lakes and tanks to overflowing before the revival ends."

As though it were a settled fact, Brother Dissey launched into the financial aspects of the enterprise. He regretted that he could not donate his services to the Lord, but since of necessity he must live in order to serve, he would labor in our midst for the meager sum of one-third of the money raised plus his board and keep. At this juncture Mother sighed. I saw that familiar look of resignation on her face.

When Father came in from seeing off Brother Dissey, Mother was at the washstand, scrubbing her face and neck.

"Are you going to let that windbag browbeat you into accepting his help in conducting a revival?"

Father smiled. "It's as possible as being browbeaten by a wind-bag. I couldn't possibly do it all myself."

The red on Mother's face was not wholly due to the scrubbing.

"It's easy enough for him to suggest building an arbor. He won't do any of the work. Easy to trust that it will rain, but that doesn't always bring one."

Father's eyes twinkled. "Sometimes we have to take our own medicine. You won't mind gulping down a little faith, will you, Mama?"

"Then I suppose it's all settled on a blind assumption."

"Not quite," Father said. "I'm taking a week to reach a de-cision unbiased by personal dislike—I hope."

Mother sighed. "I don't know how we'll feed him, now that school is out and you've no longer that extra money. You ought to give him half and let him board himself."

"That's not the Christian spirit," Father reproved.

"Perhaps not. But we haven't had the increase in salary we had expected at the end of six months."

"We won't even have a salary if my September report shows a decline in attendance, as it does now."

Mother combed her long, tan hair before the oak-bound mir-ror and coiled it smoothly on top of her head. I noticed how blue her eyes looked after she put on the blue chambray. As she placed pillows about Marjorie in the little red wagon, she gave me final household instructions, for it was Ladies Aid day.

"It's possible that some of the ladies who live far away might come home with me for an early supper. If you get out your paper dolls, see that they are put away and the house is neat."

But I was preoccupied thinking of Father, the hardships and worries of this mission field (that had brought furrows to his high forehead and flecks of white above his temples), and the wist-ful look so often in his eyes.

"Pay attention to me, Opal," Mother snapped.

When Mother had gone I dumped the contents of my shoebox of paper dolls on the floor. Lest a vagrant breeze scatter them, I got up to close the door and saw two odd-looking creatures approaching the house. Upon closer scrutiny they proved to be

Ora and Dora Slade, decked out in their mother's and Vela's discarded finery.

Plump, blonde Dora bosomed out a blue taffeta waist and also wore a green velvet pancake hat with mothy ostrich tips and a red calico skirt salvaged from some Hallowe'en costume. Ora, dark and gangling, was in a plaid basque, a blue Merry Widow sailor with a ragged willow plume, and a transparent black voile skirt without benefit of petticoat.

"Dress up and come with us," Ora invited. "The 'Flying F' outfit is camped across Lobo Creek. We'll go watch them."

From the box couch where winter clothes were stored I took Father's Prince Albert and Mother's dolman and toque and laid them on the bed. Father's red flannels I tossed on the floor, along with a worn corset belonging to Mother, a bustle, and some ruffled bust pads. The plum-colored redingote, black lace mitts, and pink wool fascinator with its top-knot of bugle beads comprised my costume.

We skirted the town and crossed Lobo below the ford. From the top of the draw we could see the "Flying F" camped in a dip of rolling land. Four chuck wagons drawn up in a semicircle, their backs toward a smouldering fire, formed the nucleus. Cow hands were lounging about, heads on saddles, or leaning against the wagons rolling "coffin nails." A dozen ponies grazed to the back of a big tarpaulin. We edged down the draw, watching the two cooks do things with iron skillets and Dutch ovens. One cowboy walked up the creek, possibly seeking to augment the pile of wood by the fire.

"Looky!" Ora pointed to a man who had swung a guitar cord over his shoulder and was idly picking the strings. We huddled down by a mesquite. As his twanging gathered form, his roving eyes picked out our bright colors on the slope. He motioned us to come down.

As we trailed down the slope one cowboy left the group and gave the wagon wheel a savage kick. The others broke into uproarious laughter. The one with the guitar spoke.

"You kids are diked out fit for a rodeo. You look mighty toney."

Dora twisted her fingers into her red skirt. "We're playing grown-ups. Our mothers are at Ladies Aid."

A cook squatting by the fire looked up. "Y'all church folks?"

"Yes," Dora piped up. "This is Opal, the preacher's daughter."

Confusion seized me. I pulled at the pink fascinator until the bugle beads caught in my hair. The guitar cowboy loosed them.

> *"There was a little girl an' she had a little curl,*
> *'Way down in de middle of her forehead,*
> *An' when she was good she was mighty, mighty good,*
> *An' when she was bad she was horrid,"*

he chanted.

"Dal sings every night till the coyotes drown him out," the cook said. "Tonight he won't have the chancet, so let him get it outen his system."

We crumpled on the dry grass while Dal fiddled with the guitar strings and sang in a pleasant, nasal tone. It was nice watching the plume of smoke from the fire break into ruffles and float away on the lazy breeze. Nice to look at the long, lean young man with the melancholy eyes and big hat pushed far back on his brown head.

And then a disgruntled voice said, "I got the badger." It was the cowboy who had wandered away and now stood tapping a large box under his arm. He tossed his cigarette into the fire and turned to the cook. "Why in hell don't you chase them off? They ain't fancy women like we first thought."

Ora's screams brought us to our feet. She was dancing up and down, frantically shaking her mother's voluminous skirt. It had undoubtedly touched an ant hill, for ants were swarming all over her. Dal picked her up, threw the skirt over her head, and brushed the ants off her legs and panties. Above the cowboys' laughter came an angry voice from the slope above.

"Ora! Dora! Come here this minute."

It was Vela—her buttercup hair fluffed by the wind, her head held high and haughty. Anger made her even prettier than usual.

Dal took us up the slope on the double, then lagged. Vela's eyes were round and dark as heliotrope. She seemed to have forgotten us and saw only Dal, turning his big hat slowly in his hands.

"Please don't scold them, ma'am," Dal begged. "We was all enjoyin' their visit. I'd like to return it someday, if I may—"

89

For an instant Vela's face lightened, then she stiffened.

"I—I don't believe I know you."

This snuffed the light out of Dal's eyes. He looked down.

"I beg your pardon, ma'am. I do for a fact."

Vela's prissiness seemed silly to me. I pinched Dal's arm.

"Maybe if you would come to church some Sunday," I said.

Vela stared at me, turned on Dal one shining, hopeful look, grabbed Ora and Dora by their arms, and yanked them up the slope. Like Lot's profligate wife, I had to look back. Dal waved his hat.

"See you in church," he called.

The Slades and I had no more than parted company when I noticed a team at our pump and recalled Mother's warning about company. Vividly came the picture of the yellowed old corset draped over a chair and the confusion of clothing scattered over the room.

I hurried into the house. Across the hot stove Mother glared at me coldly. "You left things in a pretty mess, I must say. Get off those ridiculous things before Sister Falloon sees you. You're a sight to behold."

But it was too late, for in the doorway to the front room stood little, compact Sister Falloon, with brawny, red-haired Brother Falloon looking over her shoulder. He exploded with a booming laugh.

"Howly mither! So ye dressed up and called on the cowboys."

The lobes of my ears burned. "But—how did you know?"

"I spotted ye goin' over as I was comin' back to town."

Mother gasped. "How could you do such a thing?"

"Leave her be." Brother Falloon's voice shook the thin walls. "Kids got to have their fun. What did the boys have to say?"

"They thought we were fancy women," I said proudly.

"Opal, for heaven's sake—" Mother's mouth hung open.

Brother Falloon had a fit of coughing, then boomed back at me, "I guess ye did look pretty fancy. 'Twas a foine diligation ye made. I'll see that they return the favor someday."

"Are they—your boys?" I asked.

"Sure," he answered. "The 'Flyin' F's' my outfit. They're on the way to Amarillo to drive back a herd of white-faces."

"I liked Dal the best," I told him. "He sang for us."

"Sure, an' he would. A foine lad, that. Best foreman I ever had: But 'tis lonesome he is since our Kate got herself engaged. 'Tis a cryin' shame we've not another girrul for him." Brother Falloon dropped a quarter in my palm. "Before ye take off them pretty flub-dubs, go down and ask Sim Webb for some peppermint sticks to sweeten up the sour reception the women folks gave you."

Mother nodded consent. Brother Falloon's laugh followed me down the path toward the store.

Deacon Webb was amused at my appearance. Lest he disapprove of my extravagance I was about to explain the quarter's origin when a customer came in and engaged him in conversation.

"Yes," I heard Deacon Webb say. "One of the 'Flying F' boys came and bought a—" He lowered his voice. "Probably a badger fight back of the saloon and end up by shooting up the town."

I intended relaying this news to Brother Falloon, but when I got home he and Father were conversing earnestly and I dared not interrupt.

"They must be very expensive," Father remarked.

"Faith, an' what isn't that's good?" Brother Falloon asked. "And how can one stand to gain unless he risks?"

"One must have the courage of his convictions," Father said.

" 'Tis of the future I'm thinkin'. For many years the cattlemen have driven the range cattle to market with nivver a thought to replacin' them. The Texas longhorn is vanishin' fast through ill treatment and unwise slaughter. 'Tis a sad state our children will come into unless we rebuild the herds, with better cattle than the wild ones, producin' more and better beef for the feeding of them."

"I agree with you," Father said.

"Such as yourself would be agreein', but even my own bairn Sam was of the mind to oppose the spendin' of so much money on a project nivver as yet tested and proven."

"Sam's a fine, conservative young man," Father said.

"That he is, Father Berryman, and I give heed to his opinions. But no man who cannot master his own family when he is convinced a thing is for their benefit is worthy of the name."

Knowing Brother Falloon, I was certain he would always be

the complete master of any situation he undertook. I had heard Mother say that Sister Falloon depended entirely upon her husband for all decisions of importance. She seemed a little vague and helpless when he was not about.

"But one thing has held me back," Brother Falloon continued, "and that is that it may be the cause of grave trouble."

"You mean—"

"The rustlin'. Always there is some of it goin' on. Ranchers with big herds of range cattle do not find it profitable to hunt down the small rustlers and come to grips with them. It must be proven, and a few stock now and then are not worth the trouble. But with blooded cattle, every lost cow means much, and several of them runs into money. I have been loath to encourage trouble."

"And still," Father said, "one should not encourage a thief because he indulges only in petty thievery."

" 'Tis right you are, Father Berryman. We only invite them to our land when we make it easy for them, and someday our own children will bear the hardships we have laid up for them."

"I wonder," Father said thoughtfully, "if perhaps you ranchers could not get together and plan a course of vigilance that would make it difficult for the rustlers to make off with your stock. Perhaps the trouble could be avoided rather than coped with after it has arisen."

There was admiration on Brother Falloon's red face. "Of course, Father Berryman, that we could. 'Tis a sin I've been committing not to have consulted with my priest before this. 'Tis your advice I've been needin' all the while."

Sister Falloon poked her head timidly inside the door and asked if they shouldn't be starting for home. Only after they had gone did I remember I had not told Brother Falloon about what I heard at the store.

As Mother was undressing Marjorie, Father came and laid a twenty-dollar bill on the table before her. Mother's eyes widened.

"Where on earth did it come from?"

"Brother Falloon," Father said. "For the Lord's work."

"A new suit for you, shoes for the children, perhaps even new curtains—" Mother's face shone in the lamplight.

"For the Lord's work," Father reminded her gently.

"What—what kind of work did you have in mind?"

"It would help us to feed Brother Dissey," Father suggested.
"Oh." Mother's voice fell. "I suppose it would."

It must have been well past midnight when we were awakened
by what sounded like a band of attacking Indians. Marjorie, who
slept with me now that school was out and Sammy gone home
to the Severn ranch for the summer, whimpered, then cried out
sharply. Mother appeared like a ghost in her long, white nightgown.

"Lie still, children," she soothed. "Father says it's only the cowboys on a rampage." She took Marjorie in her lap. I listened wide-
eyed to the pounding hoofs, the blood-curdling yells, and the
volleys of shots. Father went to the door, peered out into the
night.

"Be careful," Mother warned. "And to think Opal was with that
gang of outlaws. It's a wonder she ever got back alive."

Father slammed the door. "They're not fiends. They'd not
harm a child. It's as Brother Falloon said, they're all good boys.
It's the whiskey that induces such devilment."

There was a thud on the roof, then another. A shingle slid
down and hit the ground. After that the shots and yells dwindled
into the distance and all was quiet again.

"That saloon," Father said, "is so near the bank of the creek
that sometimes I'm tempted to push it down with the rest of the
garbage. But that wouldn't solve anything. Tomorrow I'll see
what we can do about arrangements for a revival meeting."

Chapter Ten

FOR Father there was no turning back once he had set his
hand to the plow. I went with him to call on Brother Craddock at the lumber yard to ask the loan of lumber for
timbers, benches, and rostrum. Brother Craddock hooked his
thumbs in his belt as he listened to Father.

"Sure," he agreed, "I'm fer it, hide and hair. We got to keep this town clean. If we ever let scallywags in, then we got a tough job gettin' them out. Looks like we already got a few, and it's high time we was rootin' 'em out, tooth and toenail."

I thought Father was a little taken aback, since his idea was not to drive the cowpunchers out of town but to impress on them the value of good conduct and maintaining order. But Father thanked Brother Craddock, and we went on to the wagon yard where the freighters put up for the night. They agreed to donate one day each week to cutting and hauling brush from the breaks below the cap rock.

The greatest difficulty was in obtaining permission to erect an arbor. None of the townspeople wanted the grass trampled from the prairie, leaving dust to be whirled about all summer. While Deacon Webb and Brother Slade endorsed it, Judge Pothast preferred to remain neutral—which was logical, since he spent much of his time in the back room of the Betz House playing "42." Father finally presented the problem at church on Sunday and Brother Falloon offered his land across Lobo Creek.

He suggested that the arbor he built at the top of the rise. In case his outfit came back while the meeting was in progress they could camp again in the same spot and disturb no one. They could use the old fire sites again and thus spoil no more range. This arrangement met with general approval, since the arbor would not be near enough to annoy, yet would be within walking distance of the town.

After church I looked for Dal, until I remembered that the "Flying F" was well on its way to Amarillo. Again I saw Ford Hamilton at the back, but by the time I got out of the church he had disappeared. Since Ora and Dora had asked me to Sunday dinner I dashed home in order to get out of my Sunday duds and into a play dress. My white dotted swiss and embroidery-trimmed petticoat were tossed on the bed and I was down to panties and panty-waist when the front door swung open. I ducked under the bed.

Father had someone with him. I peeked from under the edge of the blue peacock counterpane and saw a man's feet. Lying there, I was sweating, scarcely daring to breathe, and the homespun rug that had come in the mission box began to eat holes in my skin.

"Have a chair, Ford. We've a few minutes before my wife comes in. What was it you wanted to discuss with me?"

I could see the toes of Ford's boots hooked around the chair legs. "Well, Reverend, some lousy hombre wrote a letter to my dad and spilled his guts about me being sweet on Sammy."

"Do you know the guilty one?" Father asked.

"I'm fair certain it was Slim Breedlove, her pa's foreman. He's sweet on Sammy himself."

"What was your father's reaction to this news?"

"He wrote me a letter sayin' to get myself home pronto."

"And are you going?"

"That's what I wanted to talk to you about," Ford said.

I could stand the terrible prickling of the rug no longer. Even if they heard me, I had to turn over on my stomach.

"If I go, that wall-eyed son of a gun gets my gal. If I don't, the governor says he'll disinherit me."

"How old are you, Ford?" Father inquired.

"Nineteen, sir. I'd finished high school and was goin' to Baylor last fall, but I got to coughin' and dad sent me out here. I like ranchin'. I been figurin' someday I'd be able to run the Hamilton Ranch for dad."

"I see no reason for you to give up your plans. I'd go back home as your father requests. Go to school this coming fall. You can spend your summers out here."

"Then I lose Sammy," Ford protested. "She's not too hot on me the way it is, and if I vamoose then she forgets me."

"Sammy's barely sixteen. I think she realizes she is neither old enough nor wise enough to make a successful marriage. She has indicated to us that she intends to go to the academy in the fall. I don't think you jeopardize your chances with her by furthering your education."

"I dunno." Ford's tone was disconsolate. "Since she came home she's been actin' plumb cool to me. I guess I don't savvy women."

By this time I had to turn on my back again. My elbows felt raw and each knee was being bored to the bone.

"What was that?" Ford asked.

"Probably a warped piece of shiplapping," Father said. "When the heat hits us, these flimsy houses crack in a dozen places."

Ford laughed. "Guess I'm jumpy as an old maid. Sounded to me like somebody under the bed."

"I've been wanting to ask you," Father said, "just why you came to our house in Chicago that night. Did you really think because of the red lights in the window that it was a house of ill repute?"

"Yes, sir, Slim really did," Ford replied. "Slim Breedlove dared me to go. He razzed me every time we got to town. Called me a mama's boy and a tenderfoot that was scared of his own shadow. I called his bluff. I figured I could sit an' play the player-piano. He said they always had one with a nickel slot in it."

"Could you have resisted temptation with this man prodding you into it?" Father asked.

"Say, listen—" Ford's voice bordered on anger. "I ain't never been drunk in my life and lots of scalawags have tried to egg me into it. And I ain't tinkerin' with no loose women. I got too much self-respect."

I closed my eyes. I even forgot the biting rug.

Ford chuckled. "But the way it turned out, I kind of thought it was a pretty good joke on both of us."

"On me, yes," Father admitted. "But it didn't turn out so well for you. The women got wise to it, which might account for Sammy's chilly attitude since she went home."

"Well I'll be dog-goned," Ford exclaimed. "I told your wife myself. It wasn't nothin' to be ashamed of."

"Women aren't very tolerant of philandering men," Father said.

"And a good thing they ain't," Ford replied, "or we'd be a darned sight worse than we are." Ford pushed back his chair. "I'm goin' to tell Sammy the truth and she can take it or leave it. Then I'll hit for home. When I get back she'll marry me or there'll be hell a-poppin'."

"I think that's a logical decision." Father followed him to the door. "Let me know when you get back."

"Thanks, Reverend. You've been a lot of help to both Sammy and me, and I ain't one to forget it. Good-by."

"Good-by, Ford, and God bless you." Father closed the door and then said, "You can come out now, Opal. Our guest has departed."

I rolled out from under the bed. "How did you know I was there?" I stood like a scrawny manikin in panties and waist.

"Your dress, slippers, and underskirt are on the bed. One usually finds the denuded rose close by the fallen petals. Had Ford been more woman-wise, he too would have guessed."

I looked down my nose. "He uses terrible language."

"On the contrary, his language was quite succinct."

"Do you think he told the truth?" I asked.

"Absolutely. Now wouldn't it be a good idea for you to get into some clothes before we have another guest and you have to spend the afternoon in retirement?"

Each morning, Monday through Friday, Father went with one or another of the freighters to cut and load timber and brush in the breaks at the foot of the cap rock. Each evening Nelson and I stood on the bank of Lobo Creek watching the lengthening stack of brush in the dip of land on the opposite side, as Father and the freighters unloaded the wagons. Nelson's eagerness to join the activity expressed itself in tense shiverings and sharp yelps, climaxed by a veritable frenzy when we joined the workers as they crossed the creek.

Brother Dissey was back at the end of the week for Father's decision. Father advised him of the arrangements. Vela Slade was to move in with Ora and Dora in order to give him her room. He was to eat his meals with us.

"Praise the Lord," Brother Dissey exclaimed, "and all that is within me, bless His holy name. Where there's a will, the Lord will provide the way." Filled with phrases of celestial gratitude and one of Mother's excellent meals, Brother Dissey went on his way rejoicing and Father went back to work on the arbor.

Pondering Brother Dissey's words, it seemed to me that it was Father who had provided the way. And even more credit was due him in the days that followed, as he and Brother Slade built the arbor. The Slade girls and I shared this phase of the project, taking lunches to the workers and romping over the new benches. Watching Father lest he disapprove of this unladylike conduct, I saw how tired he looked. His hair lay in wet ringlets above his white brow. His fine, shapely hands were scratched and scarred.

Blood clotted about one nail. He worked so hard for so small a reward. I slumped a-straddle of a new pine bench.

"I do hope it will be a fine meeting," I said to Dora.

Dora shrugged. "There ought to be two from it."

"Only two converts?" I exclaimed.

"No, silly. Weddings. We always get one or two weddings from a pertracted meeting. If it's real good, we might get three."

"But who would get married?"

"Vela's old enough. Her hair's done up and she wears pointed-toed shoes. She's been castin' sheep's eyes at the boys."

Such exciting possibilities intrigued me beyond sympathy for Father. "Brother Falloon says Kate has gotten herself engaged."

Dora nodded. "To John Ellis. He works in Judge Pothast's office. He looks like pictures of ole Abe Lincoln—only younger."

Ora too had ideas. "Jim Mahoney and Link Webb are nearly old enough. And Sam Falloon. Wonder why it is most everybody is boys?"

"There's Sammy and Rose Mahoney," I said.

"They ain't hardly old enough," Dora scoffed. "And look at all the cow hands over the country. Wonder what they're all goin' to do for girls to get married to?"

I had no solution to offer for a problem very common in the West at that time.

So engrossed were we in the building of the arbor that for several days we were unaware of one of the most significant phases of the town's development. A doctor had come to La Mesa, a small, swarthy man with a clipped black mustache and bluish cheeks. He wore dapper clothes and had taken up residence at the Mahoney boarding house. His name was Dr. Nasib Mesropian, and we first met him at church. Father learned that he was a member of an Armenian Baptist Church in an eastern city and welcomed him cordially. From the first meeting Father and Dr. Mesropian took pleasure in each other's company. Mother attributed it to the fact that so few of the townspeople were their educational and intellectual equals.

But on days when Father and I went early for the mail and stopped by Dr. Mesropian's little office at Mahoney's, they did not discuss intellectual subjects but talked of things like scalding dishes, heating milk almost to boiling before children drank it, and how to eradicate flies. It was when Dr. Mesropian asked Father if he thought the people would send their children periodically for health check-ups that I began to be frightened. I wanted no association with the shiny instruments in his wall cabinet or the long, triangular tubes with the funneled end that sometimes hung about his neck.

"This is a great and growing land," he said to Father one day. "We must see to it that mental and social advances keep pace with the material advances it is bound to make."

Conversations in Deacon Webb's store at mail time seemed to bear out Dr. Mesropian's opinion. Many La Mesa citizens now considered the time ripe to put on pressure for the railroad. So far, neither our population nor our rainfall had been sufficient to convince the railroads that a line through this section would be profitable.

In order to hasten the day, a big business man up north had begun trying to make rain scientifically. Mr. Post, manufacturer of a new ready-to-eat breakfast food named Elijah's Manna, had several thousand tons of explosives delivered to his ranch northeast of us at Post City. Day after day throughout the long, hot summer, we could hear low rumblings and feel the ground quiver beneath us. Mr. Post believed that rain could be produced by systematic bombardment of the heavens. Citizens interspersed business with sky-scanning as thunderheads rose by noon and vanished before sundown. All one Friday we had signs of impending rain, signs that for once lasted through the night. On Saturday morning the skies still bore a malignant aspect, but that fact did not deter Father from leaving on his bi-monthly trip to Seminole.

By early afternoon the muddy yellow pillow supporting a great purple mass to the northwest smothered the sun. Returning from an errand to Deacon Webb's store, I found Mother fastening the windows and bolting the front door. There was a peculiar quiet in the air and a thick, dusty smell. All outdoors looked tan from the mustard-colored cloud. Mother went out, made fast the shed door, opened the chicken pen, and was herding our flock of young fryers inside, when suddenly the wind hit. It caught under the chickens' long wing-feathers, turned them wrong side out like umbrellas, and took them whither it listed. Mother's skirts skinned backward, and with her hair streaming she barely got inside the back door when the first hailstone struck. The little house creaked and quivered as Mother put Marjorie in the feather bed and drew the covers over her head.

With the breaking of a front-room window, the door between the two rooms blew open. Mother stood against it, and the crescendo increased until it sounded as though we were being bombarded with baseballs. Marjorie fought off her covers and came up with squinched eyes and stretched mouth, but her screams were inaudible. Mother motioned me to hold the covers over her. A great crack of lightning streaked across the window by the bed and was blotted out by a gust of muddy rain. Then all was quiet but for the receding roar of the hailstorm.

Mother opened the door onto a scene of complete destruction. Every window in the front room was shattered, the shades slashed. Leaves from Father's Bible littered the soggy rug, and the whole room was overlaid with slivers of glass from the windows and from the frames protecting the pictures of Grandfather and Grandmother Berryman that hung at the head of the bed. The peacock counterpane was hurled against the wall, and my big doll from the mission box lay with her feet in its folds, her bisque head shattered beneath a twisted wig.

I lunged for the door. "Marie—look at Marie!"

Mother yanked me back. "Don't set foot in that broken glass." The remainder of the day was spent in cleaning out the hailstones and salvaging what we could of the room's furnishings. Marie's head was removed along with the glass, and her kid body was laid away for the day when we might purchase a new head. But our most poignant loss was the whole flock of young fryers Mother had nurtured against the day we had to feed Brother Dissey.

By Sunday night the bedding had been dried and Mother had tacked two dish towels and an old sheet over the broken windows. Father came back from Seminole during the night, but not until morning could he appraise the damage. In contrast to Mother's depression at the expense of repairs and the loss of her chickens, Father seemed jubilant over our safety after such a harrowing experience.

"Brother Slade will help me repair the roof and replace the windows," he said at breakfast. "The damage is not nearly so great as I had feared from the devastation I saw in the path of the storm. We are extremely fortunate."

Undoubtedly feeling that Father underestimated the disaster, Mother said, "While one counts one's blessings he might as well be realistic and tally his losses. Repairing the house is simpler than replacing our chickens."

"Or getting a new head for Marie," I insisted.

"I know," Father said. "Those losses may have to be endured indefinitely. We'll ask Brother Webb to order a head for Marie, and I may be able to buy a few chickens from one of our members in Seminole. He has a bumper crop this year. And by the way, Seminole is getting to be quite a town. In some respects I believe its potential surpasses La Mesa."

"How so?" I thought I detected a note of apprehension in Mother's voice.

"They may have oil in that area. One of our members from Monument told me a geologist sent by some big oil company was working in that vicinity the past week."

"Why should an oil company want to know people's pedigrees?" I asked.

"Not a genealogist," Father corrected, "a geologist. One who analyzes the formation of the country to determine if streams or pools of oil lie in the subterranean strata."

"Isn't that rather far-fetched in so barren a country?" Mother asked.

"Lack of rain rather than lack of oil would account for the dearth of vegetation," Father said as he pushed back his empty plate.

That was my signal to accumulate the remaining scraps of biscuits and bacon, pour over them the bacon fryings, and serve Nelson his breakfast. I set the plate outside the door and called. I whistled after the manner of Tom Craddock's teaching. Henny-Penny and Cocky-Doodle, now the only occupants of the chicken pen, struggled to get through the fence, but no speckled dog came bounding from the shed. I peered under the house, opened the shed door and called. The horses turned and looked at me. I closed the door and bolted it. When I turned Father was there.

"I'm sorry, Opal," he said.

"But what's happened to him?" I quavered.

"I returned him to his owner," Father said.

"You mean—you gave him back—"

"To Wes Enright. And now I must look up Sheriff Lubeck. At last I've information that will be valuable to him."

About the only thing not effected by the hailstorm was the bedbugs. I took my sorghum pail with the tight-fitting lid to Deacon Webb's store for kerosene and found Vela buying some Octagon soap and a pound of Arbuckle's Ariosa coffee. Looking enviously at the soap wrappers and signatures on the coffee paper which brought fascinating premiums, I didn't notice the young man who came in with his arm in a sling.

"There was a little girl and she had a little curl—," he chanted.

"Dal!" I gasped. "Are you back from Amarillo already?"

"I didn't go," he said. "I had a little accident the night we camped here. Been laid up ever since." His sad-looking eyes were not on me but on Vela, lovely in a green tissue gingham and wearing a black buzzard-wing bow on her yellow hair. "So I haven't been able to get to church. Would it be all right if you introduced me to your lady friend here?"

I was anxious to oblige. "Vela this is Mr.—Mr.—"

He came to my rescue, made a low bow to Vela. "Dallas Malone."

"Pleased to meet you, Mr. Malone," Vela murmured.

"Here's your gallon of coal oil," Deacon Webb said to me. "Pretty heavy to carry on that wire bail." He poured a half-dozen whole nutmegs from a small sack into a box and handed me the sack. "Here—wrop this around your hand."

Half-way home I set down the pail to rest and looked back. Vela was coming out of the door, Dal behind her with her basket over his good arm. Once again he caught me looking back. His face broke into a wide grin.

"See you in church," he called.

While helping Father de-bug the beds, I told him about Dal.

"I had heard that one of the boys was accidentally shot," he said, "and that Mr. and Mrs. Betz were caring for him. They must be very kindly people."

I remembered seeing Mr. Betz only once. He was a small, inoffensive man with a drooping mustache and pale eyes that looked slightly bewildered. And why not? Had not Father often prayed that our enemies be confounded?

Through the freighters Father ordered large cards printed in Big Spring and also arranged for palm-leaf and cardboard fans to be donated by the businessmen there in return for the advertising printed thereon. When the cards came Father and I distributed them over town. Brother Hinkins placed one in each of his bank windows. Brother Craddock tacked several on the board fence bounding the lumber yard. Father even let me go inside the barber shop with him, where Brother Hipplehite was lowering a big armchair with back-and-forth strokes of a crank.

"Come in," he invited. "Climb right up in the chair, little lady, while I whet my shears." I sidled back of Father, even though fairly sure Brother Hipplehite was only kidding when he threatened to cut off my long, unbleached-muslin-colored hair. Father called my attention to the row of ornate mustache cups with gold-embossed names.

"One for every man in town who isn't too poor to have tailor-made shaves."

"One for everybody except Simeon Webb." Brother Hipplehite gave the razor strop a savage swipe with the bright razor blade. "I ain't puttin' no Black Republican's cup alongside of a white man's."

"Brother Webb is a good man," Father said gently. "He has a right to his own political opinion."

"But sitch an opinion ain't welcome in my tonsorial parlor. And it ain't goin' to be welcome in this here town much longer." A lock of hair that looked soaked in axle grease fell across one side of Brother Hipplehite's forehead. His negligible chin receded into his high collar as he bent to examine the razor's edge.

"I don't believe the town will take offence at a man's politics as long as he isn't offensive about them."

Brother Hipplehite dropped his voice and looked at Father through narrowed eyes. "That's whar you're wrong, Parson. Right now we're a-organizin' us a lodge to keep sitch varmints as niggers and Black Republicans out of town. Or run 'em out once they git in."

103

Father ignored this and asked Brother Hipplehite's permission to set the cards in his window.

"A revival meetin', huh? That will pleasure my wife. She's a Holiness herself, and she shore enjoys shoutin' and speakin' with tongues. Stick 'em in front of them bottles of bay rum—that's the checker. I'll hep you drum up a crowd."

Outside I asked Father why he didn't tell off the man about Deacon Webb. "He's a better man than Brother Hipplehite," I insisted. "Brother Hipplehite yap-yaps all the time."

"I think his bark is worse than his bite," Father said.

"But if he's going to try to run Deacon Webb out of town—"

"I know," Father said, "but the more you stir some things the worse they stink. Right now all he wants is a little opposition, and with that for impetus he'll really begin to make trouble."

"What lodge drives out niggers and Black Republicans?"

"I suspect he means some organization that patterns itself after the old Ku Klux Klan of Reconstruction days."

"Will they drive Deacon Webb and his family out of town?"

Father nodded. "Indirectly. Deacon Webb plans to sell and go back to Ohio. He dislikes having his wife and children snubbed because he was appointed postmaster by a Republican president."

Deacon Webb helped Father place the cards. While Link sorted the mail, Father stood looking intently at the tobaccos in the case as though he were memorizing their names, though he never smoked. Link finally handed us two letters. One was Father's check from the Board. He endorsed it and gave it to Deacon Webb, who returned the balance after deducting our monthly store bill. Then he filled a sack with tarbabies and peppermint sticks and handed it to me. I turned to offer some to Father, but he was reading the other letter. All I could see was the name of the theological seminary at the top.

"What do they want?" I asked.

"They offer me the chair of applied theology," Father said.

"Is it a rocker?" I inquired.

Father laughed. "To simplify, they are offering me a job—teaching theology at my Alma Mater. It is quite an honor."

"Are you going to take it?"

"I don't know. Would you like to go back to Louisville?"

"No," I said emphatically, and then it occurred to me that perhaps Father wanted to go. It was an honor, he had said. "But maybe it would be nice. You wouldn't have to work so hard."

"That's possible. We'll see what your mother thinks."

"I coughed the whole winter we were there," I reminded him.

"That was one of our reasons for coming west," Father agreed.

A glint caught the corner of my eye. It was the gold-mounted elk's tooth that hung on the chain across Sheriff Lubeck's vest.

Father said, "I've been trying to get hold of you at your office."

"Been away," the sheriff answered shortly. "Been checkin' up on some reports of cattle rustlin'. What did you want?"

"I wanted to know whether you had interviewed the Slothower brothers when they were in this community."

"Shore, I saw 'em. They didn't know nothin' about this here McGurk except that they'd seen him some months back, down around Fort Stockton. They told me you'd bought a team off'n them."

"Yes," Father replied. "A very good team."

The sheriff glanced toward Deacon Webb and Link, then motioned his head toward the door. Father and I followed him outside.

"Was that all you wanted to see me about?"

"No," Father said. "I thought you'd like to know that Lem Slothower was the man that came to me with Mrs. Enright under the name of William McGurk."

"But you said the snapshot was the man. That wasn't Lem. Lem always had a mustache and sideburns."

"He has now," Father said, "and he may have had before that. But the night he came to see me he was clean-shaven."

"Well I'll be—" The sheriff pulled several papers from an inside vest pocket, separated the snapshot, and studied it. "Well, I'll be a son-of-a-gun! I'd never o' knowed him—but you're right."

"It's only logical," Father said, "that a man who'd change his name would also change his appearance."

"Now lemme see." The sheriff was marshaling his thoughts aloud. "Enright knowed his wife was hobnobbin' with another man and he killed her. If he knows that man was Lem Slothower—"

"Is there anything to rule out the possibility that Slothower

105

rather than Enright might have killed Mrs. Enright?" Father asked.

"Yep," Sheriff Lubeck said. "Motive. Slothower didn't want to kill her. He wanted to marry her. Why do you think it was Lem?"

Father hesitated before he spoke. "I don't know as I should mention this, but it made a profound impression on me. The night this couple came to our door, Opal's little dog resented their approach. Again when they left he was antagonistic. The next morning he was missing. We found him later with his head bashed in."

The sheriff was impressed. "His head bashed in, you say?"

"Not by accident, I'm sure, since his body had been thrown on a rubbish dump."

The sheriff's tongue made a clicking sound. "Head bashed in. That's the way Mrs. Enright was killed." A sudden thought seemed to startle him. "Did you let Lem know you recognized him?"

"No," Father said, "I didn't. You see—on the day I went out to look at his horse, I suspected from Nelson's, that is, Enright's dog's actions that this team formerly belonged to Wes Enright. Now I know—"

"You've seen Enright?" the sheriff cut in.

Father nodded. "Yes. He contacted me on my way back from Seminole. He has identified the team. He tells me that immediately after riding home and discovering his wife's body, he went out to hitch up his horses and found them missing."

"So he figgers Lem killed his wife and stole his hosses."

"That's the way it looks to him. He asked me to urge you to find Lem Slothower."

"It ain't goin' to be easy, now that they're on the move." The sheriff glared at Father. "Besides, how do I know Enright ain't just pullin' a fast one? If he was on the up and up, he'd come to me."

"I wonder," Father said, "what one of us would do in his position, granting he is innocent. He tells me he has not been in hiding, but has been working incessantly to clear himself. He assures me he'll give himself up as soon as he or you have evidence that will clear him. Don't you feel he is due the benefit of the doubt?"

The sheriff was silent for a bit. Then he sighed heavily.

"Don't say nothin' to nobody about this, Reverend. I'll see what I can dig up on this angle. I see you don't have the dog no more. If anybody asks you, tell 'em you lost him or he ran away." Sheriff Lubeck was a very astute man.

With a half-dozen of the large cards yet to be delivered, I saw Father glance toward home—wistfully, it seemed to me. The house stood in plain view, an unpainted little box with the uneven patches of new redwood shingles spotting the already weathered roof. Rain and sun, wind and hail had beat upon it and it had held. Not only did it stand sturdy and square, but through this baptism it had been invested with a kind of beauty —the beauty of the prairie. No longer brash and bright, it had blended now with the immense *décor* of the Llano Estacado.

At the base of its dun walls on the side sheltered from the hailstorm, brave zinnias lifted bright heads; and trained by twine strings, morning glories crept across the windows. A wisp of gray smoke trailed from the chimney. Mother was getting supper.

In that moment of hesitation, I shared the longing Father must have felt for the sanctuary of that small home. We could go inside and close the door upon the problems of men who sought to drive their fellowmen from town, of men who murdered and fled, perhaps to murder again. We could even grasp the opportunity to leave this vast, unfriendly land which yielded nothing but hardships for those who sought to soften it.

Father sighed and we set out toward Judge Pothast's office to dispose of some more of our cards.

Chapter Eleven

FATHER'S arrangements for my weekly music lesson with Sister Bachellor included a half-hour of daily practice on her piano. Since it cost him fifty cents for my lessons and fifty cents a week for the practice time, I was expected not to waste a minute.

I never knew just how Dr. Bachellor and his wife arranged for the use of the front room, but seldom was there a conflict. If one did occur, Sister Bachellor cleared the room quickly, taking me with her to the kitchen, where she made tea or opened a bottle of soda pop, which they always had on hand. This little tête-à-tête was made interesting by stories from the lives of musicians, and would have been even more pleasant had Sister Bachellor not seemed so disturbed whenever her husband was in the house.

This was natural, for sometimes in the midst of a story a shriek would come from the other room, or a series of grunts and groans that made your flesh crawl. Once when we returned to the piano there was blood spattered on the white keys and a great pronged tooth with a blackened side lay on the music rack in front of my first-grade studies.

This afternoon I knocked on the rim of the door, expecting to see Sister Bachellor materialize behind the gauzy screen, her hands extended before her in graceful motions out of the lace ruffles at her wrists, her short, mincing steps barely rippling the full gathers of her skirt. Usually she was smiling above her high lace neckband (boned into points under her ears), and you could see pink or blue ribbon beneath the lace insertion in the yoke of her blouse. But today voices came from within the house. I knocked again, and still there was no response.

"—I've stood all I can. One brat after another pounding that piano all morning. And me trying to sleep." It was Dr. Bachellor's voice, sounding as though he were talking through his oatmeal.

"But Oliver—" Sister Bachellor's tones were always subdued and conciliatory. "You wanted them."

"Only for as long as we needed them."

"We still need them. Every cent you take in goes for—"

Something thumped and glass clinked. Then Dr. Bachellor spoke thunderously. "You've never gone hungry yet. After this game tonight, we'll be in the money again. I want those brats cleaned out. Mark my words, Alice. Get rid of them."

Sister Bachellor's purring tones emerged from their wrappings. "And go through the same thing we did in Cisco when that first well came in dry and all the oil men left? I'd pretended illness and let my pupils go. That didn't keep you from buying whiskey as

108

long as you could get credit. And when we had no food and no place to live—"

"For gosh sake, quit your whining. If you were a jolly sort and made up to the boys, we could be in clover all the time. But you with your mealy-mouthed prissiness—. It's enough to drive a man insane. And then to have that whanging when I am trying to sleep—"

I had heard so much I dared not knock again, lest Sister Bachellor come to the door and I be unable to face her. Tip-toeing away, I ran until the wagon-yard shed put me out of sight. Then I loitered along, wondering whether or not to tell Mother or Father. Mother would probably stop my music lessons if she knew, and now even more than before I wanted to continue. The Bachellors had suddenly become very fascinating.

During the following week I adroitly questioned Ora and Dora about the Bachellors. We met daily at the arbor which Father and Brother Slade were trying to finish by Saturday. The rostrum was completed and the benches were in. A room enclosed with tarpaulins, with flap openings, adjoined the back of the rostrum, so that mothers and babies might slip into its sanctuary for nursings and diaperings. Ora, Dora, and I went through all the motions of a revival service while Father and Brother Slade lifted the brush above the scantlings and lashed it in place. Then a line of posts was installed for hitchings and camp grounds laid out.

"Did you know," I ventured, "that sometimes when we go for our music lessons Dr. Bachellor is still in bed?"

"Sure." Dora tossed her pig-tails. "He never gets up till noon, and he's all red-faced and bleary-eyed. Sister Bachellor says he's got a terrible cold and the dust makes it worse. I think he's a drunkard."

"Vela says she and Tommy have come by there at night and they always have the shades down. Once a man came out and the door stayed open and Vela saw them playing cards around the dining table. Vela says she saw money on the table." Ora's blue eyes were shiny as glass-agates. "And who do you think one of the men at the table was? Just guess."

"Adoph Betz." He was the only really wicked man I knew of.

"No, silly. What would he want to play cards somewhere else for? He's got his own tables in the saloon."

"I give up," I said.

"Judge Pothast," Ora announced, "Vela said so."

"Judge Pothast goes to Adoph Betz's too," Dora said. "So does Brother Falloon. And I've seen Dr. Bachellor go there lots of times."

All this was almost too much for me. I began to see why Brother Dissey had urged the revival.

"Once" (Dora's voice was a loud whisper) "when I went for my music lesson Sister Bachellor had a black ring around her eye. I bet her husband beats her up when he gets drunk."

"Then why doesn't she leave him?" I asked. "Nobody'd blame her."

"Maybe she doesn't want to." Ora pursed her lips.

The meetings were to open on the third Sunday in August, in order to end before the fall roundups began. Early Saturday morning Father and I equipped ourselves with tow sacks and went far afield for cow chips. Mother was baking for the Sunday dinner at the arbor and would need more cow chips than could be found in the depleted area close to town.

We started out on the path leading to the pest house, since beyond was a ravine and a more broken terrain where cattle formerly sought a meager shelter during northers. A long-tailed chaparral bird ran down the path ahead of us until the pest house offered its unneeded protection. Beyond the pest house, Father stopped and looked at the well-defined trail leading into the ravine.

"I wonder," Father said, "if someone has been camping here?"

But in the trampled area of the ravine's floor there were no ashes of an old fire, no rusting cans or bits of rubbish such as campers always left. There were also no cow chips.

We climbed the bank and made our way between dried clumps of grass and sprangling beds of prickly pears. Beneath dried flowers the apples were turning faintly red, but I knew Father had no time to test their ripeness. Long, green beans hung from tired old mesquites, as though they had sapped all the trees' strength. But it was not yet time for the brown streaks to appear that made them deliciously sweet to chew. A jackrabbit sprang up and loped away unchallenged.

Far out in the dip of yet another draw we found the great gray discs and some roots of dead mesquites. Father tied the grotesque roots together with stout cord, the easier to drag them; and with sacks filled we began the long, tiresome trip home. Father was ever mindful of my limitations; so when a half-way point was reached, we sat on our sacks and rested. In the intimacy of these grim tasks shared with Father I could talk of things which could not be discussed in less secret places.

"Father, do you think Lem Slothower killed Mrs. Enright?"

"I think he could have, but I don't know that he did," Father replied. "That is for Sheriff Lubeck to determine."

"Did he act like a murderer when you bought the horses?"

"Not particularly. He's a braggart and a bully. He does most of the talking, but that seems necessary since his brother, Clem, scarcely opens his mouth. He seems a confirmed grouch, suspicious and sulky. They are neither of them very pleasant characters."

"You don't think Wes Enright killed his wife, do you?"

"No," Father said, "I'm quite sure he didn't. But we must reserve judgment on Lem Slothower until more facts are known." Father shouldered his sack and motioned me ahead of him, so that I would not take his dust on the well-beaten path through the ravine and toward the town.

When we reached home our kitchen looked like a commissary. On the table sat a tall, white cake, fuzzy with cocoanut, and three cinnamon-sprinkled, dried-apple pies. And Mother was baking tea cakes. Two chickens she had bought from Sister Slade were now dressed and ready for frying.

It was as though we had been holding our breaths for this Sunday morning. By nine o'clock buggies, hacks, and wagons were disgorging their loads at the arbor. The tarpaulin extension and the two tents beside it were filling with children, mothers and babies, diaper bags, lunch baskets, lap robes, and pillows. The arbor and adjacent territory looked like a giant ant-hill of activity.

Brother Dissey patted the mothers on their backs and reminded them of their noble callings by proclaiming, "All that I am I owe to my angel mother." He chucked babies under their chins and gooed at them. He encircled the young ladies with a gallant and fatherly arm, and gave the young men virile back-slaps and hand pumpings. Father distributed palm-leaf and pasteboard fans. He filled the water buckets and hung them beside the tin dippers on posts at the ends of the rostrum.

The town people came: Deacon and Sister Webb, with Lincoln, Garfield, and McKinley trailing behind them; Brother and Sister Slade, with Vela, Ora, and Dora, picking their way through the rocky creek bed; Judge and Mrs. Pothast and their niece, Ruby Tuttle, who bragged about her home on a big plantation in east Texas, where Negro servants did all the work and no white woman ever turned a hand. Brother and Sister Craddock drove the phaeton, with Mattie between them in front, and the whole Hipplehite family in the back—Millie Dee between her mother and father, and Phineas and Fredonia crouched at their feet. Even Sister Mahoney got away from the boarding house and came with Jim and Rosemary.

Soon after Dr. and Sister Bachellor arrived, Sister Bachellor had the organ going and the children gathered about it. Ora, Dora, and I, superior in our familiarity with the songs, were drowning out the other tuneless voices when Dal Malone came down the aisle, trailing from his good hand the two Betz children. Such sacrilege practically took the song from my lips. The saloon keeper's children in church! Father was quick to notice. He met Dal half way, motioned me down from the rostrum.

"Opal, this is Anna." Father placed the little girl's hand in mine. "And this is Hermann Betz. See that they get to know the other children and make them feel at home."

I was so embarrassed I could scarcely make my way back to the group, who stood with wide eyes and sagging jaws. Ora and Dora edged away gingerly. Lest she be contaminated, Ruby Tuttle slipped out.

The young Betzes tagged me like hungry mavericks. They sat with me during Sunday school, huddled beside me throughout church, clung to me in wide-eyed enchantment during the picnic dinner. I felt completely and thoroughly disgraced. The other town children who had been my friends stood about in tight little groups, whispering over this scandalous turn of events. When I attempted to join them they scattered in a hysterical game of tag, leaving the Betzes and me standing solemnly alone. I looked for Dal, that I might turn them back to him; but he and Vela, Kate Falloon, and John Ellis were all in a hack drinking lemonade and eating cake.

Late that afternoon, when the Betz children went back across Lobo Creek hand in hand, I received Mother's sympathetic permission to put Marjorie in her little red wagon and take her home. Instead of staying for the night services, we were to have some cornbread and sweet milk and go to bed. It had been a hard, bitter day, and once in bed I cried quietly over the situation and fell asleep.

Hours later, when Mother and Father returned, I awakened quite refreshed and so angry with Father that I debated getting up and telling him what I thought of his actions. But as I lay there I found that Mother was taking my part.

"What will people think? Your daughter associating all day with the saloon keeper's children. Not one of her friends would have anything to do with her. It was the most humiliating thing you could have done."

Father's voice was gentle. "I had quite forgotten that all children are snobs and cutthroats. I had deluded myself with the idea that they are sweet and innocent. But the grown folks will understand and the children will soon forget. Only the Betzes will remember."

"Remember to hang around her from now on," Mother said.

"Would you have me treat those innocent children as the other children treated them?" There were sparks in Father's voice. "Are we to exclude them from Christ's invitation to 'Suffer the little children to come unto me,' because their father owns and operates a saloon?"

"Must we always be so literal?" Mother asked impatiently.

"I'm sure we must," Father replied, "unless the Christian spirit we profess is only a pretense."

I sought refuge under the sheet. I was no longer angry with Father nor very sympathetic with Mother. Only sorry to have caused the dissension and anxious for the wound to heal. But Mother, finding this a dead-end street, detoured.

"I notice that your friend Dissey is working primarily for himself and secondarily for the Lord."

"His ways are a bit flamboyant, but if they get the desired results, we should not be critical," Father insisted.

"The result will be that once your church is firmly established, he will grab the pastorate for himself," Mother replied.

"Evangelists seldom like the monotonous grind of a pastorate. They thrive on the fanfare of revivals but become bored with the menial duties of a pastor," said Father.

"You wait and see," Mother answered. "He's making a big play for the young folks and they're silly enough to fall for it."

"Probably he's looking for a wife," Father said.

"A wife—*and* a church," Mother persisted.

I stifled a giggle. The idea that any girl would fall in love with fat and fortyish Brother Dissey was preposterous.

Chapter Twelve

Brother Dissey appeared for breakfast the next morning, smiling and rubbing his hands.

"Good morning, fellow-workers," he said. "An auspicious beginning—very auspicious, I should say. A splendid day in every respect."

"Yes," Father agreed, "it was an enjoyable occasion."

"Make friends first, I always say. As their hearts become softened and their minds receptive, then will we bear down with the writhing of the damned in hell and the shouting of the saints in heaven. Then will we see the power of the Lord made manifest."

Father shook his head dubiously. "There should be a better way to bring a loving Father into the lives of men."

"There isn't," Brother Dissey stated flatly. "My years of experience have taught me the best methods. Our first job is to herd the backsliders into the fold. Then light out after the black sheep. If they are stubborn, set the dogs on them. Better that than to have the wolves of hell devour them."

"For the most part, our people are good people," Father insisted. "Only when they become negligent does the disturbing element get the upper hand."

"Sins of omission are as bad as sins of commission," Brother Dissey declared. "Later we'll concentrate on Adolph Betz, and either pray him through or make it so hot for him he'll vamoose."

"I think the Betzes are essentially good people," Father said.

"Never compromise with the devil, Brother. You leave this in my hands, and when we get through this town will be as clean as a hound's tooth."

"If it is," Father said, "it will be something unique among west Texas towns." He snapped open the case of his watch, a signal to get on with breakfast.

Mother breathed a sigh of relief when Brother Dissey galloped through the blessing, flopped over his plate, and piled it with fried mush.

Compared to Sunday, the weekday attendance at the arbor was scanty, consisting mainly of town women and campers. Father and Brother Dissey alternated with the preaching. But while there was less excitement during the week, you could see much more of what went on about you. Sitting with Ora and Dora one evening just before services, I watched Vela and Tommy Craddock slide into a back bench. By moving, I confirmed my suspicions that they were holding hands. Remembering Vela and Dal, it seemed to me she was geing pretty flirty.

"Is Vela going to marry Tommy or Dal?" I asked.

Dora drew down her mouth in disgust. "I don't think she really wants to marry Tommy. Besides, he's going away to college. And Mama wouldn't let Vela marry a gun-totin', hell-raisin' sinner like Dal. So it don't look like she'll marry either one."

"If Dal knows that, maybe he'll get saved," I suggested.

"Who's goin' to tell him? Vela won't, because she says it's not right to bribe a man into religion. One wedding's all shot to pieces."

The more I thought about Vela's predicament the worse I felt about it. Why shouldn't someone tell Dal Malone that Mrs. Slade objected to her daughter's marrying a gun-toting, hell-raising sinner? Many times at Ladies Aid I had heard elaborate stories of the hard lives and the sad plights of sweet and gentle girls who married wild, drinking, roistering men. The ladies drew verbal pictures of the poor, bedraggled wife, one crying child clinging to her tattered skirt, a baby pressed against her hollow chest, standing in a shanty door peering hopelessly into the distance for sight of an errant husband. No heat, no food, no clothing, while the prodigal spent all his goods in riotous living. What mother wouldn't object to such a future for her daughter?

Yet Brother Falloon had called Dal the best foreman he ever had. Surely if Dal really wanted to marry Vela he'd be willing to mend his ways. Somebody ought to tip off Dal that unless he did, he would have no chance with Vela.

At noon on Saturday Sammy came galloping up to our house and asked Mother if she might stay with us over Sunday. Mother was delighted to see her. I too was delighted, for things were always exciting when she was around and I wanted to ask her several questions. Sammy, like Father, always gave me straight talk and sensible answers.

Sammy skinned out of her jeans and into a school dress.

"You know what? I'm going to school in Fort Worth, startin' the first week in September. Just two weeks to get everything ready."

"How did you happen to decide on Fort Worth?" Mother asked.

"When the Hamiltons came out to the ranch, like they always do in summer, they asked me to visit them and I did. Gee, that's a swell ranch—they've got everything, even a three-cornered piano. And Ford's sister Lucy is just my age. I taught her a lot about ridin' and ropin'. Ford's mother—she's a swell lady—she said Pa had took—taken—her son for a year and she thought it a fair exchange to take Pa's daughter for a year—" Sammy paused for lack of breath.

A very serene and knowing look came into Mother's face.

"Ford is a very sagacious young man," she said.

"And smart too," Sammy agreed. "His pa's a swell hombre. And they ain't—aren't—none of 'em a bit stuck up. Miz Hamilton said for me not to get clothes here. She'd hep me when I got to Fort Worth. But I got to have a few things, so's they won't be ashamed of me when I get off the train. What can I get?"

"Brother Webb was expecting some blue serge. Go down and see if it has come yet. A jacket suit with a dainty white blouse—" Mother turned to me. "Set the table, Opal. We must give Father and Brother Dissey something to eat before they go to afternoon services."

" 'Scuse me, please," Sammy said. "I ain't got time to eat. I got to get to the lumber yard and see Tommy pronto."

Mother was filled with consternation at a woman's taking the initiative. "I'm sure you'll see him tonight at the arbor."

"But I got to see him when Vela Slade isn't hangin' around." Sammy flew out the door and was gone before Mother could remonstrate. After dinner when Brother Dissey returned to Slade's for his nap, Mother took the opportunity to tell Father about Sammy and her plans.

"The Hamiltons seem to have taken a very wise attitude," Father commented.

Mother shook the red-checked table cloth out the back door.

"I suppose one can't blame them for trying to marry off their debauched son to a good girl."

"So far as I know," Father replied, "Ford is a good boy and he should make Sammy a fine husband."

"How can you say that?" Mother stormed. "You know his habits."

"Now, Mama." Father's tone was pacific. "Investigation and indulgence are widely separated acts. Young men have curiosity about what goes on behind closed doors, particularly when their comrades have personal knowledge. Ford handled his problem more judiciously than most."

"You whited sepulchre," Mother said. "The same sin you condone in a man, you condemn in a woman. I should think that a minister could recognize sin in his own sex as well as in the opposite."

"I think I do. But in eradicating a sin, I try not to mutilate the character of the sinner. By the way, where is Sammy now?"

"Flown off in a whirlwind to see Tommy Craddock," Mother snapped. "If she'd had any bringing up, she'd know better than to run after a boy. She might have a chance if she didn't fling herself at his head."

Father pinched the bridge of his nose where there were little grooves from the pressure of his nose glasses. "Sometimes the cloying sweetness of such feminine graces as eyelash flapping, coy smiles, mincing steps, and handkerchief dropping gets pretty irksome. Of course, I don't know how Tommy regards these things."

Mother sloshed the dishwater vigorously. "I despise trying to discuss things with you on one of your perverse days. You must have gotten out on the wrong side of the bed this morning."

Father's weariness vanished in a burst of spirit. "I'll switch sides with you any time you decide you'd rather get up and build the fire, feed and water the horses and the chickens, and milk the widow Trueblood's cow for our quart of morning milk, while I get breakfast and dress Marjorie. Is that a deal?"

"Yes," Mother said, "if you'll assume the job of finding and preparing the quantity of food necessary to stoke Brother Dissey three times a day, wash and iron and clean and sew, take care of a baby, and attend two services daily, besides leading the Ladies Prayer Meeting—" Mother plunked the dishes into the pan of hot rinse water.

I had to lift them up with a case knife and then grab them with a towel-covered hand, but the water seeped through and the scalding dishes burned my fingers. Each awkward effort led to a mounting fury with both Father and Mother.

Why, I fumed inwardly, did they try to stay together, hating one another as they did? Probably because they thought people would talk if they parted. Suppose people did talk. A mother and father who loathed each other, who spit angry words back and forth, whose criminal disregard of their own child forced her to burn her hands time and again, should quit carrying on a pretense of a happy marriage. But no—someone might talk about them. They couldn't stand that. Small matter what their child had to stand—

I glanced at Father. He was smiling—the indulgent smile I had seen often when one of us was angry. "About all we lack is a cut-worm to whittle off our gourd vine, and we could out-complain Job."

Mother laughed gaily. "That reminds me, those zinnias under the front windows look pretty sick. If you think the well will last through the summer, would you give them a little water?"

Only then did it penetrate my consciousness that the disagreements Father and Mother had, even those when a little fur flew, were in reality very superficial. Fundamentally there was solid harmony between them. Nothing could disrupt it. And the more sorely tried Father was, the more gentle and understanding Mother became. For the first time I realized that my father and my mother loved each other.

Sammy breezed in just before supper in a flurry of excitement. Tommy had asked to escort her to the evening service at the arbor. I saw Mother's surprise that Sammy's bold tactics had brought results.

"Tommy would of took—taken—Vela, but last Sunday she promised Dal Malone to go with him. Tommy thinks maybe she's sweet on Dal. I reckon he wants to make her jealous."

"If you thought that, would you go with him?" Mother asked.

Sammy shrugged. "Sure. I'd go with him if I knew that he asked me just for plain gol-danged meanness."

On the way to the arbor Sister Bachellor caught up with us and asked if she might walk home when we did. She explained that Dr. Bachellor was not feeling well enough to attend, but had insisted she not fail us as organist. Mother kept inquiring about Dr. Bachellor's illness until Father changed the subject.

I joined Ora and Dora and we scouted among the campers until we were almost late for services. We finally slipped in at the back among a group of strange people. Several men slid in, smelling of cloves and Sen-Sen. I was a bit uneasy until Dal and Vela pushed us down the bench to make room for them. The men behind us were restless, and at intervals one would turn his head and there was a squirting sound and a plop in the dust. When they mumbled, Dal looked back and all was quiet again.

It was Brother Dissey's turn to preach. He stepped up to the pulpit and announced in stentorian tones: "Since coming into this arbor tonight, I have thrown to the winds my carefully prepared sermon. There is no time to waste on high-falutin' words if we are to snatch brands from the burning. I take my text from the fourteenth chapter of the Book of Revelation, ninth and tenth verses: 'And the third angel followed them saying with a loud voice, If any man worship the beast and his image, and receive his mark in his forehead or in his hand, the same shall drink of the wine of the wrath of God, which is poured out without mixture into the cup of his indignation; and he shall be tormented with fire and brimstone in the presence of the holy angels, and in the presence of the Lord.' "

Brother Dissey flopped his Bible shut with a loud snap. In the silence that followed we could hear his deep-drawn breath, could see him bracing himself to do battle with Satan. Then with his Bible clasped to his breast, he stepped boldly out in front of the pulpit.

"There are those among us who have upon them the mark of the beast of strong drink. The brand of Satan is upon them, and verily, verily I say unto you, they shall be tormented with fire and brimstone on Judgment Day. He who delays his repentance pawns his soul with the devil. I repeat—he who delays his repentance pawns his soul with the devil—"

There was a rustling behind me and a stage whisper, "He shore goes after sin all spraddled out."

This was followed by some snickering and more whispering. It was inevitable that from his vantage point Brother Dissey would notice it.

"—this vile and infamous breeder of iniquity—the licensed saloon—must be destroyed, lock, stock, and barrel. The emissary of the devil who runs it should be run out of town for the shameful blot he has made on this fair community."

Vela's legs pushed against mine and I looked sideways. Dal had risen and drawn himself up straight and proud. He gave his pants a hitch and pressed past us, walked straight out into the night. Heads turned, whispers fluttered about. Brother Dissey paused significantly.

"Slaves of the monster rum become so hardened that the pleadings of saintly women go unheeded. Rats that they are, they prefer darkness to light."

The backs of Vela's ears were as red as prickly-pear apples.

"What did Dal leave for?" I whispered.

"Mr. Betz is his friend. Dal won't stay and listen to Brother Dissey call him all those foul names."

"Wouldn't he quit being friends with Mr. Betz if you'd ask him to?" I suggested.

Vela's chin went up. "But I think Dal is right in being loyal to his friends. Dal is a good man."

During our whispers Brother Dissey was making an impassioned plea for sinners to turn from their evil ways. He suddenly approached it conversely, asking the Christians to line up, thus embarrassing the timid sinners. "Let the redeemed of the Lord say so," he shouted.

There was an answering shout, "So," followed by one great bleat after another, like an anguished sheep. Every head turned as Sister Hannah Hipplehite went down the aisle. Suddenly she sprawled on her face and flopped from side to side, gibbering some unintelligible jargon.

"Amen, Sister," Brother Dissey's voice boomed above the ruckus. "Amen, Sister," he repeated. But Sister Hipplehite was too far gone to take the hint and end her performance. "Amen, Sister," Brother Dissey called once more, and then stood helplessly while Sister Hipplehite tossed and jabbered.

Father disappeared from the rostrum and soon Deacon Webb and Brother Craddock went down the aisle, lifted her bodily, and carried her outside. Brother Hipplehite took a dipper of water and followed.

The snickering behind us had turned into open laughs.

"Let's go tell Dal," one man said. "He'll get a hulluva wallop out of all these shenanigans."

"Where'll we find him?" the cowboy back of me asked.

"At the Betz House, of course." A half-dozen men moved out. I whispered into Vela's ear.

"Do you suppose Dal did go to the saloon?"

Vela looked down in her lap. "I've an idea he did."

"And all those men went because he did?"

Vela's voice caught on a snag. "That's just it. Wherever Dal leads, the men follow. Even if it is to the saloon."

Vela walked home with Tommy Cradock and Sammy. Or at least she started with them, but I was pretty sure I saw Dal join them at Lobo Creek. Sister Bachellor wouldn't hear of our going out of our way to take her to the door, so we stood on the path and watched until we saw her go inside. The house had looked dark, but when the door swung open we could see that it was brightly lighted inside.

"We ought to go over there," Mother exclaimed. "Dr. Bachellor must be very ill—all those lights burning—"

Father spoke up. "If Sister Bachellor wants us, she knows where to find us. Or she can get Dr. Mesropian if she needs him."

"She wouldn't dare do that," Mother said.

"Why not?" Father asked.

"Because she'd be disgraced."

"Why on earth should she be disgraced? If one needs a doctor and a doctor is available—"

"No white woman would dare to call a Negro into her home," Mother said. "You should know that."

"Who said that Dr. Mesropian is a Negro?" Father demanded.

"Sister Hipplehite," Mother replied. "She told us last week at Ladies Aid. She said Brother Hipplehite talked to some man who knew Dr. Mesropian some years ago, and that he is part Negro. She asked us to let all the ladies know, so they wouldn't make that mistake."

Father exploded. "Of all the malicious lies I ever heard, I think that is the worst. Dr. Mesropian is no more a Negro than I am."

"How do you know?" Mother asked.

"He told me. He's an Armenian. His diploma from Rush Medical College—"

"Naturally he'd tell you that," Mother said. "He's smart, and no smart man would go around saying he had Negro blood."

There was resignation in Father's voice. "I might as well tell you that Brother Hipplehite—and undoubtedly his wife also— are trying to stir up public sentiment against anyone who differs from them or their ideas. They are also trying to run out Deacon Webb."

Mother gasped. "But why? Deacon Webb is no Negro."

"He is a Republican."

"Why, that's despicable," Mother fumed. "The Webbs are fine people. They're not trying to force their politics on anyone."

"Not as despicable as spreading an untruth about Dr. Mesropian, whose only desire is to make an honest living with his skilled services. And we've real need for such services."

"If Dr. Mesropian really is a white man—" Mother began.

"He is," Father assured her, "and whenever you need a doctor, you've no reason not to call him. But even if he weren't, you'd still have no real reason not to call him if you needed him."

"You must be out of your mind," Mother told him.

"Do you think I'd hesitate to officiate at the funeral of a Negro child just because it was a Negro?" Father asked sharply. "Or that I would refuse to give aid to a Negro family in trouble?"

"I don't think you would," Mother admitted, "but I think you would lose your pastorate if you did. You don't realize how strong the sentiment is in a town like this, where there are no facilities for segregation."

"Then I'd lose it gladly," Father announced. "People like the Hipplehites are more destructive to the morals of a community than people like Adolph Betz. And I intend to make them know it."

"Before you fly off the handle, you'd better arm yourself with reliable information about Dr. Mesropian. Just why is he out in this country? Apparently he's in good health. Does he have a license to practice?"

"He does. Inconspicuously placed on the wall of his office."

"Then why, if he's capable, honest, and well, is he out here?"

"He is engaged in research in the treatment and possible cure of tuberculosis. He questions the benefit of sunshine, since germs tend to breed in moisture and heat. He's here to study this climate and its effects on victims of consumption who have come for the therapeutic value of sunshine and fresh air."

I had lagged to pick grass burrs from my stockings and ran to catch up as Father and Mother moved on. Some of the conversation escaped me, but I gathered that Mother was still unconvinced that a high scientific aim precluded Dr. Mesropian's being of mixed blood.

"You're not obligated to take up a man's personal problems. You didn't do it for Deacon Webb."

"Because Deacon Webb prefers it that way. They make no untrue charges against him. He is a Republican and proud of it. He has the right to choose whether or not he and his family shall pioneer tolerance in an intolerant community. But the charges against Dr. Mesropian are untrue. And unlike Deacon Webb, he desires to stay and conduct his research. If necessary I shall support him on the streets, in the homes, and from the pulpit."

"The day you do," Mother warned, "you'd better have your resignation ready to hand in to the church."

When we reached home, Sammy and Tommy were sitting on the steps. Tommy bounced up and opened the door for us. Mother asked him to come in but he politely refused. After he left, Sammy's face was radiant.

"Ain't he swell?" she breathed. "And you know what? He ain't only about half sweet on Vela Slade. You-all just wait until I get back from Fort Worth and see what-all happens."

When I awoke the next morning Father was standing in the kitchen door scanning the sky. A dozen times each day Father would glance upward for some indication of rain. This morning, as usual, the sky was brassy bright. The sun shimmered out across the prairie in little, eye-hurting waves.

All week I had planned to feign illness in order to stay home this Sunday, but one look at the black bread pans filled with rice pudding that Mother slid into the oven decided me. I was going to the arbor even though I served as hitching post for the Betz children throughout the day. Once there, I haunted the edges of the rostrum and tent flaps, seeking to avoid the eyes of Anna and Hermann Betz. By the time I had to take my place with the children about the organ, I was convinced that they were not coming.

Father took as his text the 117th Psalm. "Oh praise the Lord, all ye nations; praise him, all ye people. For his merciful kindness is great toward us; and the truth of the Lord endureth forever. Praise ye the Lord."

The arbor was filled. Men stood in the shade of their big hats, held between them and the burning sun. Father's voice was even and clear as he spoke of the merciful kindness of a loving Heavenly Father. Over the audience the only sound save Father's voice was the movement of the palm-leaf fans. Eager young faces, tired weatherbeaten faces were giving rapt attention.

For the first time since the meetings began I saw Brother and Sister Kelso and Henry. Sister Kelso was thinner, but in her up-turned face was a calm, steadfast look. Brother Kelso looked younger and fresher, even handsome in his blue serge suit with its black tie. I saw Brother and Sister Falloon, and with them their curly-haired, apple-cheeked daughter, Kate. Beside her was John Ellis. Surely we'd have one wedding.

124

After the sermon Father gave the invitation. Georgia Hinkins, Kate Falloon, and Rose Mahoney came to the front and clasped Father's hand. Then John Ellis and Sam Falloon and Link Webb came up. Back of them were Vela Slade, Jim Mahoney, and Tommy Craddock. Father had talked to each of them during the week, to mothers and fathers, and knew it was their desire to make public confession of faith and application to enter into the fellowship of the church. Brother Dissey bounded to his feet and welcomed each individual with a fervent, "Praise the Lord," and "Thank God, the devil has been cheated of another victim."

When the service was over and Brother Dissey had pronounced the benediction, the saw-horses were brought out and boards laid across them, making a table in the space between the rostrum and the benches. After dinner the young folks gathered in groups and some went out to the hacks and buggies. Mothers took their babies to the tents. Ora, Dora, and I were playing mumble-peg with Gar and Mac Webb when we noticed a number of men gazing into the haze of the western horizon.

"Maybe it'll rain and we can have a baptizing," Ora said.

We ran out and clustered about our respective fathers.

"There is no doubt in my mind," Brother Slade was saying. "Can't you smell it? Somebody may have tossed out a cigar stub—"

There was a general sniffing. The prairie haze had undoubtedly developed an acrid odor. The sun paled and took on a dusty glow. The words "prairie fire" leaped from lip to lip. In another half hour the men had assembled barrels of water in the wagons and stacks of gunny sacks from the lumber yard and livery stable and made a concerted exodus in the direction of the fire.

Among the children excitement was rampant over tales of prairie fires and the devastation they caused. Faces lengthened in disappointment when some two hours later the vehicles came back. The fire had been a small one, covering scarcely more than two or three sections. After unloading their barrels in town the men came across Lobo Creek and back to the arbor. Soot-smudged faces and smoky clothes lent reality to the stories of crackling grass and sweeping flames in the rising wind.

Food was once more piled on the table and pots of steaming coffee served. Brother Dissey personally complimented each returned hero, regretted his inability to be with them, and gave God the glory for the fire's having yielded to their efforts. Later in his sermon Brother Dissey painted a picture of the fire's origin. He said that a drunken cowpuncher, staggering from the saloon to his horse and spurning the arbor where divine services were in progress, must have taken off across the prairie with a lighted "coffin nail" between his lips. He had then doubtless tossed it away with no concern for the destruction it would create.

At this juncture Sammy jabbed her elbow into my ribs. But Brother Dissey was describing the leave-taking of the fire fighters.

"Behold the hosts of the Lord," he thundered. "See them going forth to battle to the death with the minions of the devil—"

I saw then what Sammy was trying to bring to my attention. Just outside the arbor a group of spooklike legs bristled in the rim of lantern glow. I heard the rasping sound of air being ejected between loose lips.

"Slim Breedlove," Sammy whispered, "festerin' up meanness."

I remembered that name as the man Ford Hamilton had suspected of causing him trouble. Brother Falloon slipped out quietly, and soon all the long legs faded away. Brother Falloon came back just as quietly.

Brother Dissey begged for sinners to fill the mourners' bench. Even though we sang *Come to Jesus* over and over again, there was no response. Everyone was too weary to undertake salvation that night.

We went home immediately after church, all of us tired to exhaustion. But sometime in the wee, small hours of the morning we were again aroused by fiendish yells and volleys of shots. One of our kitchen windows was shattered and Father's new team kicked the shed door off its hinges. Before breakfast Father went out and repaired the shed door. When he came in he sagged into his chair opposite Brother Dissey and glanced at the window where Mother had pasted brown paper to keep out the flies.

"It seems as though our labors have brought small reward," he said.

Brother Dissey's voice was reproachful. "Brother, where is your faith? We welcome persecution. It's darkest just before the dawn."

There was a twinkle in Father's eye. "And often noisiest."

Brother Dissey expanded his chest. "I welcome any challenge

126

the devil throws down before me. He will have to find a more effective tool than Dal Malone with which to dent my armor."

"Dal Malone?" Sammy blurted out. "It wasn't Dal—"

"Of course it was," Brother Dissey contradicted her. "You'd have thought that getting shot the last time would have taught him a lesson. But when the demon rum imprisons a man, it often takes more than a shot in the arm to release him."

Father's mouth twisted. "Will you return thanks?" he said.

Brother Dissey laid his arms on the table, clasped his hands above his plate, and lifted his face. Tensely I listened, determined to catch at least one more word beyond the "Kind and Indulgent Heavenly Father," but it was no use. He ripped along like a tornado down a mountain side. By the time my plate was turned over Brother Dissey already had two biscuits, butter, bacon, and a blob of sorghum. He emptied his coffee into his saucer, blew upon it, and drank with a great swishing sound.

"Nothing quite as invigorating as an excellent cup of Java," he said with great relish. "Eh, Brother Berryman?"

"I prefer Formosa-Oolong," Father said, sipping his tea.

"That's good coffee too," Brother Dissey agreed, "but not so flavorful as Java. Real coffee connoisseurs of the Orient all prefer Java."

"I'm sure they do," Father said, "if they prefer coffee."

Father and Brother Dissey left for the arbor early, so that Father could stop by the lumber yard and leave measurements for a new window glass. While Sammy and I made the front-room bed, I asked her, "Why did you say Dal Malone wasn't in on the shooting?"

"Because he rode back to the ranch Saturday night, so that Brother Falloon and Sam could come in for the services on Sunday. He wasn't even in town last night."

"How did you find that out?" I asked.

"He sent word to Vela. She told me."

"Then who do you suppose shot up the town?"

"Slim Breedlove," Sammy answered promptly. "He'd have broke up the meetin' last night if Brother Falloon hadn't stopped him. When old Pat Falloon lays down the law, they ain't no ornery cowpuncher goin' to buck him."

My opinion of jolly, blustery Brother Falloon was undergoing revision. "Is—is he dangerous?"

"Listen," Sammy straightened from pounding the feather bed, "next to Teepee Hamilton, he's the biggest rancher in these parts. A guy that starts from scratch and gets where he's got ain't no milkweed puff. Once I seen—saw—Pa throw two cans in the air and Pat Falloon shot at 'em, a six-shooter in each hand. Each can was drilled with two shots. And that's shootin', believe you me!"

I was now thoroughly convinced that Brother Falloon was indeed a man of power in the community. Only one other thing I wanted to know. "Are the Slothower brothers as bad as Slim Breedlove?"

"They don't stir up no trouble. But they're stinkers. Some folks say they hate each other but don't dare do nothin', so they just take it out on their livestock."

"You mean—they beat their horses?" I said in horror.

"Over the head. A thing no decent man would do. Pa's seen 'em."

I didn't have the stomach to ask any more questions.

Regardless of the specific knowledge Sammy and Vela had, rumors flew about. Dal was the drunken cowboy who had started the prairie fire. Dal was the leader of the gang that shot up the town. Dal was out to break up the revival meetings. So Sister Slade forbade Vela ever to see Dal Malone again.

Though the prairie fire was not large and not unusual at this season of the year, it exerted a tremendous influence on the people. The men scrutinized the sky constantly for signs of rain. The heat increased, the wind blew more constantly. The ranges were as dry as tinder, and every lighted match was a hazard. Day by day the people's spirits seemed to wither in the heat and the drought. Some of the campers, uneasy about their homes on the dry range packed their covered wagons and left.

Weariness accumulated in Father's face as the second week wore on, with no converts. Mother had lost so much weight that she was anchoring her skirts to her corset with safety pins. Marjorie whimpered from ant stings acquired in unguarded moments and from prickly heat irritated by the dust.

As I went about my Saturday morning dusting, after Mother had swept, I wished the revival meetings were over. Mother was as jumpy as a stray cat. Marjorie was cross and obstinate. Father looked so weary I wondered how he could last through another sermon. Only I was serene and unruffled. At that moment some playful urchin must have sighted his slingshot at the house and let fly. I jumped and dropped the glass nappy containing mother's resurrection plant. Fortunately neither bowl or plant was damaged. I mopped up the water, refilled the square bowl, and put them back on the claw-foot table.

Father came in with the forms for his Home Mission Board report and spread them beside his church records. In his fine Spencerian hand, with beautifully-shaded capital letters, he wrote an account of the year's work. Monday was the deadline for filling in the figures and mailing it.

"You've got nine new converts to report," I reminded him.

"Unless they can be baptized, I cannot add them to our membership," Father said, "and it isn't likely we can accomplish that within the next two days."

From Father's tone I knew that the report was not good.

"What will the board do if they don't like your report?"

"Probably assign this field to a better man who can develop it successfully," Father said.

"Then what will we do?"

"Start looking for another field, probably farther west—provided the board will extend its support."

He closed his book with a sigh, took off his glasses, and let them flip up the chain to the gold lapel button. Deep pinch-marks made his eyes drawn and forlorn. Suddenly I was angry with everyone, God included, for making things so hard for Father.

"If God won't help any, why don't you just quit Him flat?"

Father's smile was a little amused. "God is not on trial, Opal. I am. This is a test of my faith and courage in adversity."

This shamed me a bit, but I had to justify my stand.

"If you don't want to quit Him, you could at least go and sit in the chair at the seminary and let Him work it the best way He can without you."

"God could make out quite well without me," Father replied, "much better than I could manage without Him. But I shouldn't want to start a new work on the basis of a previous failure. Should the board see fit to relieve me here, I doubt if the seminary would sustain their offer. To teach Applied Theology, one must have been able to apply it."

I suspected that Mother would not relish moving to a more sparsely settled area, one even more primitive and difficult to pioneer. I began to be apprehensive about our family unity should Mother be petitioned to make such a move.

"What would Mother say about moving further west?"

Father's half-smile lifted his brows a bit. "She might have a good deal to say. But I've no doubt we'd come to an ultimate agreement."

Chapter Thirteen

MARJORIE sat in the middle of the bed and bawled. Two big tears hung just below her dark eyes. Father came in from the front room where he was preparing his sermon for Sunday night, the last night of the revival meeting.

"What's the matter with her?" he asked. "Is she ill?"

Mother took her foot off the sewing-machine treadle and the whirring noise stopped. She lifted the presser-foot, and snipped the thread. Sammy's new suit for the trip to Fort Worth was nearly finished.

"It's time for her nap. I'm too busy to rock her to sleep."

Marjorie held out her chubby hands to Father. He lifted her in his arms, went back into the front room, and sat in the rocking chair. I followed him and took the straight chair by the window. I hoped Father would sing Marjorie to sleep with one of the old plantation songs, for in them his rich baritone was superb. When Father chose *Ole Nigger Ned* I was happy.

> "Oh, dey was an' ole nigger an' his name was Ned,
>   An' he died long ago, long ago,
>   An' he had no haar on de top of his haid,
>   In de place whar de wool ought to grow.

Oh, his laigs was long lak de cane in de brake,
    An' he had no eyes for to see,
An' he had no teef for to eat a corn cake,
    So he had to let de corn cake be.

When ole Ned died missus tuk it mighty hard,
    An' de tears run down lak de rain,
An' den she wipe her apron wid de corner ob her eye,
    Kase she nebber see old Ned again.

Chorus—*Lay down de shubble an' de hoe,*
        Hang up de fiddle an' de bow,
    Kase dey's no mo wuk for po' ole Ned,
        He's gone whar de good niggers go."

While listening, I was dreaming out the window. The meetings would end tomorrow night. Like Old Nigger Ned, Father would have to "lay down de shubble an' de hoe," because there would be no more work for him here. Actually much work remained to be done. There was the Betz House still running full blast, selling whiskey that made the cowboys shoot up the town. There was the band to which Brother Hepplehite belonged, circulating lies about Dr. Mesropian and trying to run Deacon Webb out of town.

I thought that God ought to recognize these things and not just sit quietly on his throne with folded hands while the Home Mission Board proceeded to measure Father's work merely on the number of new members taken in or the increase in the church building fund. It wasn't fair. It simply wasn't fair that Father was going to have to "hang up de fiddle an' de bow" while there was still so much work that needed doing.

Suddenly I saw the Slade girls galloping toward the house. Lest they barge in and waken Marjorie, I met them at the back door.

"Come with us," Dora panted, "and see Falloon's Folly."

"Sure," Ora chimed in. "Everybody's talking about it. Brother Falloon is throwing away his money."

Remembering the quarter he had given me, I wanted to be on hand if Brother Falloon was throwing away money. I grabbed my sunbonnet and asked Mother's permission at the same time.

"Where are you going?" Mother asked.

"Just to the bank of Lobo Creek," Dora told her.

So Brother Falloon must be throwing his money down the bank of Lobo Creek. After obtaining consent we struck out on the run, straight across town and out the Big Spring road to Lobo Creek.

"See!" Dora pointed across the creek. "There they are."

Across the creek was the "Flying F" outfit, drawn up at their previous camp site below the arbor. With them now was a great herd of white-faced cattle. Riders hovered about the herd, keeping them under control as they settled.

"But where's Falloon's Folly?" I persisted.

"That's it," Dora said. "Papa says they call them Herefords. They cost a lot of money. And you can get other cattle cheap."

"Maybe he likes them with white faces," I suggested feebly.

Ora shrugged a shoulder. "What's the difference when they're dead. Papa says Herefords won't stand cold winters and hot, dry summers as well as range cattle. And beef sells for the same money. Papa says that Brother Falloon is plumb crazy."

I was unimpressed by anything except my disappointment that Brother Falloon was not throwing money down the creek bank.

Dora spoke dolefully. "Papa says it's just like pouring water down a prairie-dog hole."

Suddenly two riders that had been drawn together broke apart, and one wheeled toward the creek and down the bank sideways, scattering loose gravel. Then he climbed up the bank to us.

For the first time enthusiasm possessed me. "It's Dal!"

"Shore is," he grinned.

I was so flustered that I chewed my sunbonnet string. He drew a folded paper from behind the sack of Bull Durham in his shirt pocket and handed it to me.

"If I was real polite and said 'Pretty-please,' would you give this to Miss Sammy Severn?" he asked.

I nodded vigorously. "Sure."

"Fine an' dandy. And you girls get yourselves a treat with this." He handed over a whole half-dollar. As he whirled his horse I finally stammered a "Thank you!" He lifted his hand.

"See you in church," he called and headed down the creek.

"We'll get a sack of candy hearts." Dora was jumping up and

down, her pig-tails whipping. "I want some that say 'Love Me' and 'Be My Girl.' "

"And a packet of Kiss-Me chewing gum," Ora said. "My wad fell off the bed post and Tessie got it."

At the store we met Sammy buying some rolls of white *soutache* for the blue serge suit, and a pair of black lisle stockings.

"You know what," she said. "Brother Falloon just got in town. He brought a whole beef, all dressed. They're going to barbecue it tonight for the meeting tomorrow."

"Mother will be thankful," I told her. "She's been at her wit's end trying to get chickens." I handed her the note. "Dal Malone asked me to give it to you."

The three of us stood about her, hoping she would read it aloud. She unfolded the paper. There was another inside it. With no hesitation Sammy read the outside one.

"Dear Sammy: This is shore a roundabout way of doing things and I don't hold with it. But I ain't got no choice. Will you give this note to Vela and bring her answer to Sim Webb's store. I'll be waiting there from five to six this evening. I'd appreciate it a right smart bit, and hope to return the favor sometime. Your friend, Dal."

"Gosh," Sammy exclaimed. "I got to catch Vela 'fore she leaves for the arbor. Is she home?" Dora nodded and Sammy flung open the door and made for the Slades'.

Many campers had come back for the final week-end of the meetings. New ones too had driven in for this last big social gathering before the fall roundup, the school term, and the winter, which would tie them to their homes. That afternoon I watched the covered wagons roll in, the bed-rolls and tents being unloaded and pitched beside the wagons. Most of the wagons had an end-gate that let down on a folding leg, revealing the chuck-cupboard behind it and making a table for the cook.

Inside the cupboards were shelves of food, and beneath the wagons hung skillets and pots. Valises under the wagon seats contained clothing, but hats were pinned to the inside of the wagon-sheets, between the bows. A canvas canteen usually hung beside the driver, and a rifle or shotgun lay under the seat, along with a sack of oats for the horses.

133

Among the campers who arrived that afternoon were my Uncle Johnnie and Aunt Tennie from their ranch in the sand and shinnery. We had supper with them, thick beefsteaks and hot biscuits cooked in Dutch ovens.

"You ought to see my nut-fed razorbacks," Uncle Johnnie told Father. "Acorn-fed hogs make the finest meat in the world. About February I'll butcher and bring you some hams and bacon."

"Splendid," Father said. "How many hogs are you running?"

"All of them," Uncle Johnnie replied tartly. "But the trouble is, I can't catch them. This spring I had a dozen sows and near a hundred pigs. Now I haven't half that many. They go back wild, once they get loose in that shinnery. It's hog heaven."

Father was thoughtful. "What's the solution for that?"

"My solution has been to darn near run my pants off and to finally let them go. You can't call them to feed when they've got all the food they want. They won't come to shelter when there's abundant shelter all about. Actually the solution is pastures fenced with hog-wire. But who besides Teepee Hamilton and a few like him, can buy a hundred miles of hog wire?"

Another of Uncle Johnnie's fine schemes was apparently fizzling out. He was still talking.

"I'm trying it one more year, and then if I can't get someone interested in financing me to the extent of about $20,000, I'm going out to New Mexico and raise goats. Do you know what goats will do?"

"Butt," Father said. "At least that's been my experience."

Uncle Johnnie chuckled. "I remember the time you got lifted over the fence by brother Jimmie's pet billy goat. But seriously, I think we ought to go over into New Mexico territory and file on at least two sections of land. That would give us a start. There's free grazing all around."

"I've been over," Father told him, "around Lovington, Knowles, Monument and Eunice. It would take a thousand acres of that shaley stuff to support one goat. Free grazing is anathema with nothing to graze."

"It looks bare," said Uncle Johnnie, "but goats thrive on that growth of stunted weeds that cattle would starve on. With goats you have your annual shearing, your increase, and your market value."

"Do you know anybody who would eat a goat?" Father asked.

"They tell me"—Uncle Johnnie's voice was a trifle incredulous —"that in cities up north, they sell goat meat in butcher shops just like beef and pork. That's a fact. Now figure it this way—"

The idea of eating goats had me gagging. I left and joined Mother and Aunt Tennie, who were cleaning up the dishes and stowing them in the chuck space at the back of the wagon.

"We got five gallons of choke cherries," Aunt Tennie was saying, "and our watermelons are wonderful. I brought you some choke-cherry preserves and some watermelon pickles. Since Johnnie lined the tank with rocks we have water for everything. I even raised yellow pear tomatoes."

"How long are you and Johnnie going to stay in that forsaken spot?" Mother asked. "There's still homestead land in this area."

"You ought to see our place," Aunt Tennie said proudly. "I've grown to like it. We've lovely cottonwood and poplars planted around the tank. All I'm afraid of now is that Johnnie will get the bug to try some new experiment and we'll leave it and go trekking off to some bare and sterile spot—"

I wandered off where I couldn't hear any of them talking. I felt so depressed about poor Aunt Tennie, harnessed to visionary Uncle Johnnie, that I followed the hum of voices to the arbor, hoping to find some of the children free of their elders. Ora and Dora, or Ruby Tuttle. Even the Hipplehite children, Phineas, Fredonia, and Millie Dee, with their runny noses, would have been welcome.

Lifting the flap at the back of the rostrum, I halted because of voices—adult voices that might trap me with long-faced oldsters until the services began. I would have to be courteous to them for Father's sake.

"Well, why doesn't she come?" It was Dr. Bachellor, and from his tone he was in one of his haranguing moods.

Sister Bachellor answered in her soapy, conciliatory voice. "Georgia will be here any moment, I'm sure. She's anxious to run through her solo a time or two before church begins."

"You mean she was," the doctor mumbled. "She's probably so busy batting her eyes at Sam Falloon that she's forgotten all about it."

"Oliver," Sister Bachellor reproved, "someone might hear you."

"What if they do? I'm getting a bellyful of these simpering women and their sanctimonious husbands. I call off one of the best games I've worked up for months just to help you keep up a front with these holy-rollers. And what do I get out of it? Wait around and suck my thumb until some fly-brained filly finishes her game of tag—"

"Oliver!" The reprimand sounded through her teeth. "We agreed that it was best. You might as well be gracious about it. You were cocky like this in Cisco when everything was flying high. Then the next thing, that boy you cleaned committed suicide. That was still under investigation when the well came in dry. Then we really had a hard row to hoe. If I ever have to go through that again—"

The venom in Dr. Bachellor's voice made my skin crawl. "So whenever the going gets tough, you whine. Well, anytime you think it's easier to crawl home on your hands and knees, begging forgiveness from your stiff-necked old man, go to it. That old devil wasn't fooling when he ordered you never to darken his door again. You had your choice, but you were a smart girl. You knew the ropes—you were crazy about me."

"Oh, Oliver," the words were a moan. "I still am—you know that."

"Sure, I know it," he smacked back. "And if you weren't the cutest little thing this side of the Pecos, I'd have shaken you long ago. So now that we've called a spade a spade, suppose we—"

There was squealing and giggling and a thump. I had to see, so I poked my head above the floor of the rostrum. There were Georgia Hinkins, hands clasped, gasping and giggling, and Sam Falloon springing up by her.

"Don't let him catch me," Georgia cringed prettily. "Ohhh-h—"

Sitting on the stool, Sister Bachellor was all smiles. Dr. Bachellor lounged over the corner of the organ.

"Oh, save me!" Georgia minced backward. "Do something, somebody—" One hand hugged her throat and she blinked appealingly at Dr. Bachellor.

"Saving women is against my principles," Dr. Bachellor said. "Grab her and kiss her, Sam." His laugh was a kind of ugly throat sound.

But Sam just stood there, red-faced and breathing hard.

Georgia gasped and sank into a chair. "Aren't men terrible?" She looked at Sister Bachellor and sighed. "They're all so wicked."

Sister Bachellor smiled wanly. "But we just have to put up with them. Now get your breath and we'll run through your solo."

Sam was looking at Dr. Bachellor, half-puzzled, half-belligerent. Dr. Bachellor put a hand on his shoulder, man-to-man fashion. "Suppose we vamoose and let the girls do their yodeling."

I jumped, slid out of the flap, and strolled around the corner. I wanted to be alone to think about what I had just seen and heard. It seemed to me there was something filthy about Dr. Bachellor with his tailored clothes and soft, white hands.

Through one of the tents I saw a woman's hand holding a baby's two feet, its fat rump turned up while she slid a fresh diaper beneath it. I could hear her caressing words and little love-spanks. That helped to take the nasty taste of Dr. Bachellor out of my mouth. From the side of the arbor I saw Brother Craddock performing his nightly duties with the lamps, lighting kerosene torches with an experienced hand.

Brother Dissey circulated through the crowd, greeting all the young folks with, "Our young folks are the hope of the nation," or, "Youth is the bulwark of civilization." Just before the services he hovered over Sister Hinkins, exchanged her damaged fan for a less used one, and gallantly escorted Georgia up on the platform and to her seat. From the expression on Mother's face, I knew that all this undue solicitude for the banker's family was not passing unnoticed.

Brother Dissey gave the signal to Sister Bachellor and led the choir and congregation in a resounding rendition of *Revive Us Again*. The chorus was repeated with great, shouting "Hallelujahs," and it proved to be a great pepper-upper as an overture. After the scripture reading, Georgia Hinkins rose and sang in a high tremulo,

> *"Oh, where is my wandering boy tonight,*
> *Down in the licensed saloon."*

The thoughts of wandering boys, coupled with Georgia's wailing notes, brought out a bevy of fluttering handkerchiefs.

Brother Dissey bounded up to the pulpit and announced his

text: "Wine is a mocker, strong drink is raging and whosoever is deceived thereby is not wise." And, lest this not be forceful enough, he added, "The wages of sin is death, but the gift of God is eternal life." Between acrobatics he mopped his brow and pushed up his coat sleeves so that his white cuffs shone in the lantern light.

He dramatized the wages of sin with one gruesome story after another. The audience cringed and sweated. He made a final, impassioned plea for mourners. At this point, by prearrangement, Sister Bachellor launched into *Oh, Why Not Tonight?* The choir caught the cue and pitched in eagerly, but were toned down by Sister Bachellor's lifted hand to a softer, more persuasive urgency.

I craned about to see what was happening in other parts of the arbor. Vela and Sammy and Tommy Craddock, sitting on the other side, were conversing. Sister Hipplehite, hands clasped, eyes staring upward, moved her lips slightly. Sister Slade walked back through the aisle, stopped to talk to one after another. But it seemed everyone was cowed and beaten and hadn't the heart to make a move toward the altar. For the first time I felt sorry for Brother Dissey. He had shot the works, and he looked more puzzled than anyone that there was no response. He stepped off the rostrum, sank down on a bench, and dropped his face into his hands. It wasn't just a dramatic gesture of discouragement; the poor man was exhausted. Father pronounced the benediction.

Not until the last of the people left the arbor could we start home. Marjorie was asleep in her little red wagon. Mother and I walked ahead, Father behind us drawing the wagon. Mother was talking.

"There was a big crowd tonight. How was the offering?"

"Only fair," Father replied.

"We ought to get some substantial contributions tomorrow."

"I doubt it," Father said. "The season has been so dry, people wonder how they'll live through the winter. We can't expect liberality among those whose very existence is jeopardized."

"I know." Mother's voice fell in soft folds. "Perhaps tomorrow everything will look brighter. What we all need is a good night's sleep."

" 'Yet a little sleep, a little slumber, A little folding of the hands to sleep,' " Father quoted.

Down the slope where the "Flying F" camped, a reddish glow rose from the barbecue pit. Shadows wavered against the side of a near-by chuck wagon as a cowboy turned the spit over the fire. There was one lone tone, a soft cord on strings, and a muted voice carried on the night wind.

We had just gotten home and lighted the lamp when Sammy came in. Tightly silent, she got out of her clothes and into her nightgown. After we were in bed the explosion came, muffled by her pillow.

"That old heifer. She won't let Vela out of her sight, and Vela hasn't got the guts of a rabbit or she'd buck up to her ma."

"What did Sister Slade do?" I asked.

"Adolph Betz told Dal they were sayin' he started the prairie fire. He wanted to set Vela straight and asked her to meet him at Deacon Webb's store. But Vela's ma's got her buffaloed. So I had to deliver the bad news. She couldn't even go with me." Sammy raised up on her elbow. "That old gal is drivin' Vela right into Tom Craddock's arms. And I think that's just what she wants to do."

"But Tommy is going away," I protested.

"With his little friend bein' persecuted? Oh no, not if I know that hombre. He'll have to stay and save her. And that's exactly what Sister Slade's a workin' for. I can see the way the rope's whirlin', but I can't do nothin' about it."

Lying there pondering Sister Slade's abominable actions, it seemed to me terribly wrong that the world should be governed by old people whose predominant aim was to frustrate and defeat young folks and children.

Chapter Fourteen

THIS last Sunday of the protracted meeting was muggy and oppressive. When we reached the arbor every fan still intact was in service, together with Sunday school cards and leaflets. The arbor was overflowing; children sat on the platform and on papers spread on the ground. Brother Dissey preached the morning sermon with his usual oratorical depiction of the fate of the sinner on Judgment Day. During the invitation song, Sister Hipplehite began a high, thin wail. Brother Hipplehite, undoubtedly under orders, clapped his hand over her mouth and took her outside. One of the campers went down the aisle with his trembling little wife clinging to his arm. Brother Dissey met them and situated them at the altar, where the drab little woman collapsed. Brother Dissey called it the power of the Lord striking down sinners, and bounded back up on the rostrum to renew his pleas.

The sight of the shrinking man and his hollow-chested wife, coughing between sobs, put a damper on the congregation. There were no more mourners, and Father finally pronounced the benediction.

By the time the ladies had spread the tables, the cowpunchers from the "Flying F" arrived with tubs of barbecued beef swung between them. They sliced the quarters with long, sharp knives, placing great slabs on the plates as they were brought up. Ora, Dora, and I ate until it was impossible to hold another bite, then lolled on a blanket. I had thought I couldn't move; but when I saw Father and Sheriff Lubeck talking, I left Ora and Dora unceremoniously and ran out and stood by Father.

"—finally caught up with 'em," the sheriff was saying, "camped right under the edge of the cap rock. Looked mighty suspicious to me. They could see the whole country below them and still not be seen by anyone coming from above. I finally made Lem admit he was William McGurk and Mrs. Enright was Miss Carrie

Weatherhogg. But one look from that surly Clem and he shet up. Couldn't never get another word out of him."

"What did he say happened after he left our place?" Father asked.

"Just that he took her home and left her there. Swears to God that's all he knows. Just dumped her out and drove away."

"And how does he account for having Enright's horses?"

"Says the hosses may have been Enright's for all he knows. That they found 'em in a pocket of Palo Dura Canyon, half dead from starvation and thirst, and got 'em out. Is that what he told you?"

"Yes," Father said. "Do you believe him?"

"I reckon they could a got loose while Enright was away." The sheriff shifted his weight and hitched up his pants. "But frankly, I didn't put no stock in the story. So I took my leave and rode back up the cap rock and out of sight. After dark I circled back, hid my hoss, and sneaked up to the edge of the rock that hung over their camp. Danged near starved while they fried bacon and boiled coffee and et their supper. Then Clem starts kickin' out the fire and Lem blows up. Says he's set around in the dark all he's a-goin' to—that he ain't goin' to burrow around like a mole for nobody.

"Then Clem snarled, 'I told you the minute you started foolin' around that woman you'd get in trouble. But you wouldn't listen.' And Lem blasts back in his bullyin' voice, 'I ain't done nothin' to get in trouble about. I never married her and I never kilt her.' And Clem, he sneers back, 'That's what you say.' Then Lem swaggers over with a skillet in his hand, ready to let him have it. He cuts loose with a string of words that'd curl your hair and Clem just sets and looks at him like he was a darin' him. Then he says, 'Go on, bash my head in too.'

"Well, sir, Lem Slothower jest stood there and looked at his brother. Then he said, 'So you think I done it too. My own brother thinks I'd lie to him. Listen here, Clem'—there was real pleadin' in his voice—'I swear on a stack of Bibles a mile high I never kilt that woman. Now are you a-goin' to believe me?' And by Go—jiminy, Reverend, it sounded mighty like he was a-tellin' the truth." The sheriff spat forcibly on the ground.

"Either telling the truth," Father said, "or trying desperately to convince his brother that he was."

Sheriff Lubeck nodded. "Well, truth or not, I had no evidence to take 'em in on. So while they made the rounds of the hosses I clumb back real quiet and snuck out."

"So now they're free to go on their way," Father said.

"Not exactly. I got Sheriff Nolan posted to keep track of 'em while they're in his county, and to pass the word on to the sheriff of whatever county they move into. At the same time he's to let me know which way they're headin'. That's all I can do right now."

Father turned his attention to a group of men who were scanning the horizon and talking in tense tones. A prairie fire, I thought, as Father, the sheriff, and I joined the group.

It was not a prairie fire, but a cloud—a low, dark wall projecting from the base of the western sky. A cloud at last! But from the men's opinions, it would probably fizzle into a "blow-out" or even a sand storm. In preparation for either, Brother Slade and Brother Falloon stretched wagon-sheets over the arbor's west side. The campers backed their wagons toward the west, pulled up tents, and loaded everything inside, tying all belongings securely. Horses that were hobbled or staked out were brought in and tethered to the wagons.

As the cloud bank rose and what little breeze there was died, the tension showed in men's and women's faces. Children fussed and babies fretted; mothers were short-spoken from anxiety. Scared to death but trying hard to conceal it, I moved to the center of the arbor, where Mattie Craddock and Ruby Tuttle sat and furiously chewed gum. They always picked the best of everything. This should be the safest spot.

Mattie looked at me, stretched her gum a good twelve inches, and licked it back. "It's been a punk revival if you ask me."

Since I hadn't asked I kept still.

"If it rains," Ruby said knowingly, "the whole thing will peter out with no converts and no weddings."

This was more than I could stand. "What do you mean, no converts?"

"You can't call Vela and Georgia and Tommy and all that gang converts. They would have joined the church anyway. They weren't brands snatched from the burning."

Boiling with indignation and having no appropriate refutation,

I walked up to the rostrum and served myself some lemonade from the pail. Sitting there sipping my lemonade and brazenly ignoring everybody, I saw Vela motion to me with a crooked index finger, which she then laid against her lips. I went back to her.

"Would you do something for me?" Vela said, and without waiting for my reply went on: "The 'Flying F' is moving out to-morrow. I can't let Dal go without saying good-by. Would you take this to him?" She drew a tiny folded paper from her lace-edged handkerchief.

"But I haven't seen him all day," I protested.

"Look down there." She pointed to the herd of Herefords mill-ing restlessly. "That's Dal on the big sorrel circling the cattle. He'll see you coming. He sees everything. He'll ride up to meet you."

I began to fear what Mother might say about me taking notes from Vela to Dal, when Sister Slade had forbidden communica-tion.

"Maybe Sammy could do it better," I suggested.

Vela sniffed. "Sammy's too busy—looking after Sammy."

I craned, thinking to see Sammy somewhere about.

"She's down there too," Vela said, "showing Tommy how to bulldog a steer. She's got him going."

"You mean he's sweet on her?"

Vela shrugged. "He's so wishy-washy he doesn't know what he wants. Sammy can have him for all I care."

I looked at the square of paper in my hand and wondered why girls always folded over one corner. Vela saw my indecision.

"I'll make you a lovely sachet bag if you will."

"All right," I agreed. Back of the arbor I stopped and saw Dal lope out and turn a bolting cow back into the herd. Just watching those seething whitefaces turned me sick inside. But I couldn't flunk out now. I struck out down the slope through the heat and fine dust drifting up from the cattle and the riders about them.

There was a strange, yellow cast that reminded me of the day of the hailstorm. A blink of green lightning flashed like a fizzling firecracker. Suddenly I wanted to get this over with and hurry back to the shelter of the arbor. I lit out like a frightened spook, my skirts flying. Before I had covered half the distance, Dal came riding hard to meet me.

"Listen, kid," he called, "you get back up that hill pronto. If these cattle see you—or if that cloud hits—"

"Dal! Dal—wait," I shrieked.

"We got all we can do to keep that herd from stampedin'—"

"But I've got something for you." He drew up between me and the arbor. "It's from Vela." I held up the note.

He read it on the horn of the saddle, with one eye on the cattle. Then he tucked the note inside his shirt pocket back of the Bull Durham.

"Muchas gracias, señorita." His smile looked like Vela's. "Tell her I can't answer it now. But if I could see her once more—"

"Why can't you see her again?" I demanded.

"And get my britches tore off? Her ma said she'd set the dog on me if I so much as set foot on the place."

The thought of old Tessie's tearing anyone's britches off made me giggle. "If you'd quit being an old sinner and get converted, Sister Slade would change her mind about you."

Dal stiffened in the saddle. "I ain't that kind of a fourflusher, pretendin' something I ain't."

"You don't have to pretend. I should think if you loved Vela, you'd not want her to have an old hell-bent sinner for a husband."

He looked at me hard, quickly swept the cattle with his glance. And then he was staring at the cloud, and through and beyond it.

"Now ain't that a thought?" he said slowly. "I reckon I shouldn't want Vela to marry a reprobate no more than her ma does." He looked down at me. "Thanks, kid. Now you high-tail it back fast, before one of them crazy steers spots you." He wheeled about and rode back. I trudged up the hill and came upon Father and Brother Falloon out back of the arbor.

" 'Tis no rain we'll be gettin' from that cloud," Brother Falloon said, "all our foine supplications to the contrary."

I scrutinized the great, frowning cloud, winced at the long streaks of lightning playing across it. Thunder rumbled distantly. But even I could see that it now lay much farther to the north. Undoubtedly Brother Falloon knew west Texas clouds and it had missed us.

Ruby's prophecy as to the fizzling out of the evening service seemed to have come true, even though no rain fell. Men slumped on the benches. Women trundled fretful babies on weary knees. Children were too tired to be quarrelsome.

Father dispensed with any elaborate song service and called for but one hymn before he read the scripture—the last three verses from the seventh chapter of Micah.

"Who is a God like unto thee,
That pardoneth iniquity?
And passeth over the transgression
Of the remnant of his heritage?
He retaineth not his anger forever
Because he delighteth in loving kindness.
He will again have compassion upon us,
He will tread our iniquities under foot,
And thou wilt cast all their sins
Into the depths of the sea.
Thou wilt perform the truth to Jacob,
And the loving kindness to Abraham,
Which thou hast sworn unto our fathers
From the days of old."

Father spoke in simple words of a loving God who had made the supreme gift of his own Son that a world of men might be saved; of a God whose mercy endured forever. He asked that his hearers join their faith with his, that they walk humbly before the Lord, that they unite in their efforts for a better town and community, in which children might grow up to know Christ through the examples of the Christlike lives about them. Then he closed his Bible and waited.

Into that hush came the tinkle of little bells. Dal Malone was walking up the aisle, tall and proud, his hat under his arm, his spurs jingling. He held out his hand to Father.

"I'm with you, Reverend," he said. "I'll do my best."

In Father's face was the same joy that there would have been over a hundred men. "I'm sure you will," he told Dal.

And then a strange thing happened. Down the aisle marched more than a dozen cowboys and knelt beside Dal. And from all over the congregation came men and women, some of them campers, some who were there only for the day. People moved back

145

to make room for them. There was no weeping, no shouting, no fanfare. I felt cheated as I moved back to the vacated end of a bench to give more room at the front.

A large woman beside me was talking. "Give it up, Adolph, for the sake of the childer. We've made enough now that you can start a drug store—your old business—"

"But our stock, Bertha. There's money bound up in it."

I peered at the small, half-hidden man. It was Mr. Betz.

"Ach," she lifted her hands, "dump it in the crick. We got enough. The preacher's a fine man, Adolph. His little girl was so good to our Anna and Hermann. I want we should hold up our heads again."

The little man's hand possessed Bertha's plump one.

"For you, Bertha, I will do it—"

Bertha Betz and her husband pushed past me. They were clinging together, hand in hand, as they joined the host at the altar.

I was fairly smirking with satisfaction over my part in the deal until I remembered that Father had thrust it upon me and I had bitterly resented it. I could take no credit for that.

But there was Dal. And once again my conscience smote me. Before me was Father, beaming with confidence in his fellow man. He thought Dal was sincere. But I knew better. I had planted in his mind the idea of professing Christianity in order to get to see Vela. And the men had followed. It was all a conspiracy to help Dal. They were putting over a huge hoax on Father. I sat there ashamed and silent, wishing I were dead.

In my misery I felt kinship with Brother Dissey, sitting with mouth half-open as though the lower part of his face had slid loose from its anchorage. The kinship was more complete than I knew; for Brother Dissey, suddenly aware that he was not coming in for his proper share of the glory, jumped to his feet and signaled to Sister Bachellor. Before she could pump up the organ and locate the key he was leading the congregation in singing *The Summer Is Ended*.

At the end of the first stanza Father lifted his hand and silenced them. He spoke a few words of welcome to those who had come forward, and told them that baptismal services would be arranged as soon as facilities were available. People pressed to the front to express their happiness over those who had joined with them in

146

the Christian way. Suddenly someone shouted above the hum of voices, "Listen!"

Through the echoing silence there came a rumbling roar like some great subterranean movement or the distant thunderous pounding of a thousand hoofs. I listened, bewildered at so august and terrible a sound.

"Lobo Creek," someone yelled. "A cloudburst up above—"

With complete authority Dal spoke to his men.

"We'd best get to the herd." They filed out quickly.

Small noises blotted into the crescendo of the thundering creek. Men lighted more lanterns and went out. Sister Bachellor called the children to the rostrum, started the organ. Sleeping babies wakened and whimpered into their mothers' bosoms, as we older ones sang hymn after hymn to combat the roar of the water.

At intervals men brought reports that the creek was still rising. That meant we were marooned for the night. Blankets and lap robes were spread for the children. But Ora, Dora, and I scouted the edge of the arbor, pretending bravery when in reality we were too scared to lie down and sleep.

At dawn we joined the watchers on the creek bank. Where the water had receded the cochineal bugs were out and the moist brown earth was decorated with scarlet velvet dots. In the pearl of a new day, houses of the town across the creek stood like gray boxes. But the creek's curve was gone. It swept by the town in a straight torrent of foaming murk and debris.

Mrs. Betz was the first to exclaim, "Look, Adolph. The saloon —it is gone. Praise the Lord."

"Praise the Lord," Father said fervently.

In that moment and in a way quite unpremeditated, the Betzes made a place for themselves in the heart of the community. Bertha Betz's emotions had finally found release. She was crying quietly.

"Ach, Adolph, if you knew the nights I have prayed that something would happen to destroy that saloon, before—before some shooting fellow killed you. It is in answer to my prayer. I am so happy for our little childer—and for you, Adolph—"

Adolph patted her hand. "So, Bertha, so. It is as I have always known. So wonderful a woman you are."

Some of the men grimaced and blew their noses. The women

looked away and asked one another when the water would subside.

Father led the way down to the ford. The water spread with the road into a wider, shallower stream. He went out on the prairie and cut the bloomed-out stalk from a bear grass. Back at the creek, he took off his shoes and socks, rolled up his pants, and waded in, feeling his way with the stick.

"Is it safe for them to go home now?" I asked Mother.

"I think your father has something else in mind."

Father gauged the current and dislodged stones from around him. He came back, laid his coat and vest on the bank, and took his folded handkerchief from his pocket. He conferred with Brother Slade and Deacon Webb while the women went for wraps and blankets. Soon the whole congregation was gathered on the creek bank except for a few of the "Flying F" men.

Father walked out into the water and stood with it rippling just under his arms. Brother Dissey stood in water to his knees.

"It's a miracle," Mother said, "but it took your father to see it."

To me it was a calamity. Father would have those cowpunchers baptized before I could tell him he had been tricked.

Father quoted from memory the third chapter of the Gospel According to St. Matthew. Then he asked the candidates to group themselves and come down one by one. Brother Dissey gave them safe conduct from the water's edge until Father received them. The sun came up and blazed over the rim of the eastern sky. It shone on weary and haggard faces and gilded the surface of the muddy water. Thirty-seven times Father pronounced the words, "And now I baptize thee in the name of the Father, and of the Son, and of the Holy Spirit. Amen."

As the women emerged from the water, they were met with blankets and coats and rushed down to the camp, where big fires blazed. Brother Falloon welcomed them with cups of steaming coffee. The men pretended not to mind the wetting, shrugged into their coats and jackets, and proceeded leisurely toward the fire. Mother and I walked back with Father, who looked tired enough to drop. His teeth chattered and his lips were blue, but the lines of strain and worry had disappeared from his face.

Mother was talking. "It does indeed strengthen one's faith. I'll concede that Brother Dissey is right in saying, 'What man cannot accomplish, the Lord will provide.' Ordinarily it takes months to find convenient places and times for everyone. That flood was made to order."

"Our prayers have been answered abundantly."

"And your unceasing work has been rewarded," Mother added. "Don't forget that without your work, this baptistry would have been useless."

"We need a church building now even more than before. For that, I think we must follow Brother Dissey and have faith."

"I agree," Mother sighed. "And unfortunately Brother Dissey is using works to follow you."

We joined the group at the fire. Dal was talking with Vela. He had changed to dry clothing, but his bright brown hair was wet and slick. Vela looked fresh and dewy in spite of the fact that she had missed a whole night's sleep. Dal had none of the solemn demeanor of a man who'd just gotten religion. He seemed happy and gay and quite able to shoot up the town if he chose.

Glancing about, I located some of the other cowpunchers who had followed Dal up the aisle. They too seemed unburdened with the weight of their decision, unimpressed with the gravity of the life they had undertaken. Some sat with arms about their knees; some were even smoking "coffin nails." Others talked and laughed just as they had in their sinful days. One or two had girls beside them and seemed as frivolous as ever.

I was convinced now that they had run a whizzer on Father. And though it was too late to keep such hypocrites out of the church, I felt that I must tell Father, so that they wouldn't fool him any longer. I slipped up beside him and tucked my hand inside his.

My voice was small and weak. "Father, I think Dal did all this just so as to get around Sister Slade and see Vela again."

"Why do you think that?" Father asked.

"Dora told me her mother wouldn't let Vela marry a rootin', tootin' sinner. She wouldn't let him come on the place."

"And you think that Dal became a Christian so that he could marry Vela?" Father inquired.

I nodded miserably. "Yes, I do."

"Well, so do I," Father said. "I think that he decided it was the more honorable life for a man who desired to be the husband of a Christian girl."

"You mean he won't go right back to the saloon?"

"Not to Brother Betz's saloon," Father reminded me.

"Nor shoot up the town anymore—or maybe gamble—" I was investing Dal with vices I did not know he possessed in order to make sure Father understood the things Dal might have engaged in.

"I'm quite sure he won't," Father said. "A man of Dal's caliber, having taken a stand he believes to be right, will remain steadfast."

With all those giddy cowboys about I was still doubtful.

"Then why did all those wranglers follow Dal to the altar? They don't all have girls. They must have thought it a joke."

"No," Father said, "I talked to each of them. Dal is a leader. The men admire and respect him. Whatever he deems desirable they also wish to acquire. Men like Dal wield a tremendous influence, whether consciously or unconsciously. Fortunately, Dal is aware of this and wants his influence to count for good."

"Then you think all those men really were converted? They didn't any of them act like they were getting saved."

"Some people are so constituted emotionally that for an experience to have significance they must realize it in tumult and portray it dramatically. Others make their decisions quietly and express them simply. In each case they may have the same validity. There is nothing in the Bible that requires us to throw an emotional orgy when we accept Christ and determine to follow his teachings and example."

If Father was bound to think the cowboys sincere, there was no sense in my arguing. In fact it was quite comforting, even flattering; for had I not suggested to Dal that he quit being a sinner? I wondered if I dared tell Father this and was considering it when Dal came up to us. His glance slashed across me sharply.

"I was afraid you might think that it was only on account of Vela that I did this," he said, "but I had made up my mind to be a better man. And by the great horn spoon, I'm a-goin' to live up to it."

"I'm sure you will," Father said. "I have never doubted it."

Dal drew a deep, free breath. "From the looks of things, there's goin' to be several couples gettin' married before long."

I glanced about the crowd. There were long, tall John Ellis and rosy-cheeked Kate Falloon; and with them were Sam, Kate's brother, and coy little Georgia Hinkins. Tom Craddock and Sammy were examining the silver mountings of a saddle; and Link Webb was pouring coffee from the big pot into the bright tin cup that Rose Mahoney held.

"That will be pleasant," Father said.

Dal poked a clump of buffalo grass with his toe. "Vela hasn't set the date, but we'd like to have the first wedding—in church."

"You shall have it," Father promised. "A fine church wedding."

Dal watched us as we left for home. In the middle of the creek over which Father carried me piggy-back, I looked back. Dal's face broke into a smile as he waved his big hat. Above the noise of the water, I could not hear his words. But I knew what he was saying.

Chapter Fifteen

SEPTEMBER spread a hazy veil over the sear brown prairies and touched them with pastel beauty. Strange and subtle changes took place as the Llano Estacado armed itself for the winter. These we were scarcely aware of, but others came of which we were fully cognizant. Brother Dissey left with ingratiating words and self-congratulatory hand rubbings over his carefully counted one-third of the contributions. He promised one more visit before winter set in. Sammy rode off to the ranch to gather together her belongings and bid her father good-by before leaving for Fort Worth. Father sent his report to the board and launched immediately into a church-building campaign. Mother and the Ladies Aid pitched in to help with a program of Saturday bake sales and plans for a pre-Christmas bazaar.

Deacon Webb went back to Ohio. Quietly he negotiated the sale of his store. Then he and Sister Webb had their belongings packed in a freight wagon, and with their sons, Lincoln, Garfield, and McKinley, were ready to leave.

Their last day in La Mesa was spent with us. Father and Deacon

Webb had a long talk while the women cleaned the Webb house for the Clevangers to move in. I heard Deacon Webb say that, were he younger and without a family, nothing would please him more than to stick and fight the thing through. But he felt that such a course would impose undue hardships on his boys. He was going back where they could grow up with the equality of opportunity which he believed was their birthright in a democracy.

School opened on the first Monday in the month, with Sister Kelso as teacher. Most of us had never had a woman teacher, but we soon found that Sister Kelso did not make that long trip each day merely to mother and pamper us. She expected us to improve each shining hour and have our assignments practically letter-perfect. This would have been fairly easy had not Otho Clevanger come among us.

Otho, the son of the new store owner, was a pale-eyed, tow-haired lad who employed much of his time inventing ways to harass people. His pranks drew a condoning smile or a half-hearted reprimand from his fatuous father. Sister Clevanger had three younger children, all girls—Eunice, Anice, and Inez—and was much too busy to superintend Otho's activities.

It was primarily my fault that I got in trouble with Sister Kelso, but Otho contributed. Sister Kelso assigned us the Preamble to the Constitution to memorize, whereupon Otho told us that in up-to-date schools such as the one he had been attending pupils were never asked to memorize prose. It was unfair to ask us to memorize words that had no rhyme. He swore he would hold out for memorizing only poetry if we would stand by him. I gave my word, along with Ora, Dora, Ruby, and Mattie.

The next day when called upon to recite the Preamble, I had not learned it, but to my amazement all the others had. It then became a matter of honor with me. I had given my word. Since I could not snitch on the others, I simply professed inability to learn unrhyming words. For three days Sister Kelso and I were stymied, since if she kept me after school she could not make the long trip home. I went unpunished, maintaining an ignoramus-like attitude.

Sister Kelso took the matter to Father, and for the first time in my life Father demanded of me an accounting for such unprecedented behavior. I explained the whole situation, and to my utter amazement he supported Sister Kelso. I had felt abused before, but with a disloyal parent I became a real martyr to the principle for which I stood. On Friday Father instructed me to learn the Preamble perfectly by Monday.

Much as I longed to go to Slade's and check up on when Tessie would have puppies, I stayed at home on Saturday lest I get into an argument with the deserters of my cause. I surprised Mother by actually offering to help her. She inquired if I were ill, which implanted an idea; and on Sunday I professed illness and was permitted to stay home from church. I hunted up the copy of *St. Elmo* Mother had hidden after she read it, and was so engrossed I barely had time to tuck it between the feather bed and the shuck tick when Mother and Father came home.

Carefully ignoring Father and fraternizing with Mother, I was still feeling terribly injured and misunderstood. At bedtime I lay with a soul-smothering dread of the morrow, when in the dead stillness Father's and Mother's voices came from the other room.

"Opal must be coming down with something," Mother remarked.

"With a jolt," Father said, "since pride goes before a fall."

"She's so erratic. I don't understand what's come over her. I'm sure she spent the morning reading a paper-backed novel—*St. Elmo*."

"You read it, didn't you?" Father asked.

"But I'm not a child," Mother replied. "If we could get a new head for Marie, she might engage in more normal activities. She's been without a doll since the hailstorm. There's so little for children to do here. Perhaps we should have gone back to Louisville."

"Opal didn't care to go," Father said.

"You mean you told her about the offer at the seminary?"

"Of course," Father said. "It concerned her as vitally as it did us. She had a right to consider it from her viewpoint."

"I think," Mother said sharply, "much of Opal's trouble is due to your letting her have her head."

"She has to have it in order to learn to use it—and control it. Right now she's hanging to a warped idea of a principle in order to preserve her personal pride."

"I think she has reason to feel injured," Mother said, which brought to my breast a great surge of affection for her.

"She has," Father agreed, "but she needn't take it out on Sister Kelso and try to turn her schoolroom into a battlefield."

I heard Mother say, "You're making it hard on her."

"She's making it hard on herself," Father replied sternly.

I expected Sister Kelso to initiate the day with a demand that I recite the loathsome Preamble. But nothing was said. At recess I stood aloof, avoiding my perfidious contemporaries, and saw Sister Kelso in the door, apparently watching us in a casual manner. Otho used this unguarded moment to slip up behind me and loose a huge grasshopper on my neck with the shriek, "Spit tobacco juice on her!" In a frenzy I clawed at my hair until Sister Kelso assured me the grasshopper had flown away as soon as it was released.

About a half hour before school was to be dismissed, Sister Kelso asked me to recite the Preamble. Something shut down fast inside me and I stood tight-lipped and silent. She took me by the arm, opened the closet where supplies and coats were stored, and pushed me inside. The lock snapped as I decided I could stay as long as Sister Kelso could keep me there. There was a window which I might open later and escape.

But suddenly on the window I saw a half-dozen wasps climbing up the panes, then dropping back, buzzing angrily in frustration. One made a sortie out into the room, narrowly missing my hair. I shrieked and beat on the locked door. It opened immediately and Sister Kelso stood by while I came out and immediately launched into a verbatim recitation of the Preamble. Titters and laughter spread over the room.

"School is dismissed for the day," Sister Kelso said sharply.

The acid of embarrassment burned my face as I loitered along the way home from school. I made a wide detour of the town to avoid any who might waylay me and torment me about the episode. This took me past the pest house, which since Father's explanation I no longer feared—or so I thought until I heard a noise inside it. Visions of a horrible, purple-faced plague victim assailed me. My skin crawled and the roots of my hair tightened as the door swung open. I took out for home on a dead run.

At a safe distance I looked back and saw Dr. Mesropian emerge from the shed and make his way toward the town. I could scarcely wait to ask Father who was in the pest house and what plague had descended on the town. But when I reached home, Mother was reading a letter from Sammy.

"See what lovely paper." She held out the twice-folded sheet. It was heavy and looked like linen, and had her name "Samantha Clark Severn," across the top in gold letters. Then Mother read:

"Dear Brother and Sister Berryman and Opal: Aunt Fanny—that's Mrs. Hamilton—took me with her and we bought a whole gob of new clothes. I've a fur neck piece and a little muff and button shoes with gray tops and curved heels. My new gray coat is gored with puffs at the tops of the sleeves. Aunt Fanny gave a tea for me and Lucy invited all her girl friends, and you know what? They all crooked their little fingers real elegant, just like Tom. And speaking of Tom, he sent me a postal with a cowpuncher on it all diked out in a swallowtail coat and a plug hat, riding up the steps of some big building, and it said, 'Oh, you kid.' Do you reckon he was trying to guy me?

"Ford's pa took us all to the Fat Stock Show. Was them critters fancy! Some of them looked just like them whitefaces Pat Falloon bought. And sell high—I'll bet that guy makes a pile of spondulicks. And some they called Holsteins were black and white pied, and you'd ought to see the milk you can squeeze out of them. Honest, such cattle and horses as you never seen in all your life.

"Opal, I left my perfume heart lying in the conch shell on the front room table. You can have it because Aunt Fanny got me a nice gold breastpin for my sixteenth birthday. A bowknot and a wishbone and an honest-to-goodness pearl set in the middle. Anyway, I'm through with Slim Breedlove. Ford give me a big box of bonbons and Lucy give me a little pocketbook of wire, like mosquito netting, all lined in silk. They call them mesh bags, and if they aint too costly, I'm going to send you one.

"Brother Berryman, I found out from Pa that Slim Breedlove is fixing to stir up trouble because of the saloon being gone. He blames you for praying the water down the crick, and aims to chase you out of town. If I was you, I'd be on the lookout for him. If he gets too rambunctious, you might as well shoot him, because he aint no good anyway."

Mother laughed at this, but it was a tremulous laugh. Father came in, took the milk pail, and went to milk the Widow True-blood's cow. Mother wrinkled her nose at the aroma of carbolic and went on reading.

"Lucy and I go to Miss Morrow's School for Girls. I don't tucker to it much. They call geography 'travel' and grammar 'English' and arithmetic 'mathematics.' I take painting, which they call 'art,' and music, which is both singing and piano playing. I reckon if I make good grades I won't have time for much else. But you folks write to me. I get lonesomer than all get out. I love you all. Sammy."

Mother sighed. "I do hope she doesn't get fed up and tear out for home, like she did at the end of her first week with us."

I went to get the perfumed heart. It was down inside the conch shell. I held the shell to my ear to listen to the roar of the ocean whose memory lay forever in the pink heart of the shell. I pinned the perfumed heart on my shepherd-check school dress and wondered if ever I'd have a sweetheart who would give me such beautiful gifts. Father came in with our portion of the milk for milking the Widow Trueblood's cow.

"I greased the chickens' heads and under their wings yesterday," Mother was saying. "I only found a few lice. You didn't need to creosote the whole hen house."

"I didn't," Father replied.

"Then it was Sister Trueblood's cow shed—"

"Sister Trueblood's cow shed smells, but not of creosote," Father told her. "I'll have to clean it tomorrow."

"Then where does that carbolic smell come from?" Mother demanded.

"The pest house."

Mother gasped. "For heaven's sake! Is somebody—"

Father nodded. "Rose Mahoney has the smallpox."

"Oh, my Lord! Now we're in for an epidemic. I suppose someone who came to the protracted meeting—"

"It could be," Father said, "but Sister Mahoney thinks it was a drummer that stayed at the boarding house overnight after the meetings closed. He'd hired a rig out of Big Spring and was so ill the next day he had to get a driver to take him back." Father was searching the clothes that hung behind the cornerwise curtain.

"Where is that old pair of pants—the one with the patch in the seat?"

"I washed them and put them in the box couch to make comfort pieces. What do you want them for?"

"To wear." Father got them out of the box couch.

"Don't tell me you're going to nurse Rose Mahoney?" Mother's voice was a mixture of anger and unbelief.

"Of course," Father said. "I've had the smallpox."

"But Opal and Marjorie haven't. Surely you wouldn't risk bringing it to them. Let someone else do it."

"Could I ask another to do what I would not be willing to do myself? There's no real hazard. Dr. Mesropian and I will take turns. Sister Mahoney has a houseful of boarders that can't very well shift for themselves."

"So you risk the lives of your own children. Let Sister Mahoney quit her work—"

"I tell you, Mama," Father said in exasperation, "I'm not risking anything. Dr. Mesropian has given me explicit instructions. Doctors have to go from patient to patient. They know the procedure."

"Besides," Mother asked, "what will people say? Two men nursing an unmarried girl—it's simply out of the question."

"Would people rather she died?" Father demanded. "Do you think for a minute that either Dr. Mesropian or I would harm a girl who was fighting for her life?"

"You mark my words," Mother declared, "you'll never hear the last of this. If Rose dies, you will get the blame. If she lives, you and that foreigner will be the talk of the town. It will ruin you."

"I can't believe," Father said, "that people are that malicious. But I'll have to take my chances and do my duty as I see it. We discussed the matter with Sister Mahoney. Dr. Mesropian says her heart is in such condition it's likely she could not stand the nursing. She'll prepare and send out Jim with our meals and the proper diet for Rose. If I refused and Sister Mahoney's heart gave way—perhaps causing both her death and Rose's—I would have only myself to blame. That is a risk I can't take."

"You'll do things your own way, of course," Mother told him.

"But when the storm breaks, just remember that I warned you."

"I'm sure I shall," Father said calmly, "much as I might desire to forget it." There was no rancor in his voice.

"It's quite evident where Opal gets her stubbornness," Mother fired back. "You should have a great deal of sympathy for her."

"I have," Father said. "I hope she has as much for me."

This business was getting a little thick for my limited comprehension. I was confused in my allegiance. It seemed to me that Mother was right; but Father was standing on a principle, and he definitely had my sympathy, for the memory of the thankless job of defending an ideal was with me strongly. Into this tortuous battle of the validity of claims came a knock on the front door. I opened it, and there stood Brother Adolph Betz.

Father spoke from behind me. "Come in, Brother Betz." Brother Betz came in, his head tilted a little forward so that his bald spot showed through the sparse tan hair. "Have a chair," Father offered.

"*Ach*," Brother Betz shook his head, "I shist hert about the young lady, Miss Mahoney. Smallpox—*nicht sehr gut*."

"She's a very sick girl," Father said, "and likely will be worse before she is better."

"Iss it as I heard that no one can help care for her?"

Father hesitated. "Very few people are willing. Mrs. Berryman and I have had smallpox. Dr. Mesropian is coming over this evening to vaccinate Opal and Marjorie. But many are not willing to be vaccinated or to have their children take the vaccine."

I was no longer confused as to whose side I was on. This was ridiculous—Father's deciding to have Marjorie and me vaccinated. The idea that he would subject us to this awful experience just to be able to take care of Rose Mahoney was incredible. I was petrified.

Brother Betz was talking. "Me—I have had the smallpox. And Bertha and Anna and Hermann were vaccinated in St. Louis. They all took. Bertha and me would like to help you take care of the young lady. That iss, should it be all right with her mother."

"That's extremely kind of you," Father replied. "I'm sure that Sister Mahoney would appreciate it. I was wondering how Dr. Mesropian and I would manage. Each of us has other duties that cannot be totally disregarded. But we can divide the time between the four of us and it will be no great hardship. Also Rose will ob-

158

tain much better care." Father got his hat and coat and put them on. "Suppose we go down and talk to Sister Mahoney about it."

Mother came in, her hand extended. Brother Betz bowed a bit stiffly. But Mother was adept at putting people at ease.

"I heard your offer to Mr. Berryman. I think that's splendid of you and Sister Betz. I was just wondering how we were ever going to get along if Mr. Berryman had to spend most of his time being nurse."

Brother Betz's blue eyes lighted like bright Indian beads.

"Ach, it iss not gut that one should bear all the burden. We are in the church to help one another, *nicht wahr?*"

"We are indeed," Mother agreed, "but so few people seem to remember it when there is a hard job ahead. This is so good of you and Sister Betz. If the children get along well with their vaccination, I too shall be able to help, making it less difficult for all."

I could only stand and gape at Mother after this reversal.

"Bertha and me—we got to be busy. We're not used to being with our hands folded. Until Brother Slade gets the new drug store built, we got time to trow away. Und"—he shrugged and looked at Mother with a sheepish twinkle in his eyes—"maybe we're shist being smart already. Maybe it will bring a little business when the store is opened."

Mother laughed. "If it doesn't, I'll lose my faith in humanity. But even so, you and Sister Betz are very generous."

Brother Betz had lost his meekness. Pride bloomed forth.

"Bertha, she likes to keep her hand in. She was a nurse when she married me. She likes to bring back health to the sick ones."

"That's wonderful," Mother said, "having a trained nurse in the community. It almost makes illness a temptation."

"Rose has first claim," Father warned. "Shall we go, Brother Betz, before my wife collapses for a rest?"

Mother was laughing as she closed the door behind them. Then she saw me cringing in the corner. "What's the matter with you? You look like the one who's collapsing."

I gulped and swallowed. "I—I think I'm going to puke."

"Then for heaven's sake, get to the door." Mother grabbed my arm and hurried me out into the evening air. The strong prairie wind whipped away my nausea, leaving me bug-eyed and speechless.

"Did you eat something at school?" she asked.

I shook my head.

"Have you taken cold?" She pressed her lips to my forehead. "You've no fever."

Two big tears rolled down my cheeks.

"What in the world is ailing you?" Mother demanded.

I pushed to get the words past the enormous lump in my throat. "Will—will vaccination hurt much?"

"Well, I'll be switched!" Mother exclaimed. "Are you standing there sweating like a nigger at election because of a measly little vaccination?" I nodded miserably and swallowed back a sob. "A great, big girl practically nine years old"—Mother rolled her hands into her checked apron—"who can recite the Preamble to the Constitution without fumbling a single word, sniffling like a baby over a little scratch on the arm. I'm simply stumped."

My back stiffened as though she had run a shingle down it. "How did you know I recited the Preamble?" I demanded.

"Sister Kelso came by right after school and told us what a splendid job you did. She had intended to dismiss the school while you were in seclusion, but you were so prompt in your decision—"

"She's a nasty old tattletale," I stormed.

"She had promised to let your father know when the matter was settled. Now hereafter don't permit Otho Clevanger to lead you astray."

"That boob," I snorted, "isn't going to lead me any place."

"And try to remember"—Mother's arm went about my shoulders—"when you find you are in the wrong and have to retract, do it just as quickly and gracefully as possible. It's so much easier on your pride and your poise not to rip your self-esteem to shreds."

It dawned on me then that Mother herself had just furnished a classic example of what to do when you found yourself in the wrong. In that moment I took one whole step upward in growth and understanding. Above all I wanted to show Mother that I too could be brave.

"I don't mind being vaccinated. Even if it does h-hurt." I swallowed. "I was just mostly 'sprised—"

Mother's hands went outward in a quick, gay gesture. "All women are alike. Most of our fright is surprise. It takes a moment to adjust ourselves. I doubt if you scarcely notice the vaccination."

"Honest?" All my wishful hopes bounced up.

"There's one sure thing, if the Betz children can take it I'm certain that my daughter can."

"Sure, I can," I swaggered. And the confidence Mother had inspired in me fortified me for the infinitesimal ordeal of having my arm scratched and the smallpox virus introduced, and a small, neat dressing plastered above it. Dr. Mesropian complimented me on my equanimity, saying that many children were nervous, though he couldn't see why. I agreed with him that it was very silly to be nervous about so simple a thing.

But some four days later it was no simple thing to have an arm as sore as a boil and a temperature that sent me into crazy dreams. I dreamt about masked faces at windows, and Father chasing Slim Breedlove over the prairie and shooting him, and Sammy Severn galloping up on a black-and-white Holstein cow, from whose pendulous bag Father milked a tubful of milk, then dunked Otho's head into it while he recited the Preamble.

Only one item emerged from this kaleidoscope as having a basis of fact. Father, Dr. Mesropian, and Brother and Sister Betz divided the day into six-hour shifts in caring for Rose Mahoney. Sister Betz left Anna and Hermann with Mother on her way to the pest house to relieve Father. Mother had them busy playing tiddle-de-winks on the front-room floor when Father came in to his breakfast. I lay on the kitchen bed.

"I think Rose has finally taken a turn for the better," Father said. "Dr. Mesropian is sure that the crisis is past. I've never seen a man work harder to pull a patient through. He's a fine doctor."

"He stopped to see Opal," Mother informed him. "He said to keep her warm and she'd be all right in a day or so."

"We're fortunate in having such a good physician," Father smiled. "If things go well, he wants to bring his family out by Christmas."

"Will Rose be very pitted?" Mother asked. "It's such a tragedy for a young girl to have a pock-marked face."

"She won't have a pit on her face. While she was delirious, Sister Betz kept her hands tied to the sides of the bed with strips of muslin. After she became rational, Rose asked that we keep them

161

tied lest she scratch in her sleep. Sister Betz is a fine nurse—so kind and patient, yet absolutely rigid about necessary things. Dr. Mesropian says he never worked with a better nurse."

"Sister Mahoney can certainly be thankful," Mother said. "Let's see—you take a daytime shift this coming week. As soon as Opal is up, we'll de-bug the beds. Marjorie has a welt on her arm."

"We'd better postpone it," Father said. "Dr. Mesropian and I have decided to stay on the night shifts."

"Sister Betz insists she's not afraid," Mother said.

"She isn't. But you remember a few days ago I told you that we had seen a masked face peering in at the window?"

Mother nodded. "Some curious person who took the additional precaution of tying a handkerchief over his nose and mouth."

"Well, last night when I relieved Dr. Mesropian he told me that the same visitor had been there again. This time he had a white sack or a pillow case over his head, with holes for eyes and mouth. Dr. Mesropian went outside, and there were not one but three white-robed figures that ran away when he made his appearance. I wouldn't want to subject Sister Betz to such an experience. These people are evidently up to no good."

Mother stopped half-way between the stove and the table, the syrup pitcher in one hand and the teapot in the other. "Do you suppose that some sneaking coward is still after Dr. Mesropian?"

"Possibly," Father affirmed, "but as long as there is no proof, we must guard our suspicions. After all, there were three of them last night. Regardless of our suppositions, two of them are anonymous. So we must consider all three of them as such."

"But can't something be done?"

"What, for instance? I have preached against hate and intolerance of race, creed, or color. Apparently it has borne no fruit. Presumably all three of these men sat through my sermons with blank, innocent faces—probably complimented me after services on the fine message I had delivered." There was bitterness in Father's voice. "Such are the hypocrites who go about under masks and hoods and bed sheets."

"But this one man—he expressed his opinion to you—even boasted about what they intended to do," Mother reminded him.

"That alone makes me think that he is not the leader. The instigator would be too shrewd to ever commit himself to me, knowing my convictions on such matters."

I was seething with excitement. Father did not think that Brother Hipplehite was the leader, but only a tool. I checked off swiftly the men I knew. It couldn't be Brother Slade, Father's best friend, or Brother Craddock, whom we had known from old Chicago days. Brother Hinkins, the banker, was much too uppity-up; and Judge Pothast's being the County Judge let him out. It wasn't Brother Falloon, because he lived out of town, as did Brother Severn and Brother Kelso. So it had to be Brother Clevanger or Dr. Bachellor, mainly because I disliked them. Of course there was Brother Betz, who had run a saloon, but he'd not risk scaring his big wife. And Dal Malone and all Brother Falloon's and Brother Severn's cowboys and the wranglers from Teepee Hamilton's ranch—I had to admit they could be guilty, but it was too big a job to pick three men from all that bunch.

Only two I was sure of—Father and Dr. Mesropian. Of course Dr. Mesropian could be lying—he'd certainly lied to me about vaccination being of minor importance. Or at least passed it off lightly.

"Could Dr. Mesropian determine anything by their size or build?" Mother asked. "I suppose it would be almost impossible."

"Only that two were tall and could run like antelope. And the other was short, probably fat, since he had to lag behind. They ran over the rise toward the ravine. Perhaps they held a conclave there, or possibly they simply wanted to change clothes."

"Can't we do anything? Do we have to just let them run good people out of town like they did the Webbs?"

"In order to do anything, we first must ascertain positively who the leader is. If I find out, you may be sure that I'll go to him personally. If that has no effect, I'll use other means."

Rarely, away from the pulpit, had I heard Father's voice vibrate with the strength of his convictions as it did now.

Chapter Sixteen

HE ladies abandoned their plans for the Saturday bake sales and pre-Christmas bazaar. All of them were nervous about food or handwork from the homes of Sister Mahoney, Sister Betz, and Mother. And of course without these contributions such enterprises were impossible. When rumors of a small-pox epidemic got about, the farmers and ranchers reduced their trips to town. Church attendance decreased, as did the town's business.

Father's quietness about the house was not entirely due to the strain of six hours' additional duties as nurse. The impetus the revival had given to his work was diminishing day by day. With business declining, the town people could not meet their pledges and the country people stayed away. Father no longer went to the bank on Monday morning with a deposit for the church building fund.

Vela came over and talked to Father. She and Dal wanted to be married before spring—possibly at the Easter season, when most of the young people now away at school might be home for a few days. Did Father think they would have a new church building by spring? Father shook his head. It didn't seem likely that any progress would be made throughout the winter. Vela and Dal had better not plan on a church wedding unless they could arrange to have it in the schoolhouse.

It was strange how things kept right on happening when you were laid up. When I resumed my music lessons at Sister Bachellor's, my knock on the door was answered by a bedlam of barking dogs. I was on the point of turning and fleeing when the door opened. I edged in gingerly and two big black-and-white dogs with fringed ears and plumed tails sprang forward, licking my face and wagging their bodies. Sister Bachellor grabbed their collars.

"Sometimes," she sighed, "they're almost too much for me. But they're a great protection. Oliver insists I keep them in the house."

"Has someone been bothering you?" I piped up, eager to find out if she had seen masked faces at the window.

"No. But you can't be too careful when you are alone."

"Is Dr. Bachellor gone?" I asked, thinking what a break it would be for her if he had absconded, and how nice it would be with no blood spattered on the keyboard or snaggled teeth on the music rack.

"Oliver had to make a trip east." Her smile was wistful, her eyes dreamy. "Gracious, but it's lonesome without him. But he had to get his new business started—breeding and raising pointers. There's pedigrees and registries and so many complicated things to do."

"What are pointers?" I asked.

"Bird dogs. Oliver is a great sportsman. He isn't happy unless he's surrounded with hunting and fishing trophies—you know, dogs and horses and guns and things."

I soon learned that a music lesson with two dogs was even worse than a music lesson with Dr. Bachellor. Sister Bachellor shut them in the bedroom. They barked and whined and clawed until she opened the door, whereupon they dashed out and knocked over a rack of pipes, and she had to shut them up again. Midway through my rendition of Beethoven's *Für Elise*, there was a terrific crash. Both Sister Bachellor and I dashed to the door. In a crumble on the floor lay the long battenberg dresser scarf, and splattered about it a broken mirror, a comb and brush, a nail buffer, and two shattered bottles of cologne—besides innumerable yellow hairpins and a barette from an up-side-down pin tray.

"I'll be so glad when Oliver gets the kennel built," she moaned.

"So will I," I agreed and sincerely meant it.

We salvaged some of the cologne by dipping Sister Bachellor's handkerchiefs in it. I swabbed up the remainder with the ruffle of my petticoat and went around smelling like a bevy of Modjeska Bouquets.

As soon as Dr. Bachellor came home, Brother Slade set his helpers to work building the kennel. After school, Ora, Dora, and I watched its progress. There were but two dog houses, and a big storage room that fastened with a hasp and padlock. A few days later one of the freighters drove his wagon up to the kennel, unloaded several big boxes into the storeroom, and bolted and locked the door. Evidently the Bachellor dogs were not to lack for food for a long time to come.

The latter part of October, Rose Mahoney went home from the pest house. The next day Father and Sister Mahony burned the bedding—mattress, quilts, and pillows. They washed the inside of the house with carbolic water, then closed the door, leaving a smudge burning in a saucer on the floor. The pest house was ready for its next patient.

When the purplish look cleared from Rose's skin, her face was as satiny as a lily petal. With her curly black hair and long-lashed blue eyes, her quick smile and easy ways, she was soon again the belle of all the play-parties and box socials. Yet her illness had changed her. She was now determined to be a nurse. Daily after school she went to the Betz home for instructions in first aid, home nursing, rolling bandages and making dressings, and how to feed sick people. She talked constantly about going to some hospital and taking nurse's training.

When Brother Betz's drug store was completed, she helped him and Sister Betz put the stock on the shelves. On Saturdays she spent the whole day learning how to mix medicines. And when Dr. Mesropian set up a laboratory in the back room of the drug store, she helped him with test tubes, beakers, retorts, smears, slides, bacteria, and germ cultures. Smallpox had certainly changed Rose Mahoney.

After the fall roundup Brother Slade went out to Falloon's and with the help of the cowboys built a house for Dal. It was in a pasture where Brother Falloon already had a well, windmill, and tank for the cattle. Vela and Dal now had plans for a Christmas wedding in the schoolhouse. Mother was sewing daily on Vela's trousseau. One by one she made use of all the attachments in the little wooden box—the tucker, and the gatherer to make the fine eyelet embroidery flounces to the petticoats, the shirrer, and the extra presser-foots for fine hemming and hemstitching.

Vela ordered pale pink batiste from Fort Worth, because it was very new to have pale pink underwear. Sister Slade held out for white for the drawers petticoats, and corset covers, but let Vela have a pink nightgown. But when the package came and the batiste was a bright scarlet, Vela was almost in tears.

"I'll buy it from you," Mother told her. "It will make Opal a nice summer dress—with a white net guimpe and trimmed in black velvet baby ribbon. I'll write Sammy and have her pick out some pale pink batiste and send it to you right away."

So Vela had her pale pink nightgown, trimmed in fine val lace, with white beading and pink ribbon rosettes at each corner of the neck. The day Mother finished it I delivered it to Vela. Ora and Dora followed me outside with some *sub rosa* remarks about a bride's first night.

"Why couldn't Vela wear a red nightgown?" I asked.

"Silly!" Ora showed complete disgust. "Only fancy women wear red nightgowns."

"Honest?" I said. "How do you know?"

Dora's look of horror set me to thinking. Remembering the disappointment of the "Flying F" boys, I had pictured fancy women as something pretty special. Maybe I'd been wrong.

"Did you ever see one in a red nightgown?" I asked.

"Of course not," Ora snorted. "Fancy women never go outdoors. They always stay inside fancy houses."

Back at home I hunted up Father's rabbit-skinning knife and engaged in improving my game of mumble-peg, all the while trying to devise a way to augment my store of knowledge without exposing my ignorance.

A week before Christmas we had a bad norther and Vela decided to be married at home. Only the Falloons and our family and the Slades were there for the wedding; but at the reception afterward most of the church members came in to congratulate the groom, felicitate the bride, and have a glass of punch and a piece of cake. Right in the middle of the festivities a horrible racket broke loose in front of the house. It sounded like a gang of hoodlums beating dishpans, blowing horns, and shooting guns.

"The cowboys—on a rampage again—" I gasped to Father.

"No. It's a charivari. The people who know Dal and Vela have gathered to salute them. Dal must either pass out treats or give them money for a celebration party. Otherwise the bedlam will keep up until he does. It's one of matrimony's first penalties." His smile met Mother's.

The crowd had called for the bride and groom. We followed them to the porch, and the din broke forth in even greater fury. Suddenly Sheriff Lubeck rode up, firing his six-shooter into the air.

"Break it up! Break it up!" he yelled. "What's going on here?" He swung down from his horse. Father stepped off the porch and pushed through the crowd to him, with me at his heels.

"It's all right, sheriff," he said. "It's only a charivari."

"A what?" the sheriff barked.

"A *shiveree*," Father amended the pronunciation. "You must have known that the boys were gathering. It's quite harmless."

"I just this minute rid into town," the sheriff said, "and for the past mile all I could hear was this dad-blasted racket."

Dal had come up beside us. "Let 'em have their fun, sheriff," he said. "I don't 'spect to ever get married but once. And anyways, they wasn't aimin' to get rough."

"Shore," the sheriff agreed. "I reckon in my business a man gets old and jittery before his time. What you givin' 'em, son?"

"They want to have a watch party down at Mahoney's on New Year's Eve. I reckon ten bucks ought to furnish the grub."

"Shore as shootin'," the sheriff agreed. "Miz Mahoney will put out more coffee and doughnuts than you can shake a stick at for that."

"It's all right, fellows," Dal called. "Who's the banker, and how much is it goin' to cost me to restore peace to the community?"

Dal moved back into the crowd. Sheriff Lubeck spoke to Father, who followed him out to where his horse stood with the reins over his head.

"I was aimin' on seein' you tonight anyway," the sheriff said. He took his Bull Durham from his pocket, made a trough with a paper, and sifted tobacco into it. "Several days ago I got word from Sheriff Nolan of Colorado County to come down to Colorado City. Seems like the boys on a ranch up this way had been scourin' the breaks below the cap rock for dogies. They spotted a flock of turkey buzzards circlin' and figured a cow was down —maybe dead. Instead they found the body of a man."

The sheriff paused to lick the paper and press it down.

"Well, I went and saw the body. It had been out in the weather and wa'n't in too good shape, but still 'twasn't no trouble for a man who'd knowed him to tell that it was Lem Slothower."

"Lem Slothower!" Father exclaimed in a low tone.

"Yep," the sheriff said. "His head was bashed in."

"So now," Father said slowly, "you are convinced that Enright killed his wife, tracked down Lem Slothower, and killed him."

" 'Pears to me like there ain't no other way to figger it."

"Then," Father said, "how do you account for my dog's having his head bashed in?"

"There's an answer for that too," the sheriff replied. "Enright was probably snoopin' about, spyin' on his wife and Lem. He done away with the dog because he made a fuss."

Father was silent for a moment. "What does Lem's brother, Clem, have to say about how Lem died?"

"That's the only hitch," the sheriff admitted. "Ole Clem seems to have faded plumb out of the pitcher. Either he's dead too, or he's given Sheriff Nolan the slip and got clean away. But"— the sheriff's voice sounded as though it came between his teeth— "I got my dander up now. I'll find that son of a gun, dead or alive, if it takes me till doomsday."

Father stood there staring into the night after Sheriff Lubeck had ridden away. Suddenly he turned to me. "Opal, think back carefully. Did you hear any sounds outside the house on the night Lem Slothower and Mrs. Enright requested me to marry them? Any sounds of someone prowling about the place?"

The very chill of that December night seemed to help reconstruct the scene Father asked me to recall. But I could remember no sound of movement outside, so intently had I focused my attention on the would-be bride and groom.

"All I remember was how hard it was to hear everything you folks said, with Shep yelping and growling outside."

"You mean," Father emphasized each word, "that Shep was still growling after our visitors came inside?"

"Yes," I said. "Once he yelped loud, like a strange dog was fooling around him."

"Or a strange man." Father stood a moment longer, then said, "We'd better go in."

The freighters from Big Spring brought us a Christmas tree, a sprangling pine some eight feet tall cut from the scrub pines that grew below the cap rock. Father and Brother Slade set it up in the schoolhouse. The Ladies Aid spent a whole afternoon dipping apples and stringing popcorn on twine and making little socks out of red mosquito netting. These they filled with candies and cookies, and tagged each with a child's name. Brother Clevanger brought over a tow sack full of goobers, which were put into red-and-green-striped bags and tied at the top.

We children gathered at Sister Bachellor's to practice Christmas carols, and she drilled us in our recitations. Otho Clevanger was to recite "The Boy Stood On the Burning Deck." Ora had difficulty in learning all the verses to " 'Twas the Night Before Christmas." Georgia Hinkins had written from Simmons College in Abilene that she would be home and would sing *The Holy City*. Sister Betz had taught Anna and Hermann *Stille Nacht, Heilege Nacht*. They were so well trained they needed no rehearsals. Henry Kelso would recite "Sail On, Sail On, Oh Ship Of State." Sister Kelso would see to it that he was letter-perfect.

Christmas Eve was cold with a nipping wind, but the sky was clear and bristling with jewels. All day long at intervals young men and young ladies slipped into the schoolhouse and deposited gifts there, enjoining the strictest secrecy from Mother or Sister Slade or whoever was tending the tree. After the closing of stores and offices the men came, their arms loaded with family gifts. People drove in from the country bringing presents to be hung on the tree or laid at its cotton base.

Father wore his Prince Albert; Mother had on her black mohair suit trimmed in bias folds of black velvet; Marjorie wore a rose cashmere dress; and I had on a spanking new white cashmere with pleated skirt and collar and cuffs banded with red. Red stars shone in the corners of the sailor collar and a red anchor rode on the sleeve.

The schoolhouse was packed with people. Just before the opening song, Father lighted the little red candles clamped to the tree with spring-toothed holders. As a precaution, several buckets of water sat against the wall. Three or four couples that had been outside in buggies, spooning under lap robes, came inside. Sister Bachellor started the organ and we sang *Oh, Come All Ye Faithful*.

The program went well, considering that Otho had to be prompted by Sister Bachellor at the beginning of each verse of his recitation. Ora chanted her poem with her eyes fixed on the ceiling, lest the sight of friends distract her. Anna and Hermann stood hand in hand, singing like two fair cherubs, with sweet high voices. Henry did himself proud with his oratorical rendition of "Sail On."

When this part of the program was finished, Father quietly stepped back of the tree and we heard the sound of a window sliding upward. Then from back of the loaded tree bounded a short, fat man in a red suit trimmed with fluffy cotton bands.

"Hello, everybody—Merry Christmas!" he said in a high falsetto voice.

"Santa Claus!" we shrieked.

He put his pack on the floor, reached in, and tossed out bags of popcorn and peanuts—the same striped bags we had filled and carefully tied.

I looked about back of me. Everyone was still there—no, now only Tommy and Rose sat together back of the double desk which previously had held the two of them and Dr. Mesropian. But of course he could have moved to another seat. Throughout the unloading of the tree I kept glancing back. But aside from Brother and Sister Craddock and Mattie, who left early, everyone else was there. It was quite apparent that Sister Craddock felt this gathering a bit too bourgeois for her newly acquired elegance. When all the presents were distributed, Santa Claus yelled, "Merry Christmas to all, and to all a good-night," and disappeared through the back window.

Later I saw Dr. Mesropian in the crowd, and his bluish cheeks had a peculiar pink cast. I was certain then that my identification was correct.

There was much robust fun over the presents that young men and ladies received. Accusations flew back and forth along with the popcorn and the peanut shells. Everyone had a fine time, but I think that Brother and Sister Betz enjoyed themselves the most. Sister Betz brought out a great tray of *pfeffernuesse* and gave each child a tidbit she had made. Before we left she reminded Mother that we had promised to eat Christmas dinner with them.

When the tree was bare and all the papers gathered up, lest

some presents be lost, Father extinguished each candle and piled the papers in the closet for use in making fires. Each of us carried away his load of apples, candy, and various and sundry presents. Still reluctant to go home and bring this jolly gathering to a close, we stood about outside—the children tagging one another, the grown folks calling back and forth to their neighbors starting their teams for home.

Father had just turned the key in the lock when someone yelled, "Fire!"

All faces turned toward the schoolhouse, expecting to see flame bursting through a window. Father jabbed the key back in the lock.

"No. Over there—across town. Look!"

We turned and looked across the town to the rise of ground bordering the ravine that lay beyond the pest house. And there, swelling into brilliant flame, biting a lurid chunk from the Christmas sky, was a huge fiery cross.

Chapter Seventeen

In the middle of December Sammy had written that she would not be home for Christmas. Brother Severn had been late with his fall shipping. T. P. Hamilton had persuaded him to spend Christmas in Fort Worth, make the rounds of the stockyards, and purchase a few head of blooded stock to build up his herd. They were going to have a Christmas tree right in the Hamilton parlor, Sammy said.

Brother Severn's lateness in marketing, Sammy hinted, had been due to trouble with Slim Breedlove. Slim was homesteading a ranch of his own and stocking it little by little while working for Brother Severn. The stock were ostensibly bought with his wages, but his herd was increasing more than his wages could provide for. T. P. Hamilton, who owned so many cattle, had not been disposed to make any issue of the few that might be getting into Slim's herd by mistake or intent. But Brother Severn, having noted some messed-up brands, had brought the matter into the open. Slim left Brother Severn's employ and some of the boys quit with him.

From the time Sammy's letter came I had worried for fear Tom Craddock would be so disappointed over Sammy's absense that his Christmas vacation would be spoiled. I might as well have spared myself; for from the moment Tom saw Rose Mahoney he was a changed lad. He hadn't been as wishy-washy as Vela thought him. He just hadn't found in Vela or in Sammy the girl he really wanted. It was as if he were seeing Rose for the first time, and that no one before her had counted at all.

Tom practically lived at Sister Mahoney's boarding house; he hung around the drug store where Rose worked for Brother Betz; and he haunted Dr. Mesropian's laboratory. This was natural, since Tommy was studying to be a doctor. He and Rose had identical interests and seemed crazy about each other.

Brother and Sister Craddock, who had approved of Vela as a potential daughter-in-law, were not nearly as sold on a boarding-house keeper's daughter. Sister Craddock blamed Rose because Tommy spent so little time at home during his vacation, and she openly resented the fact that Tommy had preferred to sit with Rose and Dr. Mesropian and the Betzes at the Christmas program. Mother said that that was what people might expect when their children fell in love. But Father was more sympathetic, remembering that Tommy had always been Sister Craddock's special pride and joy.

On Christmas Day we diked out in our Sunday-go-to-meeting clothes and went to Brother Betz's. I had never been in their home before, and it charmed and awed me. Built in the form of an "L," it had three big rooms: a living room and a bedroom across the front, with the kitchen and screened porch behind. There were hand-loomed carpets on the two front rooms, and the kitchen floor was as white as snow. Sister Betz had tatting-edged curtains at all the windows.

The living-room beds for the children were built in, one above the other, with a ladder to get to the upper ones. They were great, puffy beds, and Sister Betz said they were filled with goose down. In the kitchen was a stove as high as Father's head with red and blue and yellow flowers on the doors. Brother Betz called it a *Porzellanofen* and said that his father had brought it over from the old country.

To look at Sister Betz's table you'd never have known that food was scarce in west Texas. We had a roast goose with little *Mettwursts* circling it on top of the dressing, Irish potatoes whipped to a creamy mountain, and apple strudel with velvety cream to pour on it. After dinner Mother and Sister Betz did dishes and Father and Brother Betz went to the front room. Brother Betz bit off the end of his cigar, and sat in the carpet-covered platform rocker while Father stretched out in the Morris chair with the lace tidy on its back. Anna and Hermann and I played jacks in the middle of the floor. Brother Betz watched us and rubbed his hands together.

"*Siehst du die kleinen Kinder? Sehr gut, nicht wahr?*"

Father nodded. "*Ja, es ist sehr gut.*"

Brother Betz's face brightened. "*Sprechen Sie Deutsch?*"

"*Nein, nicht sehr gut, aber ich verstehe ein klein wenig.*"

For a while they conversed in German. When they changed to English I discovered they were talking about Admiral Peary and his expedition, which was leaving shortly to try to locate the North Pole. From that they switched to a discussion of the masked faces that had appeared at the pest house windows.

"Bertha says you and the Herr Doktor were too kind. If she had seen them it might be she should know something. Bertha iss smart." There was always pride in Brother Betz's voice when he spoke of his wife.

"Sister Betz is indeed smart, and much too valuable to subject to possible danger," Father told him.

Brother Betz leaned forward. "*Ich weiss nicht*—not for sure. But many people talk their troubles to the bartender when they are a little loose of tongue. Always I have let it go into one ear and come out from the other yet. But now I try to remember and maybe piece together."

"After last night's demonstration," Father said, "I consider it our duty to find out who's responsible and take action. We can't live intimidated by a gang of hooded men, any more than we could tolerate a band of roistering, drunken cowboys."

"*Ja, das ist richtig.* For who should be the next, maybe you or maybe me—maybe some other man who is trying to live right. I am thinking now that Dal came to see us on his wedding day. You know my Bertha, she took care of him like a son."

"I know," Father replied, "and he loves you like a son."

"He is worried. Brother Falloon has found that Slim Breedlove has—wat you call it—rustled some of his fine Hereford cows. He knows Slim has talked much over my bar. He wanted I should tell Slim it is better to drive them back to the 'Flying F.' He thinks no one else would dare speak."

"And have you seen Slim since then?" Father asked.

"*Nein*. Only before, when he came to try to persuade me to start another saloon once. He brought with him the dentist, Dr. Bachellor."

"He'll likely be back to put on more pressure," Father said.

"*Nein*, I think not." Brother Betz shook his head sadly. "Now it iss that the good *Doktor* sells it from his back door. Into the leg of his boot the cowboy slips the bottle. Ach, what a *Spitzbub* the poor wrangler iss! Two prices he pays, the liquor iss bad, and the Herr Doktor gets it all, since he pays no license to sell."

Father sighed. "I imagine it is difficult to make a living extracting and repairing teeth in these sparsely settled areas. But he certainly could have gotten along without those big, hungry dogs."

"Ach, the dogs are a—wat you say—blind. *Das Hundehaus* iss his liquor storehouse. Also he pulls teeth as a blind. The gambling iss his real business. Ach, the poor boys he takes. The poor, homeless boys—" Brother Betz threw out his hands, let them fall into his lap. "Bertha and me, we tried to make it nice for them. So hard she worked cooking good food for them to eat. Und me, always I watched that they did not get too much under their belts. Only for small stakes were the games played, making it fun. Then comes this *Herr Doktor* in his checkered coat. Drinks he buys them, and plays cards with them. Always he loses and laughs and iss jolly. Such a good fellow, they think him. Und when he asks them to his home, with eagerness they go. Ach, the poor boys, always lonesome for a home."

Father gazed at the floor. Finally he spoke. "I have never asked a man this question before, but I have never had such doubts. Actually, Brother Betz, do you think that a saloon such as you ran is an asset to a town—at least such a town as this one?"

Brother Betz answered decisively. "*Nein.* It iss evil. I worked to keep the evil small and bring some good from it. But it worried me and it worried my Bertha. I would not want it back again."

"Thank you, Brother Betz," Father said humbly. "I am glad you confirm what has always been my opinion. Now what are we to do about this greater evil in our midst?"

"*Es ist schwer.* To get the money for one license—to pick up one offender who maybe could not be convicted—the state cannot afford the expense. So we in far places must many things do for ourselves. Und maybe get us a bad name sometimes."

"Our church is stronger now. We ought to be able to accomplish more, with God's help," Father said. "We must pray—"

"*Und wir müssen arbeiten,*" Brother Betz added vigorously. "*Und denken—ja,* we have got to think. That is what the brain iss for already."

For many days thereafter, I knew that Father was thinking hard. And what was more, he was working hard. With no new cases of smallpox, the danger of an epidemic was past. Father called upon the men in their places of business and urgently presented the advantages of having a church building. With the money already in the bank six lots were purchased a block off the main street. This was long-range planning and would eventually accommodate both church and parsonage buildings. With the building fund now nonexistent, both Father and Mother redoubled their efforts. Mother induced the ladies to undertake the Saturday bake sales and set the bazaar for Easter. She made country calls with Father. Together they helped families plan their budgets to allow for tithing. But the incomes of most farmers and homesteaders were pitifully small and precarious. In each gathering both Mother and Father listened for bits of information that might lead to the identity of the leader of the gang that burned the cross on Christmas Eve.

One evening after supper when I was doing my sums in long division, Father came and sat across the table from me.

"Opal, your mother and I feel it necessary to discontinue your music lessons for a while. If we had a piano I'd let you continue the weekly lessons. But I think the daily practice hour had better be dispensed with, and without practice the lessons are futile."

For an instant I was bitterly disappointed. My chief desire at this stage was to be able to ripple my fingers over the keyboard in Chaminade's *La Lisonjera* the way Sister Bachellor did. But then I would have more time to play when I didn't have to practice daily.

"Do you think that Dr. Bachellor is one of the masked men?" I asked. It had been my private opinion that he was.

"No. I don't think Dr. Bachellor is prejudicial to any race, creed, color, or political belief, as long as he can profit from them."

This was a blow to my astute deductions.

"Brother Slade called Deacon Webb a Black Republican."

"I know. But not in a derogatory sense. He often joshed Deacon Webb about pulling off political plums such as his appointment as postmaster. But he and Deacon Webb were close friends. He felt strongly against the undercover campaign that drove the Webbs from us."

This took more wind from my sails. But I couldn't admit that I had gotten nowhere with my studious thinking.

"I wouldn't put it past Brother Clevanger," I said.

"I wouldn't either." Father smiled on the bias, and I knew he was no fonder of the Clevangers than I was. "But in all fairness, we have to remember that things were well under way before Brother Clevanger came to town. I think that lets him out as the leader."

Our conversation was interrupted by a howl from the front room. It was Marjorie, unsuccessfully trying to walk from chair to chair. Father rushed into the front room. Shortly I could hear the rocker creaking, and then he sang—at first loud and clear to drown Marjorie's howls, then more softly as she quieted down.

> "So cold, so cold, said the poor little girl,
>   As she stood at the rich man's door—"

Mother's voice cut in sharply. "For heaven's sake let's at least keep it cheerful. You'll have her back in tears again."

"I'd forgotten," Father said, "that you like your music on the rollicking side." He launched into a blatant rendition of,

"Old Dan Tucker came to town,
  Ridin' up a goat and a leadin' up a houn',
Houn' gave a leap and the goat gave a jump,
  An' throwed Dan Tucker a-straddle of a stump.

Old Dan Tucker was a mean ole man,
  He washed his face in the fryin' pan,
Combed his hair with the wagon wheel,
  Died with the toothache in his heel.

Chorus— *Get out of the way for Old Dan Tucker,*
  Came too late to git his supper,
  Out of the way for Daniel Tucker,
  Came too late for his supper."

"Give her to me," Mother said, "before she's sound asleep. I want to wash her up and put her to bed. You know" (she hesitated a moment) "I'd love to go to a play-party again. We used to have such fun playing Skip-to-My-Lou—remember?

"Flies in the sugar bowl, two by two,
  Skip-to-my-Lou, my darling."

Father smiled. "I remember well."

"Don't you suppose"—there was a wistful note in Mother's voice—"we could go to the next play-party the young folks have?"

"As sure as we do," Father replied, "someone would write to the Board and make the accusation that we were dancing."

"Oh dear," Mother sighed. "I suppose they would. But it was all so innocent, and we used to have such good times."

The queerest feeling came over me: the realization that my mother and father were not old and stodgy, not separated by choice and by temperament from life's pleasures. They were young and spirited, loved gay, good times, and had the normal zest for living that any young couple had. Yes, "young," for Mother was only thirty and Father was thirty-nine—nearer the ages of Dal and Vela than those of Brother and Sister Slade.

Mother had been reared graciously, with great attention to social amenities. Yet in this crude and primitive country there were few occasions when one might employ any but the simplest courtesies. Father, I remembered, had made athletic records, was a fine swimmer. But not since we came to the Llano Estacado had we seen a pool or a stream; never did men exercise for fun, since this hard land was apt at any time to exact more strength and endurance than they possessed.

What then had motivated Father and Mother to sacrifice so much they held dear and come to a place that offered nothing but privations, uncongenial surroundings, and frustration?

Right out of my thoughts came Father's words.

"It's worked a great injustice on you, giving up your youth and fun to take part of the load off the shoulders of a poor missionary who'll never be able to give you things you deserve."

"Don't be silly," Mother sniffed. "I wouldn't for a minute change places with any girl I ever knew. I've everything in the world I really want. I'd make a pretty spectacle of myself, old as I am, prancing around at a play-party."

The look of tenderness on Father's face was not for me.

"Every accomplishment of yours," he said, "has been made with grace and beauty. I'm sure it will always be so."

Looking at Mother with Marjorie in her arms, I knew what Father meant. Swift color came into her cheeks, and she turned and went into the kitchen. I then asked Father a question long puzzling me.

"If you and Mother had not married, or if each of you had married someone else, where would I be?"

A slow smile came over Father's face. "That is something that I with my limited knowledge have never been able to figure out." He took my scrawny hand between his two palms. "Our most precious possessions in life are miracles that originate with God and find their fulfillment in love. My greatest hope is that someday you may know this for yourself."

School began again, with all of us wearing new mittens, caps, dresses, and coats that expressed the practical side of Santa Claus's nature. The Christmas festivities, injudicious eating, later hours, and exposure in family gatherings induced a wave of grippe. I

179

was one of the unfortunates and Father marched me straight to Dr. Mesropian.

Dr. Mesropian put a stick on my tongue, pushed down, and succeeded in gagging me, while I gazed in trepidation at the three-pronged tube hanging from his ears. I was never quite convinced that it had fulfilled its purpose with mere tappings of its metal cone against my chest and back. He swabbed my throat, took my temperature, and suggested to Father that cod-liver oil in emulsion form would be a good builder-upper. He wrote some hieroglyphics for Father to present to Brother Betz.

"Before you go," he said to Father, "take a look at this."

Father took the rough, grayish sheet of paper and read it.

"When did this come?"

"Yesterday." Dr. Mesropian stood by the window and looked out into the street, straight toward the window of Brother Hipplehite's barber shop on the other side. "It was under my door when I returned from a call on Ruby Tuttle, Judge Pothast's niece."

"Was Judge Pothast at home when you called?" Father asked.

"No. He came from his office and asked me to see the little girl as soon as possible. I went almost at once."

"Do you have any idea as to who left it here?"

"Any number of people might have known I was out. For that matter I'm out most of the time, either on calls or at my laboratory."

Father studied it. "Printed with a red crayon on pencil paper, materials available to anyone. Those with children probably always have it about. Not much of a clue."

"Exactly," Dr. Mesropian replied in his clipped, precise voice. Father handed back the paper. "I hope you ignore it."

"I am perplexed. I don't know what to do."

"Help me to find out who is responsible and put a stop to it. Should you leave, you only play into their hands."

Dr. Mesropian lifted his short, square body to its full height. "I desire to carry on my work. But I should not want to disrupt a whole town if they do not wish me here."

"I can assure you that is not a majority opinion. I am trying to find out who is back of this. But I'm a poor detective. Perhaps if we work together, we will have more success."

For a fleeting second Dr. Mesropian's teeth gleamed in his swarthy face. "We shall try." He dismissed the matter with a gesture of his hand. "Get the prescription and take the little girl home and put her to bed. She will recover faster that way."

The moment we were out I asked, "What did the paper say?"

Father quoted. " 'This is a white man's town. Unless you get out of your own free will, you'll go with a coat of tar and feathers.' It was signed with three large 'K's.' "

"Whose initials are they?" I asked.

"Originally they stood for Ku Klux Klan. This may be either a branch or a purely local mob using their symbols for prestige."

At the drug store Rose was reading a letter. She took our slip back of the partition to Brother Betz, leaving the letter face down on the counter. I saw Father inspecting the envelope beside it. It was nice paper, and the handwriting had shaded capitals like those in my copy book. Before I could read the writing in the upper left corner, Rose came back with a bottle.

"A bottle of Scott's Emulsion too," Father told her.

"Not two bad medicines at once," I protested.

"This one is good," Rose said. "It's nice and sweet. But you mustn't drink it like water, or you'll be drunker than Slim Breedlove was yesterday afternoon."

Father spoke up. "Was Breedlove in town yesterday?"

Rose wrapped the two bottles in slick paper. "Yes, and sicker than a locoed horse. Brother Betz said he'd gotten some awful bad liquor. He sent him to Dr. Mesropian, but the doctor was out, Slim said. So Brother Betz gave him an emetic and fixed him a pallet in the back room. Before long he was able to get on his horse and light out for home."

Brother Betz came from the back with a small tin of salve.

"Spread this on her throat and chest once. Then cover it with a flannel cloth. It will not make any blister." He handed the tin to Father.

"Thank you. Her mother usually melts lard and adds camphor and a little kerosene and a few drops of turpentine. It's inclined to irritate."

"Ach" (Brother Betz shrugged) "much better this iss—with goose grease. Shist smell once. *Sehr gut, nicht wahr?* That iss eucalyptus oil. Someday I get my own patent and have it in drug stores all over the country."

Brother Betz followed us to the door. Father spoke in a low tone. "Someone slipped a note under Dr. Mesropian's door yesterday. It warned him to leave town under penalty of being tarred and feathered."

"Tch, tch. It iss getting vorse all the time."

"Could Slim Breedlove have left it there?" Father asked.

"*Ja*, but yesterday I think he was too sick to write notes. He was so green like a ghost."

"I suppose he could have written it before he got sick and have delivered it afterward."

"*Ja*. Only I was the one who made him go to the *Doktor*. He was trying to straddle his horse, but I argued he should see the doctor first."

Father sighed. "I was just trying to chase down every possible suspect. Sometimes it looks pretty hopeless."

"*Ja*," Brother Betz agreed. "We got to think harder."

After that we all thought harder, but apparently nothing came of it. Brother Hipplehite knew that Dr. Mesropian was out of his office. So did Judge Pothast and Slim Breedlove. But for that matter Brother Hinkins could see it from his bank, and any one of a dozen others.

My grippe furnished Mother with an excuse for discontinuing the music lessons. Sister Bachellor came to see me and brought some of the pink and green fondant she made so well. The Slade girls came as far as the door and informed me that Tessie had six puppies. I spent the time in bed cutting hearts and arrows from red paper, pasting them on lacy white cut-outs. Sister Kelso had promised to turn the last half-hour of school on February 14 into a valentine party. My sentence to bed produced a home-made valentine for each of the girls in school.

A week of rain the latter part of January transformed the prairies from a grayish-brown to a timid green. Fuzzy new leaves came in the buds of old loco stalks, greening primrose leaves pushed through the earth, and fresh buds appeared on the cat-claws. The chaparral twigs brightened and mesquites poked pale pea-green fingers into the moist, chill air. The farmers drove their plows deep into virgin soil. The cowboys rode day and night to set new-born calves on their feet and lift their fallen mothers, lest they be left by the migrating herd and fall victims to hungry coyotes.

Spring brought nests of baby cottontails in burrows of grass beneath the catclaw bushes, and famished rattlers uncoiled their shrunken hides and crawled out in search of food. Spring brought seed catalogues, sarsparilla bottles, and sand storms.

It also brought Mrs. Tuttle, Ruby's mother, to our midst. She was a bright, chirping woman whose conversation flew from person to person like electric sparks. She wore fluffy clothes and laughed a great deal, particularly at remarks made by the men. At Ladies Aid she ate her tea cakes with taps of her napkin against her lips, and I was horrified to see part of the color of her lips on the napkin afterward.

On the way home I mentioned it to Mother.

"Mrs. Tuttle's lips must be awful chapped. They're so red—they even made spots on her napkin."

"The kind of chaps Mrs. Tuttle gets on her lips won't rub off on a napkin," Mother replied tartly. "If that stuff comes off on one thing, it will on another. And when that happens—"

"You mean—it's lip paint?"

Mother's head jerked assent. "Or possibly war paint."

Chapter Eighteen

WITH the departure of the rains came the arrival of Brother Dissey on a Saturday noon. Mother saw him from the kitchen window as he drove up and halted close to the pump. She called to Father, who was in the front room working on his sermon.

"Mr. Berryman, here comes your grape-picker who works the Lord's vineyard on a percentage basis."

Father came in and looked at Mother a little wistfully.

"I hope that this is one of your more amiable days."

"If it weren't," she said, "I'd have been out there with the broom before he left the buggy."

Father went out and greeted Brother Dissey. When they came in there was a gleam in Father's eyes as he said, "I'm sure you remember Brother Dissey—"

Mother extended her hand. "How could I ever forget him? But where have you been all winter?"

Brother Dissey clasped Mother's hand. "It is gratifying indeed to be once more among the open-hearted people of the great West. I spent the winter with my sister in south Texas. She had need of me."

"How nice to be able to escape our rigorous winter."

"Oh, I should never have deserted my work except that duty called. My sister's husband was down with lumbago. I hastened back here in order that the carefully knit threads of evangelism might not be unraveled during my enforced absence."

Mother's smile was a trifle brittle and Father hurried Brother Dissey to the front room to await dinner.

After I had set the table with the red-bordered cloth and the bone-handled knives and forks I edged into the other room. Mother was frying calf's liver that Dal and Vela had brought us that morning. From time to time Brother Dissey lifted his head, looked toward the kitchen, and breathed deeply of the aroma of liver and onions.

"I was afraid of that," Brother Dissey was saying, "when we didn't make an example of that saloon keeper and run him out of town."

Father's reply was spirited. "Brother Betz is a fine man. He has nothing to do with this. It was going on before we had the meetings, though we didn't know it. Now that the saloon is gone, it has taken on new customers, new impetus, and even new significance."

I realized they were discussing Dr. Bachellor's activities.

"I'm not convinced," Brother Dissey argued, "that this fellow Betz isn't back of it. Once a saloon keeper, always a saloon keeper. You can't change the leopard's spots."

Rather than convert a discussion into an argument, Father sought to dismiss the subject. "I shouldn't have worried you with

184

this problem, since we residents of La Mesa have to work it out for ourselves."

Brother Dissey reared back. "Sister Hinkins wrote me all about it, urging me to return before things got out of hand. I asked Brother Kelso and Brother Severn and Brother Falloon about it this morning. I ran into the three of them at Joyner's Well. Only Brother Falloon was indifferent to my solicitude."

"What were the three of them doing at Joyner's Well?"

"They were examining the ground about the windmill and tank," Brother Dissey said. "They seemed gratified over their findings. By watching through the glass in the back of the buggy, I saw them follow a trail to the northeast, probably toward the cap rock and the breaks."

"There are ranchers in that direction. They may call on them," Father commented.

"I can understand Severn's and Falloon's interest," said Brother Dissey, "but Brother Kelso has few cattle. Why should he meddle in their problems?"

"This winter at intervals Brother Kelso worked for T. P. Hamilton, his wife's uncle, as he has in years past. It is possible he gleaned information that only he could follow up."

Brother Dissey sighed voluminously. "It looks to me like sin is flourishing in this community as never before. Drinking, gambling, cattle stealing—even murder. It takes an able man to knit his flock together. He must unceasingly pursue the devil and fearlessly engage him, if he expects to rout him and keep him routed."

"Quite so." I knew that Father was aware that Brother Dissey considered him unable to keep the devil routed.

"But one must recognize him in his many masks," Brother Dissey continued. "For instance, there is Brother Falloon. Probably a good man but a papist and one of the devil's own tools."

"Would you suggest that one rout Brother Falloon?"

"Not until every means has been exhausted to make him see the light, to make him realize the error of his ways. Failing in that, yes. We cannot be soft with sin. We must go after it tooth and nail. We should drive iniquity from the community as we would a lewd woman."

"By what authority," Father asked, "do we condemn a Catholic merely because he is a Catholic?"

Brother Dissey brought down an authoritative palm on the Bible lying on the table. "By the Bible. That is our guide. I believe with Pastor Russell that the Church is the beast that appeared to John in the Revelations of St. John the Divine."

"Pastor Russell doesn't limit his interpretation to the Catholic Church," Father pointed out. "He includes all forms of organized Christianity, of which we are one."

"And he should. The Roman Catholic Hierarchy is symbolical of the Church of Revelations. We with our dogmas and creeds and doctrines are in the same category. To be a follower of the true religion, one need only be a witness for Jehovah. That is my aim, to be Jehovah's Witness. We are in the days of Armageddon. We can not arbitrate with sin."

Father was riled. "When we start driving out such men as Brother Falloon because he differs from us in belief, we might as well return to the days of witchcraft. That is pure, heathenish intolerance."

"What is tolerance," Brother Dissey bellowed, "but a lack of principle and moral courage? Right is right, and wrong is wrong, no matter how deceptive in appearance. If Brother Falloon will not be set right, we have but one duty—to rid the community of such as him."

"Opal," Mother's interruption was deliberately timely, "tell your father and Brother Dissey that dinner is practically ready."

When we finished eating, Brother Dissey unbuttoned his vest, let out a notch in his belt, and rubbed his hands together.

"A splendid repast, Sister Berryman. I am fortunate to have such friends gathering sheaves beside me in the vineyard of the Lord."

I caught Father's amused expression.

"With such cooking ability," Brother Dissey winked at Father, "it's not hard to see how your wife found her way to your heart."

"There are other ways also," Father said gently. "My wife never cooked a meal before we were married. Cooking is but one of the hardships she assumed as the wife of a missionary pastor."

"You overestimate the hardships." Brother Dissey waved them

aside. "I've had more than my share, but the joy and satisfaction of a strong, well-knit flock more than compensates for the inconveniences."

Father and Mother exchanged glances.

"We're not complaining," Mother said, "but sometimes one does find flock-knitting arduous work, don't you think?"

"I never find the Lord's work arduous," Brother Dissey asserted. "However difficult the task, I attack it with rejoicing."

"That's splendid," Mother agreed, "and this absolute devotion to your work would eliminate any need for a wife—which is fortunate, since a woman is rarely interested in a man of such complete singleness of purpose. Or if she were, she'd be silly."

Brother Dissey bristled. "I'm not so sure about that. Only this winter an estimable young lady was, to put it lightly, very interested in me. You misjudge your sex."

"I still think she's silly to try to come between a man and his all-sufficient love for his work."

It seemed to me there was a quirk to Mother's argument, that each flat statement curled at the edges. It was so unlike her usual realistic logic that I was annoyed. So was Brother Dissey. His face was growing steadily redder.

"But this woman isn't," he contended. "She is a staunch Christian, one of Jehovah's Witnesses in the community where my sister lives. She is a true disciple of Pastor Russell. She has no desire to divorce me from my work."

"Oh dear," Mother sighed, "don't tell me you're thinking of bringing a tender eastern girl to this country—to travel from place to place—no home in which to take root. She must be a peculiar woman to want that kind of life."

"She's not at all peculiar. Naturally she'd want a home. We'd not expect to live in a couple of valises strapped to a buggy."

Mother's eyes sought Father's, with an "I told you so" look.

"Of course," Mother said brightly, "you could take up a homestead in the middle of your territory, raise a garden and chickens, even get a cow. Your wife could take care of things while you were away."

Brother Dissey's face was livid. "I don't intend to change my career to farming or ranching. Angelica would be as violently opposed to that as I am. She and I can best serve as ministers."

187

"Angelica," Mother murmured. "That's a kind of wine, isn't it?"

"Certainly not. It means angel-like." Brother Dissey buttoned his vest. "I think I must be getting on."

Father looked surprised. "Aren't you staying over Sunday?"

"I've promised Sister Hinkins to spend the night in their home." Brother Dissey stood up, fastened his belt. "Good-day, Sister Berryman."

With Brother Dissey gone, Mother and I attacked the dishes. I dwelt on his wanting to run Brother Falloon out, until I let one of Mother's good primrose-pattern cups slip out of my hand and crash to the floor. I held my breath and waited for the reprimand.

"What a shame," Mother said, "that you couldn't have broken it over his head."

"Do you think," I asked quickly, "that Brother Dissey could be the one who is trying to run Dr. Mesropian out of town?"

Mother shook her head. "Not Dr. Mesropian. Your father."

"Is that why he and Sister Hinkins are as thick as three in a bed?"

Mother chuckled. "Being a minister's daughter, it would be more tactful to say 'as thick as molasses in January,' but the idea is the same."

"If Sister Hinkins is that stinking," I sputtered, "then I'll bet she'd try to run out Dr. Mesropian too."

Mother paused with the dishpan in her hands. "I wonder," she said. Then she went out and poured the dishwater on the zinnia bed.

On Saturday I helped Father put in the garden. Brother Douthitt, who ran the livery stable, plowed all the town gardens. He would not charge Father for the patch he plowed for us. Father then worked the rich, sandy loam with the hoe and rake and threw out all the clumps of buffalo grass. He made long furrows for lettuce, radishes, and onion sets, which were first to be planted. I went along behind him and distributed the lettuce and radish seeds with conservative care down the long straight rows Father made with the aid of two stakes and a stretched string.

While we were thus engaged Sheriff Lubeck rode up on his

big roan stallion. It was the first time we had seen him since before Christmas—on the night of Dal and Vela's wedding. It seemed to me the lines of his long face had deepened and his eyes had receded into his head. He looked older and sadder and much more tired.

"Well, Reverend," he said from high in the saddle, " 'pears like both of us get to the end of a row once in a while."

"Yes." Father leaned on his hoe. He was studying the sheriff's face as he spoke. "If we are fortunate, we finish before night comes. In that event we can claim that 'Something accomplished, something done, has earned a night's repose.' "

"And sometimes," the sheriff said, "you wish you hadn't accomplished what you set out to do—you druther be hoein' the ole long hard row—not knowin'—" His shoulders slumped, his hands rested one upon the other on the saddle horn, every line of his body drooped in complete dejection.

"I take it you've reached the end of the trail on the Enright case." Father's voice was tempered to a near-whisper.

"I reckon I got no business bein' a sheriff. I got no stummick for turnin' a man over to the law, knowin' all he's got to go through afore he hangs for his crimes. It's more humane to string him up when you ketch him."

Father was uneasy. "Where is Enright now?"

"I dunno. He said he was goin' back to work for Hamilton."

I could hear the breath Father had been holding as he released it. The sheriff continued talking.

"I ran into him at his cabin and we searched every inch of the place. About a hunnerd yards away we found what we was lookin' for—a pair of slashed hobbles and a jackknife with a broken blade. Ole Clem Slothower's initials was cut in the bone handle."

"So it was Clem Slothower," Father said.

"Yep. I tuk out down through Colorado County, and by hook and crook I caught up with him. He was hell-bent for the Davis Mountain country. If he'd a got there we couldn't a got him in a month of Sundays."

"That was good work," Father said. "I don't feel that you need have any compunction about putting a man like that where he belongs."

"I reckon not," the sheriff said, "but it's a little different when you've knowed somebody since he was a kid. I reckon you deserve part of that reward for gettin' a line-up on that team of Enright's—"

"No," Father said. "To you is due the credit for your unceasing efforts in behalf of justice. If the reward is to be shared, it should be with Wes Enright. At best it is but fractional compensation for the loss he has suffered. If you see him before I do, tell him to come in and get his team. I should be able to find another within a month or so."

"It's a good thing you mentioned that. I'd a forgot it. Wes told me to tell you to keep them hosses. He's got no use for a drivin' team now."

"That wouldn't be right—"

"If I was you, I'd do it, Reverend. It'll make Wes feel better. It's the only way he's got to show you how he appreciates your having faith in him whilst the rest of us was a doubtin' him."

Father was deeply touched. His gaze sought the distance and his lips pressed together over words he could not say. The sheriff saw this and drew himself up in the saddle.

"Well, any way you look at it, it's bad business. And it's best it's over an' done with." He wheeled his horse and headed toward home.

Father watched until the lumber yard fence hid him from view. Then he looked down at the trench with radish seeds like a string of small tan beads. He picked up the rake and drew over them a blanket of dirt.

Before we had finished the freighters came in. I went to the house to mind Marjorie while Mother got supper and Father went down to Brother Clevanger's store for the mail. He came back with a letter from Sammy. We gathered about the table while Mother opened the fat envelope with a paring knife. She took particular note of the script.

"Sammy's penmanship is improving. I hope as much can be said for her manners."

"If only they don't destroy her spirit," Father said. "The wild horse whose spirit is broken in the taming is a sorry thing."

"I doubt if the Hamiltons are too refined," Mother said. She flattened the thick pages with her hand and spread them on the table.

"Dearest folks," she read. "To be polite I should say I take my pen in hand to say that I am well and hope you are the same. But I ain't so well in my mind. This trying to learn to talk Frenchified is all silliness, and I got no business spending my time cube-rooting. If I had my druthers, I druther sing *Red River Valley* or *Frankie And Johnnie* than *My Mother Bids Me Bind My Hair*. That's a plumb silly song. And Lucy's friends are always having teas and they ain't my style of parties. I got a couple of beaux, but they make me sick to my stummick, always being so nasty nice where there's company and the minute they get you by yourself wanting to start sparking and spooning.

"Ford has got him a hootchy-kootchy girl from a show at one of the theaters here. Aunt Fanny is on her ear, but Teepee laughs and says a little acting ability in the family might be a good thing. I ain't saying what I think, but it just shows you what men are, toadying to a girl that kicks up her legs in public. I'm mighty disappointed in Ford.

"Pa says Slim Breedlove is cutting didos. That guy's a dogie from locoed stock. You'd ought to have killed him like I told you and saved all the trouble. He used to be a good man, but I reckon he's got too big for his britches. Pa says it's partly Teepee's fault because he was never of a mind to make a ruckus over a few head of range cattle. But if Pat Falloon gets the proof he's looking for, there's sure going to be hell a-poppin' or I miss my guess.

"I reckon you folks are tuckered out listening to all this belly-aching. If I don't get to feeling more peart pretty soon, I'm a-going to high-tail it for home. Tell everybody hello for me. An ocean of love to you all. Sammy."

Mother folded the letter and slipped it back in the envelope. "Sammy's terribly homesick. I hope she doesn't give in to it."

"Seems to me," Father said, "it might be just as well if she came home. She's doing herself no particular good there."

Mother stared at Father. "Fine sentiments from a man who has always advocated education for men and women alike. Tommy Craddock doesn't want a larruping woman like Sammy for a wife. She'd be a laughingstock."

"The kind of man Sammy will marry will like her as she is. He won't want her with a lot of airs and foibles."

"Sammy's set her cap for Tommy and won't give up easily," Mother told him. "Ford Hamilton is turning out to be the kind of fellow I knew he was. Crazy over fast women."

A little smile came and went on Father's lips. "He's the kind of man I thought he was. Sammy isn't fast enough to keep up with him. But his father is."

Mother snorted. "His father is probably a woman-chaser too. Everybody says he was wild as a maverick when he was young. He's not likely to have changed very much."

Father pushed back his chair. "While I was at the post office, Rose Mahoney came in for the mail. She got two letters—both of them from Tommy. It doesn't look much as though Sammy needs to be refashioning herself on that account."

"Puppy love," Mother sniffed. "Probably only temporary. Tommy has no record of steadfastness."

Sometimes it seemed to me that Mother could be far more contrary and exasperating than Father.

Chapter Nineteen

Brother Dissey made his March visit on a Saturday, and because so much time had elapsed since he had filled our pulpit, Father asked him to preach the Sunday morning sermon. Brother Dissey must have verified his information regarding the drinking, gambling, and cattle rustling, for he used the morning service to deliver a tirade against such vices. The next morning he drove blissfully on, leaving Father to take whatever repercussions there might be. I knew that Father was not afraid of reprisals but that he also expected some definite reaction to this blatant name-calling in the crusade against crime.

It was not long in coming. On Wednesday night, well after midnight, there was a violent knocking on our front door. Father pulled on his pants over his nightshirt. Mother came scampering into the kitchen. The front room had to be clear for visitors. Father went to the door with the lamp in his hand. He spoke pleasantly to the caller and invited him in. Some words ensued and Father set the lamp back on the center table and went outside, closing the door.

Mother crawled in bed beside me. We lay there breathing lightly. But all we could hear was the muffled murmur of voices, followed by the clatter of horse-hoofs, and Father came back inside and closed the door.

"Who was it," Mother asked, "and what did he want?"

Father's voice was tight with anger. "It was Slim Breedlove, delivering his ultimatum that there must be no more insinuations against him from my pulpit, or else—"

"Or else what?"

"Or else he'll git me!" Father mimicked.

"You mean—he'll murder you?"

"He seems to favor arson as a more suitable punishment."

"Oh, my gracious," Mother gasped. "What'll we do?"

"Do our duty, whatever it may be, regardless of Slim Breedlove or any other bully. Things are crucial when a man like Slim Breedlove thinks he can dictate the words a minister shall say from his pulpit."

"But the children—if he should burn our house—"

"We'll do everything in our power to protect our children," Father answered, "from, among other things, parents without courage."

Mother got up and tucked the covers about Marjorie and me. Then she went back to her own bed. Soon Father blew out the light.

After that Father was even more determined—made more pastoral calls, stayed an extra day on his bi-monthly trip to Seminole, and increased his efforts to get contributions to the building fund. Always considerate of Mother when she was troubled, Father tried to make her life as the wife of a missionary pastor less harassing. He revealed that he had taken some concrete means of allaying her fears about Slim Breedlove.

"I talked the whole matter over with Judge Pothast," he said.

Mother's face brightened. "What did he have to say?"

"It seems there's nothing he can do, as Slim Breedlove's land is over the line in Borden County, taking it out of his jurisdiction. Any action would have to come from the authorities in Borden County."

The saggy lines returned beside Mother's mouth. "Then I suppose we just sit quietly and let him proceed as he chooses."

"Citizens are not helpless. State and federal laws prevail in all counties alike, but it takes longer to set those wheels in motion."

"How does Judge Pothast advise you to go about it?"

"Judge Pothast seems disinclined to put out any advice. He is an attorney and conducts a private practice, which he expects to be paid for. He's loath to donate much of his salable stock."

"Didn't you offer to pay him?"

"At the close of our consultation, yes. Just as I offer the doctor his fee at the end of a call. Judge Pothast refused quite genially, which I felt was no more than right, since he had given me nothing of value."

"Then what are we to do?"

"On the spur of the moment, I don't know," Father said.

While they were talking, Mother had gone to the window.

"Here comes Mrs. Tuttle. What in the world can she want?"

Mrs. Tuttle was having difficulty on the narrow path. She held her full skirts above her high-heeled laced shoes in order to avoid filling them with grass burrs and at the same time tried to hang onto a ruffled rose parasol which was tossing about in the strong prairie wind. She finally made it by what Father termed a series of fits and starts. Mother opened the door and welcomed her.

"Dear Mrs. Berryman." Mrs. Tuttle took Mother's hand with the tips of her gloved fingers. "It's heavenly to get inside out of this ferocious wind." She dropped into the rocker, glanced at Father, and her eyelids went up and down. "Of course you big, rugged men don't mind. But for a woman who's lived such a sheltered life—" she sighed—"I much prefer it back home. But Maudie—Mrs. Pothast—simply won't hear to it. 'Delia Tuttle,' she says, 'it's positively sinful for you and Ruby, two helpless, unprotected girls, to live all alone—'"

"We understand," Mother said briskly. "If you will pardon me, I'll make some tea."

"Please—" (Mrs. Tuttle lifted her fingers) "don't go to a particle of trouble for little me—" But Mother had the tea kettle on

194

the front of the stove and motioned me to chuck in some cow chips.

Over the tea and tea cakes Mrs. Tuttle stated the purpose of her visit: an invitation for me to come to a party she was giving for Ruby. She had ordered a packing case of ice cream to be sent out from Big Spring. She and Mrs. Pothast were making favors of Easter baskets with colored candy eggs. By the time Mrs. Tuttle was ready to go I was so charmed with her that I didn't mind if she did leave part of her lips on the napkin. Mother thanked her graciously for the invitation and promised that if possible I would come. Mother had to be cautious and investigate lest we go to parties where card games were played.

The next day Ora and Dora told me that Ruby had said they would play Flinch at the party. I knew that this must be reported to Mother, since Flinch was played with cards.

"I probably won't get to go," I told them.

"But Flinch doesn't count. It's not played with real playing cards."

"I'll have to ask Mother anyway," I replied.

"Better not," Dora warned. "She might think any cards was cards."

I was pretty sure that that was exactly the attitude Mother would take. Deeply depressed, I took out for home.

I had decided to tackle Mother when she returned from Ladies Aid, but Father brought in some letters and made preparation to answer them on the kitchen table. By a little surreptitious peeping I saw the printed heading of the American Medical Association on one of the letters and the Office of the United States Marshal on the other. While I wondered what business Father had with these austere organizations, Mother came in with a bundle of news garnered from the ladies.

"Georgia Hinkins and Sam Falloon got engaged during vacation," Mother said. "Now Sister Falloon and Sister Hinkins have decided to have a double wedding for Kate and Georgia at the Falloon's ranch."

"Really?" Father said. "That should be quite an event."

"Quite the biggest social event this community has ever had."

I jumped from my seat on the bed. "Mother, will you make up that red batiste Vela got for a nightgown? And may I have some new slippers and hair ribbons to wear to the wedding?"

I saw the light fade from Mother's eyes. "Sister Falloon isn't sure she can have the children. There are so many grown folks that they may not be able to seat and feed the children. And anyway, it's possible that none of us will get to go."

Father looked perplexed. "You have always gone to the weddings where I have officiated."

"That's just it," Mother said. "From the way Sister Hinkins acted—avoiding any mention of your officiating—I suspect that she will insist on asking Brother Dissey."

"But I am their pastor," Father said.

"Mind you, nothing has been said," Mother put in. "But I've a hunch Sister Hinkins will hold out for her dear friend Dissey."

"I doubt if Brother Falloon will stand for it," Father said. "There is no love lost between him and P. Sylvester Dissey."

Mother sighed. "We'll see. I just wanted to put you on guard. What do we have here—some mail?"

Father nodded. "A reply to my letter to the American Medical Association." He handed her the letter. "It is as I had thought. Dr. Mesropian is making quite a name for himself in his research on T.B. Even when he came here he was one of their best men in the field."

Mother read the letter through. The light came back to her blue eyes. She looked at Father and they smiled at each other.

"Now I suppose you'll send this on to Tommy Craddock?"

Father nodded. "Together with a letter from me."

"Splendid. He ought to be able to do something with this."

I wondered why Tom Craddock, only a first-year student, would benefit by knowing a big man in the medical world. But perhaps he wanted to impress his teachers. It was vague, but Father and Mother seemed very pleased about it.

"And the other one?" Mother was asking.

"A reply to my letter to the United States Marshal. It looks as though we might get some cooperation from there."

Mother read the letter and laid it back on the table. "We aren't as isolated and forgotten as we sometimes feel. Our government tries to look after its citizens. It is much the better way."

"I've never been a believer in pulpit pyrotechnics as a weapon of warfare," Father said. "One should use the pulpit to put the love of God into men's hearts, not engender hate for his fellowmen, no matter how depraved they may be. We have legal provisions for the punishment of crime. It is a dangerous practice to leave it up to the community. They do not differentiate between hatred of the crime and hatred of the man who perpetrates it. A mob of church people can be just as dangerous as any other mob."

Father licked the red stamps and pressed one on each envelope with his fist. He glanced at me drooped over the foot of the bed.

"Want to go along, Petey?"

I bounced up and grabbed my sunbonnet.

A field lark sat on a fence post and tootled as we went by. Dr. Bachellor came from his house and whistled to his bird dogs, that were running out on the prairie, their noses to the ground. They lifted their heads and came back to him, their plumey tails waving in the breeze. He threw them two bones and then awkwardly tried to go in through the side of the house before he finally located the door.

"I wish there was some way," Father said, "that we could get a piano. I regret your losing so much time from your music."

"If we had the money," I said, "we could ask Sammy to pick one out for us while she's in Fort Worth. Then we could rent out practice time on it to help pay for it."

"That's an idea. I'll take it up with your mother, and we'll write Sammy and have her find out what one would cost us."

As we passed Dr. Mesropian's office he invited us to come in. I hung back, lest upon a routine check of my chest he discover something that might call for a throat-swabbing or a bottle of some putrid concoction from Brother Betz's drug store. But today he looked only at Father.

"Adolph wants to double the size of his drug store. He wishes to include an office and additional laboratory space for me."

"Splendid," Father replied. "Your practice is large now and you need more space. You could then install the X-ray equipment you've been wanting."

Dr. Mesropian's bright, black eyes focused on Father. His small, black mustache spread into a line above his lips. "It would be fine—just what I have been hoping for. But yesterday I got another of those notes. This time it is a demand, allowing me but one week to shake the dust of La Mesa from my feet."

Father was silent. His face became as grim as the doctor's.

"I can't be positive," he said, "but I think I know the instigator of this business. And I've taken steps to put a stop to it. I am reasonably sure that within a week we'll know the answer. If it takes longer, I'll arm myself and act as your bodyguard until this thing is settled beyond any doubt."

Dr. Mesropian bristled. "I too know the man and I am not afraid. But I will not subject my profession to such indignities. There are civilized communities in which one may work in peace."

"I agree," Father said. "My profession is also one of dignity. But I am willing to abandon that dignity in order to establish the rights of a free man to live and work honorably in a free land."

Dr. Mesropian's back was as straight as a ramrod. His knuckles were white where his fingers gripped the desk's edge.

"This too," Father continued, "is a job for a physician. And oftentimes more difficult is the healing of a diseased mind than the repair of a ravaged body. But the benefits will reach on to generations yet to come. You must do it, Doctor."

"Very well." The doctor rose and smiled. "You have never let me down, nor will I fail you now."

"Thank you," Father said. He got up and I darted for the door lest Dr. Mesropian remember the stethoscope dangling down the front of his coat. "I'll keep in close touch with you. Let me know if anything suspicious takes place. After Monday I'll be around each day."

"Thank you. And how is the little girl today?"

"Oh, I'm fine." I skipped down the steps and out of reach, caught the heel of my shoe on a loose board, and sprawled on the ground. Father lifted me out of the dust, and before I could say "scat" we were back in Dr. Mesropian's office and he was examining my elbows and knees and had the cups of his stethoscope poked inside his ears.

At Brother Clevanger's store, Father bought a special-delivery stamp to go on the letter to Tom Craddock and mailed both letters.

When we'd finished our errands I got my first chance to relieve my consuming curiosity.

"Dr. Mesropian already knows, and you said you were pretty sure. Brother Hipplehite is the head of the mob, isn't he?"

"No," Father said, "only an eager assistant."

This rocked me back. "Then who is it?"

"I'd rather not express myself until the proof is conclusive. There is still a margin for error."

"But if it's not Brother Hipplehite or Dr. Bachellor or Brother Dissey or Brother Clevanger, then it's Slim Breedlove or—"

"Let's not conjecture," Father advised. "Let's await developments."

Chapter Twenty

THE old antagonism between Sister Kelso and me had long since vanished, and since janitor duties devolved upon the teacher I frequently offered to stay after school and help her dust erasers, clean blackboards and windows, sweep the room, and dust the desks. For a general cleaning Henry carried water and kept the fire high in the pot-bellied stove while Sister Kelso and I washed windows. It was when she teetered on the stepladder and quickly sat down on its top until the dizziness passed that I noticed how pale and tired she looked.

"You mustn't get sick," I warned her, for school without Sister Kelso would be a dreary thing.

She came down from the stepladder and sat on a chair.

"You've been a wonderful help. I don't know how I could have managed without you. I'm going to tell you a secret. I've not told another soul but Emmett."

"I love secrets," I exclaimed. Being somewhat doubtful of my ability to keep one, I added, "And I try awfully hard to keep them. I'll try extra hard on this one."

Sister Kelso laughed. "You won't need to keep it long. I am going to have a baby next fall—about October, I think."

"That's wonderful," I said earnestly, thinking of little Harry and how sweet he was, his curly golden hair and blue eyes and plump little legs and arms. "I hope it's a lovely boy baby—" I stopped short, fearing that the memory of Harry would make Sister Kelso sad.

"I love little boys." She looked through the window and across Lobo Creek and into the lowering sun, the way she did the day we buried Harry. Then she turned to me. "But I love little girls too." She drew me into the bend of her arm. "I should be so happy to have a little girl who would grow up to be like you."

A compliment can be very painful to an awkward child with scrawny arms and legs, with hair the color of faded hemp, with some of her teeth out and some only half in. I was miserably tongue-tied and afraid to try to speak lest I cry.

"Thank you," I gulped, "but if you have a little girl I know that she'll be pretty—like you—"

She held me away from her. "Why Opal, whatever made you think you aren't pretty? You're a lovely child. You are honest and truthful. Those are beautiful qualities. You've nice manners and a great deal of spirit. You're loyal and intelligent and co-operative and never seek to hurt people. Those are the genuine beauties."

"My hair is straight and ugly and my teeth are all snaggled. I look like a rabbit" (I swallowed hard) "and sometimes I even step on my own feet and trip myself."

Sister Kelso laughed again, but it was a kind laugh. "Let me tell you something. In a few years you'll have chestnut hair—a light brown with red in it. Your eyes that are neither blue or brown will be hazel—a shade of green. That is a stunning combination. Your teeth will come in and you'll be neither fat nor skinny, but delicately rounded. And then—remember that I was the first to tell you—you will be a real beauty, not the ordinary kind, but something special."

I fairly gasped at the picture. "Oh, I hope so—"

"You will be," she said confidently. "Now do you see why I'd be proud to have a little girl growing up like you?"

I nodded, too choked up to speak even one word.

"We're going to build a new house this summer. Brother Craddock has already hauled out several loads of lumber. We want to have it completed and be moved in by fall—before the new baby comes."

Suddenly an alarming thought came. "But the school—"

"I like to teach. I have been so grateful to your father for help-ing me get the school and making the new house possible. But I like my home better. I'm handing in my official notice right away so they can have another teacher by fall. I hope you like her and make it as pleasant for her as you have for me."

"I won't like her as well. But I'll try to be good."

"If you're not, I'll put a bug in her ear—or should I put it in your hair?" We went back to the window washing, and finally we gathered our things and locked the schoolhouse while Henry hitched up the team for the long trip home.

"I heard you outside a half-hour ago," Sister Kelso said. "Why didn't you come in and help us finish the windows?"

"I broke my top string," Henry told her, "and went to Brother Clevanger's for a new one. I didn't aim to be gone so long, but I saw Father's horse in front of Mahoney's boarding house."

"Had your uncle Teepee sent him in for something?"

Henry fumbled with the tugs. "No. He was at Dr. Mesropian's getting his arm fixed up."

The color drained from Sister Kelso's face. "A snake bite—"

Henry shook his head. "Dr. Mesropian said he'd be all right. It just went through the flesh above his elbow."

She grabbed Henry's arm. "But what happened?"

"Somebody shot him. But honest, he's all right. The doctor said so. He's already gone on home."

I ran most of the way to my home, bursting to tell Father the news. But he already knew it. He had been at Dr. Mesropian's when Brother Kelso came in with a tourniquet just below his shoulder. Then I remembered that this was the day Dr. Mesropian was supposed to get out of town. I longed for Father to tell me how things stood, but he said nothing. By supper's end I had to know.

"Father, what is Dr. Mesropian going to do?"

Father's thoughts were on something else. "About what?"

"About leaving town. The week is up today."

"I accompanied him on his calls today. Brother Betz is staying with him tonight. If an emergency call comes during the night, Jim Mahoney will come for me and the three of us will go with Dr. Mesropian."

"I'm scared out of my wits that you'll get into trouble before this is over," Mother said. "They may kill all of you."

Father's voice was grim. "That's what they'll have to do before they get a chance to tar and feather Dr. Mesropian."

Even before it became dark, Mother lighted the two lamps and carried one into the front room. I helped do the dishes while Father read his Baptist Standard. Once or twice Mother stopped washing dishes to listen. When a coyote howled, she stifled a little cry.

Father looked up from his reading. "There's really nothing to be alarmed about. Each man we suspect is a friend of ours. There is no reason to believe anyone would wilfully harm us. I don't think Dr. Mesropian will be molested unless he is alone."

After that both Mother and I felt more at ease.

We were at Evening Devotion when the idea came to me, full-blown from the brow of Jove: why not present my request to Mother tonight? She was always loath to refuse without due deliberation, and this night other things were on her mind and she might more readily consent. I could not postpone its settlement much longer.

Father was at the clawfoot table, his Bible open before him. Mother sat in the sewing rocker with Marjorie on her lap. I perched primly on a chair. A miniature pink-globed parlor lamp was reflected in each lens of Father's glasses. They pinched the bridge of his nose and were tethered to his ear by a fine gold chain.

Father closed his Bible. We knelt by our chairs. I was dutifully reverent at first, but Father's prayer was longer and more fervent than usual. I shifted back on my heels to ease my knees.

"—and Father, we have labored faithfully and not without a measure of success. Increase our strength and our faith. And if it be Thy will, guide us that we may succeed in confounding our enemies."

Confound our enemies, I thought, and let Father say, "Amen," quickly so that I could raise my knees from that torturing home-spun rug which was Mother's pride and joy. When Father had finished and Mother began unbuttoning Marjorie's clothes, I crossed my fingers and took a deep breath.

"Mother, may I go to Ruby Tuttle's party?"

"I understand they're going to play cards," Mother said.

"Not real cards. Just Flinch."

"That's real enough to cause criticism from those who are of a mind. Right now we can't risk it." She skinned off Marjorie's dress.

Lest Mother order me to bed, I blurted out, "Then may I go to the double wedding at Falloon's?"

Mother stripped off Marjorie's panties and panty-waist. "Sister Falloon made it quite definite this afternoon at Ladies Aid that the children were to be left at home. She can only seat and feed the grown folks. Sister Hinkins agreed with her on it."

"Just one child wouldn't matter," I pleaded.

"If you went, they'd all go. And—" Mother added vehemently —"it would serve them right if the children went. Now go to bed —unless you want a spanking. That's a request I'm not in the mood to refuse."

I marched stiffly into the other room. By the time she came in with Marjorie I had plopped into the feather bed, pretending sleep. If I could stay awake and quiet I might hear Mother and Father talking and learn why she was angry. I had certainly chosen a bad time to ask a favor. Usually Mother let down the coil of long tan hair, slipped out the rats, and made a braid. But tonight she went straight into the other room. The joints in the sewing rocker creaked.

"Do you still intend going to that wedding?" she asked.

"I am their pastor. They'll expect me," said Father.

"You'd think they'd expect you to perform the ceremony. But no! They get that back-biting, two-faced Dissey."

"That was Sister Hinkin's idea. I doubt if Brother Falloon would have consented if he were here. He doesn't know what has gone on in his absence. Or if he does, Schuyler Hinkins is his banker."

Mother's voice was contemptuous. "Brother Falloon could buy the bank if he chose. They don't need to toady to that silly little Hinkins girl just because she is marrying Sam Falloon."

As usual Father was patient. "Brother Falloon is in Fort Worth buying cattle—among other things. I don't think he'd have done it if he were here."

"I've told you all along that Brother Dissey was sneaking around trying to take this church away from you. I hope that you believe me now." The rocker squeaked faster.

"I've believed you all along," Father said, "but I didn't know any way to circumvent him. Did you?"

I could hear Mother sigh. "And any day now he'll be driving in for food and fellowship. It's like harboring a viper to your bosom."

Father's voice sounded sad. "Because Brother Dissey ignores Christian behavior is no reason for me to do likewise."

"That cad," Mother said. "Too lazy to pioneer a church. Wants to bring his bride to a ready-made berth, then twist the congregation over to the Russellites. He'll divide the membership, of course. But in any case both we and the church are done for. This town can support barely one church, with the Board's help. If we could only get a church building to hold the people together in joint ownership—"

"That's another reason for keeping faith with Brother Falloon. Upon his generosity may rest our fate."

"You're so meek!" Mother exploded. "If you spunked up and told them off, they'd have more respect for you."

"I find no scriptural authority for spunking up," Father said, "though I do remember, 'Charity vaunteth not itself, is not puffed up.' I have prayed over the matter unceasingly—"

"But you've got to *do* something! Don't you realize that this is crucial? If Brother Dissey performs that ceremony, it will indicate that he has the Falloons' support. That's all these sheep need to make them flock to his side. Dissey can then write his own ticket."

"In that case," Father conceded, "we'll probably see his handwriting on the wall before the wedding is over."

"You may. But I won't. I'm not going."

Everything was terribly quiet. Then Father spoke: "That's for you to decide. I have to proceed according to my lights."

"Then—" The rocker creaked loudly. It sounded as though she said, "I shall proceed according to my lights." But it may have been that the words drowsed through my mind repetitiously as I fell asleep.

The next morning at breakfast Father said to me, "You'd better stay home today. I'll send word to Sister Kelso to excuse you."

"But why?" After last night I did not like Mother well enough to want to spend the day with her.

"I'm making calls with Dr. Mesropian again today. If your mother should need me she can send you for me. I'm quite sure that the whole matter will be settled today—not later than to-morrow."

When Father had gone Mother said, "If you'll do the house-work I'll make up that red batiste for you." This astonished me, since I was not going to Ruby Tuttle's party or to the Falloon wedding. But a new dress was not to be passed up. While I did the dishes Mother lay the pattern on the bed and set the scissors into the beautiful red batiste. When the material lay in a stack of odd-shaped pieces she took the white net ruffles (left over from the mission box dress she had remade for Sammy) and washed and starched them to new crispness for a guimpe with short puffy sleeves. She oiled the sewing machine and set the bottle of lemon-colored oil back in the safe, lest Marjorie find it and sample its contents.

I patted the feather beds into smoothness with the broom, then used it to better advantage by giving the rug a few savage licks. While I was shining the brass knobs on the enamel bed in the front room Mother called me to go to the store for rice and bacon and a nickel's worth of horehound drops for Marjorie, who had the sniffles.

Returning from the store on the path through the buffalo grass I loitered to sympathize with a tumblebug rolling his obnoxious burden, when a rig went by in a cloud of dust. It was Brother Dissey, his visit as usual timed for noon. Before last night I had only disliked him. Now I actively hated him. As one viper to an-other, I stuck out my tongue at the retreating vehicle.

Scarcely was I inside our door when Mother grabbed the rice from my basket. "I declare, it's hard enough to feed him anytime —but today, of all days, when I'm sewing. Hand me the lemon flavoring from the safe." That meant but one thing—Mother's de-licious rice pudding.

I opened the safe door and took out a tall, thin bottle with a yellow label. Just as I was about to hand it to Mother I noticed that it was not lemon flavoring, but the lemon-colored machine oil. I started to replace it when, like Abraham, it seemed the Lord stayed my hand. If it would make Marjorie ill, it should do no less for Brother Dissey. He would then be unable to perform the ceremony for the double wedding. The fact that Mother did not catch my error assured me that I had acted under providential tutelage. She flavored the pudding generously.

"The mercerized table cloth is good enough," she said, "but use the bone-handled knives and forks. And drop more cow chips in the stove."

Father came home to lunch while Brother Dissey was feeding and watering his horses. When they came in together the kitchen was as hot as Daniel's furnace, but the pudding was done and as brown as cinnamon. Brother Dissey needed a shave and his celluloid collar looked as though it had not been scrubbed for a month. He fairly beamed at the bacon, hot biscuits, and sorghum; the radishes, lettuce, and onions from our garden.

"Your usual de luxe table d'hôte," he said to Mother. "Without friends like you, Sister Berryman, I should be poor indeed."

"You should be," Mother replied.

Brother Dissey talked little while he ate. As he finished he looked at Father and deliberately launched into the Falloon matter.

"Sister Hinkins tells me that you have not yet garnered Brother Falloon into the fold. Is he proving to be tougher than you expected?"

"I don't know," Father said. "I haven't tried."

Brother Dissey's look was reproachful. "You're making a grave mistake when you don't seek out every sinner and point out to him the error of his ways. The Good Book makes plain the way when it says to 'suffer the little children.' " He waved a magnanimous hand. "No one should be left out. Everyone should be invited to the wedding of the Lamb and the Bride. Ahem—speaking of weddings—" He glanced modestly at his empty plate. "I suppose you know I have been asked to perform the ceremony for the double wedding."

"Yes, I know." Something in Father's voice caused me to look at him. Only then did I realize how grievous was his hurt.

"I did not seek this honor. It was thrust upon me. Only at Sister Hinkins' insistence did I give my reluctant consent."

Mother's eyes were almost black. She shoved a dish of pudding under Brother Dissey's nose. He glanced down, lifted all his spoon would hold into his mouth, smacked his lips. But immediately a startled look spread over the loose flesh of his face, and his jaw sagged. From his pocket he pulled a handkerchief that had evidently seen service as a shoe-polisher, and mopped moisture from his forehead. He pushed back his chair.

"If you'll excuse me," (he ran his finger around inside his collar) "I need a breath of fresh air. I'm afraid I'm inclined to eat too fast."

From the doorway came a voluminous belch. Sounds of Brother Dissey disgorging his ample dinner made crinkles between my shoulder blades. I sat with clenched hands and closed eyes, rendering silent thanks. Now Father would get to perform the ceremony for the wedding.

Mother's gasp brought me to life. Her face was bewildered. She dipped into the pan of pudding, savored it. Her eyes came to rest on me, sharp with understanding. Her words were low and incisive.

"If it weren't that it might make you deathly ill, I'd make you eat every bite of it."

Father's face was impassive, but there were glints in his eyes. He got up and took his hat from its nail by the back door.

"About three o'clock," he said to me, "go down and call for our mail. It should be out by then. Bring any letters to me. If I'm not in Dr. Mesropian's office, wait for me there."

Brother Dissey came in, looking weak-eyed and spent, but scarcely ill at all. His leave-taking with Mother was more frosty than any heretofore. His parting shot was deliberately malicious.

"If I shouldn't see you again before, I'll see you at the wedding."

Mother laughed and tossed her head. "I doubt it. It's such a relief not to have to attend a wedding. If you had performed as many wedding ceremonies as Mr. Berryman has, you'd be bored with them too." It was hard to get ahead of Mother when she got the bit between her teeth.

When he was gone I turned to Mother. "He sure said that 'I'll see you at the wedding' in a nasty way."

"Can you blame him? He thought I had tried to poison him. He might even take it up with Sheriff Lubeck."

"No!" I cried. "I'll tell him—" I bolted for the door.

Mother grabbed my arm. "I don't think he will go to such lengths. But why ever did you do such a thing?"

Thoroughly frightened and very penitent, I told Mother how it had happened, confessed my intentions, and revealed her own carelessness.

"I'm sorry if he thinks it was you," I told her. In all honesty I still couldn't say I was sorry for what I had done.

"In a way it was," Mother said. "If I'd not been so angry and resentful, I'd have caught the error. Anyway"—she was smiling around her eyes—"it was a nice try. But hereafter let's stick to the legitimate weapons and fight fairly—if possible."

While we did the dishes Mother bemoaned the time which should have been spent on my dress. "It's still more than an hour before you have to go for the mail. Suppose you get the lap robe from the buggy, spread it on the ground, and take Marjorie outside to play. I need every minute I can get on that dress."

I opened my mouth to protest. The new dress was proving far more costly than I had anticipated. But one look at the sheer red batiste and the lacy white net, and my lips clamped together. With grim determination I picked up the chubby baby and lugged her outside.

Chapter Twenty-one

SOMETIMES knowledge comes early in life that the most lonesome roads in the world are not foreign highways or unexplored trails but familiar paths from which the familiar faces have vanished. Never before had anything other than illness kept me from school. A dozen steps along the dusty path toward town and a loneliness born of forgottenness settled upon me. At intervals on each side were small, box-like houses where not a single child played on a porch or romped out to meet one.

Shades were drawn against the afternoon sun, babies were taking siestas, mothers availing themselves of a rest period or a chance to catch up on quiet duties. It was as though the whole town had drawn in its banners, folded its hands, and passed into a deathlike lassitude. A compelling nostalgia for the schoolhouse across the town sucked at me like the core of a whirlwind. Not for many a day would I long to stay home from school.

As I stepped up to the post office window, Brother Clevanger peered in the cubbyholes and shook his head.

"But there must be," I blurted out. "Father's expecting—"

"Come to think of it," Brother Clevanger peered at me over the top of his gold-rimmed glasses, "your pa was here and got it."

"Are you sure?" I asked.

"Course I'm sure," he barked. "Leastwise I think I am."

I turned away and fumbled with the handle on the screen door. Suppose Father hadn't been there. Then I had better go to Dr. Mesropian's office and tell him there was nothing. And if he had been there—but to make sure, I had better go.

Dr. Mesropian was in his office. He opened the door. I took one glance at the pendant stethoscope and backed away.

"I'd like to see my father, please," I told him.

"I'm so sorry, he is not here." Dr. Mesropian gave a little bow. "But I will be glad to check you over, listen to your heart—"

There were little crinkles about his eyes, but I took no chances. I backed out the door. "Can you tell me where he is? I've got to see him." My heels slipped off the edge of the porch and I'd have landed on my back had not Dr. Mesropian grabbed my arm.

"Ah, that was close, was it not? Your father has gone to the lumber yard, to see Mr. Craddock, I think."

I leaped off the porch, then thought of my manners. "Thank you," I said. Dr. Mesropian was bent over, laughing.

The door to the lumber yard office was open and I went in. It was uninhabited and quiet save for the leaves of an open book on the table, fluttering in the breeze. I passed through and into the yard where there were stacks of lumber, two-by-fours, shiplapping, and bundles of redwood and cypress shingles piled high.

I circled several piles and finally heard voices on the far side of a stack of box siding. I listened, for if it were not Father, there was no need to let Brother Craddock know that I was wandering uninvited around his premises.

Brother Craddock was speaking. "Here's what he says. Dear Father: I am well and enjoying my pre-medic work more every day. I cannot thank you and Mother enough for making it possible for me to study medicine. My one ambition is to be a great doctor and make an outstanding contribution in the field of medicine. Do you know that you have right in La Mesa one of the nation's greatest doctors? I have just learned this from no less an authority than the American Medical Association, and I know it will make you proud to live in the same town with such a man. Any help that you can give him will advance the cause of medicine and give you a part in a great work. And too, it will assure me an opportunity that money could not buy—the privilege of working with him when I come back home. Dr. Mesropian has offered to take me each summer, and when I have graduated and passed my state board exams, to become a partner with him. Please do everything in your power to guard this opportunity for me. It is something more precious than anything I had ever hoped for. Perhaps some day, with Dr. Mesropian's help, I can become the fine doctor that he is—something I have heretofore only hoped and dreamed I might be."

Everything was quiet and then Father spoke. His voice was like the lash of a whip, bitterly sharp. "And that is the man you sought to tar and feather and run out of town."

Brother Craddock's voice trailed out in a whine. "But how was a man to know—"

"Why does a man need to know? All you need be interested in is whether a man is a decent, law-abiding citizen. If so, he's as much right to live in this town as you have."

"A lot of us don't like furriners and niggers—"

"Columbus was a foreigner; Lafayette was a foreigner; you yourself are not an Indian, are you?"

"I shore ain't," Brother Craddock shot right back at him.

"Then you are a foreigner. Your father probably was English —and your mother—what was she?"

Brother Craddock hesitated. "She was Creole. But that ain't part nigger like you think. It's French and—"

"I know what a Creole is," Father snapped. "Dr. Mesropian is from the Caucasus, the birthplace of the Caucasian race—and he's just as white as you and I with our mixed origin. But you were so afraid someone might find out your mother was a Creole that you instituted an inquisition to hide your inferiority. You're not inferior by birth. It is of your own making—of your own thinking, which manifests itself in skulking around in the dark, threatening and intimidating honest men who've nothing to hide and nothing to fear."

I was appalled at Father's vitrolic words. I thought Brother Craddock would haul off and flatten him by the lumber pile. But I was astounded to hear him say in a meek and humble voice, "What do you suggest that I do? Apologize to the doctor?"

"By all means," Father replied, "and apologize to every man that you have inveigled into your rotten mob. Disband it and renounce everything for which it has stood."

"What will the doctor think when he learns that I am the one back of it all—" Brother Craddock mumbled.

"Dr. Mesropian knows. He wouldn't be the fine doctor he is if he weren't a better judge of human nature and individual characteristics than you or I. He is also a fine enough man—I hope— to forgive you the miserable things you have done."

I heard the movement of feet and scampered back to the office. Waiting primly on a chair, I regretted my haste in abandoning my listening post, for Father and Brother Craddock did not come in. I dwelt on the astonishing news that Brother Craddock was the head of the mob. And ever since he had prevented Sister Craddock's dosing me with sulphur and molasses I had thought him such a nice man. How could I ever look him in the face again, knowing all the skulduggery he had engaged in? Suddenly I decided I couldn't—not right then anyway. I jumped up and tore out of the office and made a beeline for home.

The last few steps I lagged, wondering whether or not to tell Mother, in case she questioned me. I might as well have saved the troublesome thoughts, for Mother was fidgeting because my lateness was delaying progress on the dress.

"Where in the world have you been all this time?" she demanded, and without waiting for a reply grabbed up the dress. "I can't put in the hem until you try it on."

She put the crisp white guimpe on me, slipped the red bodice edged in black velvet ribbon over it, then the full red skirt, which without the hem came halfway to my ankles. It was beautiful, and I extended my arms to admire the puffy sleeves.

"Step up on that chair," Mother said, "so that I can gauge the length. I think you're old enough to wear your dresses below the knees."

I bounded up on the chair, caught the bottom of the skirt under my foot. The frail batiste parted in an ugly, shredded tear.

"Oh!" Mother's tired nerves gave way. She buried her face in her hands. "It's ruined. Opal, how could you be so stupid?"

I gazed at the hole in horrified fascination. I had to make Mother understand that I hadn't intended to do it.

"I guess—I must have inherited it," I choked, and two tears went trickling down the sides of my nose.

Mother stepped back and looked at me. And then she began to laugh. I had to laugh too, though I couldn't imagine why we laughed.

"You're absolutely right," she said. "Out of the mouths of babes—" She examined the hole. "It's low. It will turn under if we make it the same length you now wear. Then we'll put three little bands of black velvet ribbon at the top of the hem and no one will be the wiser."

Mother put in the hem, stitched on the velvet ribbon, then shoved the sad iron on the front of the stove. She pressed the dress on a folded sheet on the table. It was the most beautiful dress I'd ever had.

Father came in to supper and I hastened to explain that I had carried out his instructions about calling for his mail.

"I went to the post office, but Brother Clevanger thought you'd called for your mail. So I went to Dr. Mesropian's to find out for sure, but you weren't there."

"So you came on to the lumber yard," Father added.

"How did you know?"

"I saw the tail of your dress switching around a stack of shingles. Did you hear our conversation?"

"Some of it," I admitted.

"Enough to satisfy you?" Father asked.

I nodded "yes," then shook my head "no." "Why did Tommy Craddock write all that to his father just this very day?"

Father laughed. "You're smarter than Brother Craddock. He never asked me that. But I didn't give him much chance."

And even as Father spoke I began to see the whole thing.

"I wrote to the American Medical Association, then forwarded their reply to Tom. Together with it I sent a letter explaining what was going on here and asking him to write his father immediately, telling him of the correspondence he was having with Dr. Mesropian. Tom had intended to save that as a surprise for his father when he came home. But Tom, being the good boy that he is, fired a letter right back saying—"

I nodded. "I heard it."

"You two have more secrets than the K.K.K.," Mother said.

Saturday morning at breakfast Mother astonished me so that I could not eat my oatmeal porridge.

"I think Opal should go to the wedding in my place."

Father was troubled. "You said no children were to attend."

"They aren't," Mother agreed, "but if Opal went in my place she would not go in a child's capacity. Don't you see?"

"I suppose you might draw a fine line of distinction. But we can't well explain that to the other parents, can we?"

"We shan't need to. You can just tell Sister Falloon that Marjorie had a cold and that I had to stay at home with her."

Father looked at me, his brown eyes warm with pleasure.

"Want to go, Petey?"

"Oh, Father—I'd love it."

"Finish your breakfast," Mother admonished, "then run down to the store and get a new pair of white lisle stockings and two yards of red ribbon to match your dress. Here's a sample."

Mother followed me to the door. She looked across the gently waving green of the prairie toward a clump of lacy mesquites.

"You'd better not tell any of the girls," she said.

My spirits fell. "Not even Ora and Dora?"

"Only if they ask you point-blank. You mustn't lie."

These drastic limitations failed to depress me greatly. I was going to the double wedding. I could crow for months afterward. Something in my attitude must have aroused Mother's suspicions.

"Remember," she warned, "don't get in any fuss with Otho."

I found the Slade girls on the back porch, half-hidden by baskets of cotton, from which they were removing the seeds, preparing it for Sister Slade to make into comfort batting. Two pairs of stilts stood handily against the porch post.

Dora tossed her head. "Bet you're not going to Ruby's party. Bet your mother wouldn't let you."

I dug my toe into the ground and shook my head. I fought the temptation to say I didn't care—that I was going to the double wedding. But she hadn't asked me point-blank.

The calf bell on Brother Clevanger's screen door clanked as I drew it open. Otho's .22 rifle leaned against the door and I looked about furtively to see if Otho lurked behind a counter. Suddenly he rose up from behind a keg of ginger snaps he was opening. I addressed Brother Clevanger with the air of a queen. Otho listened to my order.

"You can't go to Ruby's party," he taunted through a mouthful of cookies. "Are you getting all diked out just to sit at home and twiddle your thumbs?"

I arched my brows. "I'm going someplace better."

His eyes widened. "Where's that?"

I smiled sweetly. "Wouldn't you like to know?"

"You're fibbing or you'd tell." He swallowed, scoured his teeth with his tongue, and the cookies oozed out at the corners of his mouth.

Mother hadn't instructed me not to tell the boys. "Well, Mr. Smarty, I'm going to the double wedding at Brother Falloon's. So there!"

Only for an instant was Otho stunned into silence. Then he came back with the cutting retort: "Why should you want to go? Your pa's not going to get to marry them?"

"That's all you know about it," I lashed back, and as soon as that ill-considered statement was out I knew I had to do something. If Father didn't perform the ceremony Otho Clevanger would taunt me for the rest of my life.

All the way home I kept one eye on the trail and the other

squinted shut in fervent prayer to God that he not hold my failure with the machine-oil against me but give me another chance.
"God," I told Him, "I'm not as incompetent as you probably
think. Show me the way and this time I'll be careful to make a
success of it."

As the days passed I considered various fantastic lines of action.
Ruby Tuttle's party came and went. School ended with a nice
party where Sister Kelso gave each pupil a gift and we all chipped
in and gave her an ashes-of-roses shawl. And now the day of
the wedding was at hand and still I didn't know how I was going
to make it possible for Father to perform the ceremony.

The Falloon ranch was some twenty-five miles distant and
Father wanted to be there by noon. The lamp shone brightly on
the table where Mother made biscuits for breakfast. After calling
me she poured water from the teakettle into the wash tub at
the foot of the bed. I lay for a moment blinking my eyes, orien-
tating myself.

"Wake up, Jacob, day's a-breakin', peas in the pot and pancakes a-bakin'," Mother said. "Get up and take your bath before
Father comes in from harnessing Duke and Don. Here"—she laid
out clean panties, panty-waist, petticoat, and dress on the bed—
"wear this checked gingham. I'll put another change of underwear and your new dress in the valise."

While I bathed, Mother put the clothes in the valise, carefully
smoothing out Father's fine suit. "It's a blessing they sent this
Prince Albert," she smiled at Father as he came in from emptying
my bath water on the morning-glory vines and zinnias under the
windows. "That suit you are wearing is getting pretty tacky."

Father inspected the thin spots on his black serge.

"I had about prayed the knees out of this one when the new
one came. Should that contain some kind of lesson?"

Mother laughed. "How about work? It might have contributed
something to both the wear—and the results."

Outside the sky was pearly, with two fluffy clouds as pink
as the inside of a conch shell. Father put the valise under the
spring lid in the back of the buggy. Then he got in the buggy
and took the lines.

"Help Father all you can," Mother whispered as she lifted me
up beside him. "He has so much to bear." She turned to Father.

"Don't eat too much wedding supper or you'll be as paunchy as Brother Dissey."

Father laughed and clucked to the horses.

As we traveled the sun rose and threw long, stringy shadows of the horses' legs and the buggy wheels beside us. After some miles Father turned off on a road of one deep rut and one shallow one, originally a cow trail. He took the whip from its socket and examined it. It was not the ordinary light buggy whip to flick the horses, for Duke and Don never required urging. It was a heavy, leather-wound one, ending in thongs. "There's a jack in the next pasture," Father explained. "We're not likely to see him, but we'd best be prepared."

He replaced the whip. The horses kept their steady gait mile after mile. Don, a little longer-legged and higher strung than Duke, tossed his head impatiently. We skirted the edge of a section where reeds and tall grass grew, a lagoon when the rains came. Now it was bumpy with cattle tracks. A half-mile beyond the dry lagoon we reached a fence. Father alighted from the buggy, held out his arms to me.

"May I drive them across the drop gate?" I asked.

Father was diplomatic. "I need your help to hold the wire down." I didn't let him know that I had heard him promise Mother not to leave me in the buggy alone, for Mother had never trusted Duke and Don.

Father unhooked the three strands of barbed wire from the post while I did the same with the next down the line. We held them to the ground while Father spoke to the horses to go over. They had just cleared the wire when there was a sharp squeal like that of a pig caught in a fence. I looked up, and coming over the top of the draw ahead was the jack—coal black and shining in the sun. His long ears were laid back and he was making a bee-line for the horses. Both horses threw their heads upward.

Don snorted, leaped forward. Father dashed to the buggy, grabbed for the lines, and missed. The lines flew up in loops above the horses' backs. Father grabbed again, caught the whip. The force with which it parted from the socket almost threw him to the ground. The horses were on a dead run, following the fence, the buggy bouncing and rocking, its wheels scarcely touching clumps of grass and catclaws.

The next thing I knew Father was beside me, the whip in his hand. The jack having chased the team out of sight, let out a bray of triumph and came trotting back toward us. Father lashed out at him with the whip, once, twice, and again. The jack kicked his heels in the air and squealed. Then he took out over the ravine in the direction from which he had come.

Father's breath came fast. Sweat trickled from under his hat. "Fiddlesticks!" It was the strongest expletive in his vocabulary. "If we'd had a good dog, that would never have happened. He'd have chased the jack away before it reached the horses. Now we're in a pretty mess."

"What'll we do?" I quavered.

"Shank it." Only complete exasperation drove him to slang.

"But my red batiste—your beautiful Prince Albert—"

Father's lips twisted a little. "Perhaps after all it is better that Brother Dissey is officiating. I shouldn't enhance a wedding party in this raiment."

I could scarcely keep back the tears. Should my sketchy plans bear fruit, Father would now have the humiliation of conducting the ceremony in a soiled and threadbare suit.

The sun was a sizzling copper plate in a cloudless sky. Father took off his Stetson and set it on my head. I noticed how handsome were the scallops of black against his white forehead. At the top of a slope I stopped at the sight of a house beside a shimmering blue lake.

"We're almost there," I burbled happily. "See?"

Father shook his head. "Falloons don't live on a lake. That's a mirage—a false hope—a delusion. We still have miles to go."

Miles to go—miles to go. We might even be too late for the wedding. Once more in my extremity I resorted to a silent bombardment of the Almighty. "God, if you'll just let us get there in time, I promise I won't ever ask you for anything else. Honest, I won't—or will I? I might be in a tight spot again. Well, maybe I would, but I'll try to lay off after this. God, help me out just this once. I'll try to keep out of trouble after this. Just get us there in time—"

It was mid-afternoon when a dejected child half-hidden under a ten-gallon hat and a bareheaded man carrying a Simon Legree whip stumbled into the Falloon yard. Sister Falloon and Kate met us on the porch. Father related our story, then explained, "Opal came in her mother's place. I hope that doesn't inconvenience you, Sister Falloon."

"We're happy to have her," Sister Falloon said. "My husband still isn't here, but we'll send the boys to find your team and buggy."

Kate Falloon put her arm about me and led me into the house. Both Father and I felt better after a lunch of cornbread, turnip greens, and cool clabber from the well house. Kate then took me to her bedroom to see her wedding gown—soft blue china silk with an enormous shadow-lace bertha. Georgia's was identical in style, only pink, and each had four yards of satin ribbon in its sash. I had never seen anything so beautiful except my red batiste. Once more out on the porch, Father came and sat by me.

Buggies, hacks, and wagons drove in, unloaded, and went back to the corrals. Women stepped out in the splendor of twenty-gored black voile skirts over rustling silk petticoats. Hopping out of the Slade surrey were Ora and Dora, like primroses in pink dotted swiss—brand-new dresses. And Ruby Tuttle, her blue sailor suit banded in red, her red kid slippers straight from Fort Worth or Dallas. I dared not let my thoughts dwell on my lovely red batiste somewhere on the darkening prairie, shredded by jagged catclaws, because I still had a job to do. Somehow I had to help Father perform the ceremony, since God had let me get to the wedding in time.

"Heavenly Day!" It was Sister Falloon's amazed, futile voice. "They promised no children. Who could have changed all our plans?"

Promptly I piped up. "I heard Brother Dissey say that the children—everyone should be invited to the wedding."

"But Opal," Father remonstrated, "he didn't mean—"

"See," Kate flung at her mother. "I told you that he was conniving and presumptuous. You should never have consented—"

"It was Sister Hinkins' idea." Sister Falloon twisted her hands. "With your father not here to decide, I didn't know what we should do."

Brother and Sister Betz came in a hired hack, with Anna and Hermann in the back seat. Brother and Sister Hipplehite were in the phaeton with Brother and Sister Craddock, the three children tucked between the seats, while Mattie rode between her mother and father.

"My goodness gracious," Sister Falloon wailed, "whatever can be delaying your father. He was supposed to get to La Mesa early this morning. Will someone please tell me what to do with all these children?"

"Here comes Brother Dissey." Kate motioned. "Ask him. He got you into it. Let him get you out of it."

But Brother Dissey sought no back-door entrance. He marched up to the front porch, smiling, shaking hands, genial and hearty—one hand clasping his Bible to his chest, the other busy in extending cordiality.

The Clevanger buckboard drew up and out of the end rolled Eunice, Anice, and Inez. Otho balanced himself on the wheel, teetering while he ogled the Berrymans' drab apparel and scuffed shoes. With a fishy stare aimed directly at me he jumped nimbly down and swaggered away. Father took my hand in his.

"I'm sorry. We are certainly the Lazaruses at this feast."

My eyes brimmed, not for my humiliation but for Father, who had no handsome Prince Albert in which to lead a wedding.

Kate swooped down and took me off to a bedroom where I could freshen up. I lifted my eyes to her beseechingly.

"Miss Kate, you aren't going to let that horrid Brother Dissey marry you, are you? You'll never be happy if you start out being married by somebody you don't like."

"Why—" The apples in Kate's cheeks spread all over.

"Honest, Miss Kate, he's sneaking around trying to take Father's church. That's why he worked Sister Hinkins to let him marry you. It's like—like harboring a viper to your bosom," I stated ponderously.

"I know." Kate spoke quickly. "I told Mother that. But she was afraid to stand up against Sister Hinkins—unless Father were here to back her up. But now—why, it's just too late to do anything."

"No, it's not," I protested. "Not if you just wouldn't marry."

Kate patted my shoulder. "Honey, you don't understand. I'd like to do it, but I can't turn everything upside down at the last minute." At the door she turned and smiled back wistfully, "Honest, I'm sorry."

That left me limp and numb. I had failed miserably. Neither supplication nor effort had availed. I turned to the wash stand, slopped water from the big china pitcher into the bowl, dipped it up on my sun-scorched face. I rerolled my braids behind each ear and retied the black ribbons, thinking of the new red ribbons, the fine white lisle hose, and the beautiful red batiste—fit now only to line an eagle's nest or a coyote's den. My eyes blurred when I heard a commotion. Someone was coming pell-mell down the hall. Kate burst into the room.

"Opal, the boys found your team and buggy. Here's your valise. They also saw my father back on the road. He'll be here very shortly. Dress quickly and let your father have this room to change in. Hurry." She dropped the valise and was gone.

For an instant I stared at our valise. It didn't matter much now, for no one would notice Father, with Brother Dissey up in front. And soon Brother Dissey would have Father's church and we would be gone and no one would care. We might even be a laughingstock. For Otho would tell everyone how I had bragged that Father was going to perform the ceremony.

But if I had to go down before Otho's ridicule, it might as well be with colors flying. I tugged at the straps, loosed the buckles. There beneath the lid were the gleaming red ribbons, the black patent-leather slippers, the fine white lisle hose, and the shining new dress—plumage as fine as that of any proud bird that ever went under the axe.

Chapter Twenty-two

I HUNG back until Father came from his dressing, then we two slipped into the back row of folding chairs. By peering around the edge of the assembly I could see the painted globe of the lamp lighting the blue plush album on the parlor table. When the breeze puffed out the Nottingham curtains, the crystal pendants on the globe tinkled. Sister Bachellor seated herself at the organ. She glanced in the mirror, fluffed her skirts. The bellows breathed as she pedaled up the wind.

Brother and Sister Kelso sat in front of us, with Henry on Brother Kelso's lap. Dal and Vela were beside them. All about us children were on laps and hugging the walls. Packed solidly back of us, all standing, were the "Flying F" boys. Suddenly there were whispers and Brother Falloon was standing in the door. Strains of the *Lohengrin Wedding March* sang out. Brother Falloon edged to the vacant chair beside Sister Falloon, slid his big Stetson hat under the chair, and cramped his high-heeled boots against its rounds. His red head bobbed up as Brother Dissey marched in and came to a stop before the windows. Then came lovely Kate, her curly hair fluffing over its rats, with tall John Ellis, her groom. Sam Falloon, wiry and strong as a rancher should be, stood by little Georgia Hinkins, of the flapping eyelashes.

The music stopped and Brother Dissey opened his Bible.

"Dearly beloved, we are gathered together—"

"Faith, and we are that!" Brother Falloon's big voice boomed out, "but not to have you sayin' thim sacred words. We'll have our own priest or we'll have no wedding at all." He stood up, scanned the assembly.

Brother Dissey's loosely upholstered face became mottled.

"I assume that you didn't know—" he began stiffly.

"I know enough to govern what goes on in my own house," Brother Falloon said. "Father Berryman, where are ye? Your team is in the corral—ah, there ye are. Will ye be comin' up here where you belong? 'Tis right and proper my own children should be married by their own priest."

Father rose and squeezed past the chairs up to the front. I could scarcely watch him for craning to see Brother Dissey, who seemed to have shrunk as he sagged into the seat Dr. Bachellor vacated for him.

I have never seen anyone so beautiful as Father was that day in his lustrous Prince Albert, his deep resonant voice saying the words that pronounced Kate and John and Sam and Georgia each man and wife.

"What God hath joined together, let no man put asunder."

After that all the men were kissing the brides and Sister Falloon and Sister Hinkins were crying and everyone was laughing and shaking hands. And in the melee Otho Clevanger set his heel squarely on the toe of my patent-leather slipper and bore down with a twisting motion. I grabbed my foot and howled.

"Well, Miss Smarty Berryman," Otho smirked, "I told all the kids, and everyone of us got to come to the double wedding."

Fighting mad, I threw caution to the winds. "And my father married them! So there, Mr. Stinky Clevanger."

Brother Falloon's big hand fell on my head. Terrified, I looked up. Laughter crinkled his bright eyes. "Bravo, macushla. Times there are when forbearance is the devil's own device. I said as much to your foine mither this noon, over a dish of her ilegant rice pudding."

Father had come up beside us. I thought there was a strange and tender light in his eyes. His lips parted as though he intended to speak, but Brother Falloon continued, "'Tis nice to look about and see all the children, the only ones of us who've grown up in this land, who'll carry on when we are gone and make a great country of it."

"I agree with you," Father said.

"Ah, and 'tis well I know it, Father Berryman. You and Opal will stay the night with us. I have need of your counsel before you lave."

"Thank you," Father said. Then Sister Falloon came with word that the wedding supper was ready. She requested that Father sit at the table with the wedding party and offer grace.

It was a gala evening and even Otho could not spoil it. We played drop-the-handkerchief outside while the grown-ups ate, and even for us there was plenty and to spare, from luscious brown fried chicken and barbecued beef to generous pieces of the wedding cake. One by one the guests departed, and Sister Falloon finally tucked me into a trundle bed which she insisted she had been keeping just for the time when I would spend the night with them.

I tried to stay awake watching the narrow bar of light under the door separating my room from that in which Father and Brother Falloon were conversing. But I could not distinguish more than an occasional word and the strenuous day proved too much for me. I never knew when Father came to bed.

While we breakfasted, one of the hands brought our team and buggy to the back door. We bade farewell to Kate and John,

Georgia and Sam; and Brother and Sister Falloon accompanied us to the buggy. Father held out his hand to Brother Falloon.

"When I try to thank you for all you have done, words fail me."

"'Tis I who owe thanks to the Blessed Virgin and to yourself for such wise and kindly counsel," Brother Falloon replied.

Praise made Father humble. He said, "Though I am a minister of the gospel, I am only a man and fallible. Mine is but a man's opinion."

"Call yourself by whatever name ye wish, but ye are the foinest priest it has iver been my privilege to know. Your wisdom is of the spirit, while ours is of the flesh only."

The two men grasped hands for a moment. Father's voice was low and he had difficulty with his words. I could only hear something about "—great shall be your reward in heaven."

As Father drove away, I remembered again that marvelous moment when he marched up to perform the wedding ceremony. "It was sure fine that Brother Falloon came back when he did."

"Yes," Father said. "Getting that elaborate altar hauled out from Big Spring consumed much time—that and visiting with your mother." Father's smile was amused but kindly. "Perhaps your mother used her rice pudding more advantageously with Brother Falloon than you did with Brother Dissey. But certainly your purposes were the same."

I was slightly embarrassed at Father's left-handed commendation, but more puzzled about the altar.

"I don't think there's any room in the schoolhouse for an elaborate altar."

"I'd forgotten you didn't know. Through Brother Falloon, the Lord is bestowing on us a new church building."

It was no wonder that Father's face shone, saint-like, in the soft morning sunshine. The Lord had indeed been good to Father —all through Brother Falloon, the man Brother Dissey had called a tool of the devil. It seemed to me there should be some fitting way that we might honor Brother Falloon; but we were poor and he was rich, and we had so little of value which we might give him.

The warmth of beginning summer was in the gentle breeze carrying the perfume of blooming primrose and loco and many little wildflowers that came into secluded glory between the tufts of buffalo grass. The bear grass showed nubs of bloom-stems centering their rosettes of spines, and the prickly pears had greened. There was the touch and the smell of the land, a land that had accepted us. It lay upon me, a lethargic peace. I knew Father felt it too when he began to sing, "What wondrous love is this, Oh my soul, oh my soul—"

I relaxed against his shoulder. All the clouds of fear and tense apprehension were gone. We were to have a new church building and Brother Dissey would not be able to usurp Father's church and drive us out.

"Father," I said, "when will we get the new church?"

"It will be started soon and should be completed before the fall roundups begin. We will start with a main unit that can be added to later. I sketched the plans and Brother Falloon approved them heartily."

"Was that what he was thanking you for?" I asked.

"No. For my efforts in behalf of the ranchers—my appeal for governmental cooperation."

I sat up straight in the seat, remembering a menace not yet disposed of. "Against Slim Breedlove?"

"Against anyone robbing owners of valuable property or harming unprotected citizens."

"Did Slim Breedlove shoot Brother Kelso?"

"Brother Kelso doesn't know who shot him. The ranchers have inaugurated a kind of patrol to keep watch on their outlying borders. Brother Kelso was riding for T. P. Hamilton. He was shot from ambush."

"Didn't he see anybody at all?" I persisted.

"No. He saw a half-dozen whitefaces in the draw and rode toward them to find out why they were so far from the main herd and to drive them back. He was shot before he reached them. He put a tourniquet on his arm and came to the doctor as fast as he could."

"That was a low-down, dirty trick," I exclaimed.

"It was more than that. It was attempted murder. And that has me puzzled. I don't believe Slim Breedlove is a murderer, or he would have threatened me with murder rather than arson."

"Is the government sending a posse to help the ranchers?"

"The government has not revealed its plans as yet, but I look for some kind of assistance." He gave me a piercing look. "But this is strictly our secret. If it leaked out, all our efforts would end in defeat. I don't want the least hint of this to go any further."

"I can keep a secret," I said, remembering having kept Sister Kelso's secret and thus proving to myself that I could.

We drove in home just after noon. Mother came to the door.

"Welcome," she called. "You're earlier than I expected. The jack must have missed connections with you on your return trip."

"How did you know about it?" I demanded.

"Ora and Dora and Otho were here even before Marjorie and I had our breakfasts, bursting to tell us all about it."

Few days in the life of a missionary are pure and unalloyed joy. This day approached such perfection, with our family together, Mother relating the particulars of her visit with Brother Falloon, Father telling the details of our adventure on the prairie, our despair, and Brother Falloon's magnificent coup. Within an hour the sparkle had come back to Mother's eyes—eyes that had dulled through evenings at the poorly lighted sewing machine. Gaiety was in her voice and buoyancy in her step. Once again Father's words contained sly humor, and his laugh, so seldom heard in past weeks, was spontaneous. The lines of weariness in his face seemed miraculously to be fading, restoring to us the handsome, vigorous man who had, less than two years before, brought all the strength of his youth to this new field.

As for me, never had it seemed so good to be living in a wide, free land and to be the daughter of a missionary pastor in whom the Lord was well pleased, on whom He poured out His blessings.

The joy was dimmed a fraction when Father remarked at supper that he had seen Sheriff Lubeck ride in and must go over and take up some matters with him.

Mother laid her hand against her throat. "You think—"

"I don't think," Father said, "that cleaning up the hooded hoodlums in the town or our plans for a new church building have appreciably discouraged the cattle rustlers. Probably the most vital part of our work remains yet to be done."

Mother sighed. "I'd quite forgotten for the moment that Slim Breedlove and Dr. Bachellor were still to be dealt with."

Longingly I watched Father leave, knowing that this time I would not get to listen in on his conversation with Sheriff Lubeck.

One of my summer jobs was to watch Mother's hens with their broods of young chicks, lest they wander too far and a hawk swoop down and carry away a prospective fryer. Henny-Penny with her mottled feathers and miniature children had a way of escaping my intermittent attention.

A day or two after the wedding she gave me the slip. I had walked for miles, it seemed, when just before dusk I met her and her tiny quail-like babies chasing each grasshopper and bug on the long trail home. I plodded behind them, and as we passed Dr. Bachellor's house I noticed a freighter's wagon drawn up with its end-gate touching the back door. I told Father about it when I reached home.

"Probably another load of rot-gut whiskey," Father said. The worried look came into his face. "Sheriff Lubeck is in touch with the proper authorities. Shortly they'll be able to do something about that gambling den."

The next morning, who should ride into the yard but Sammy Severn, duded out like the cowgirls in pictures of highfaluting rodeos. She had on fancy boots, a short divided skirt with leather fringe, a beaded buckskin jacket, and a hat with a chin strap dangling tassels. Her hair lay in waves and curls and shone like polished cherry wood. Her cheeks were no longer like saddle leather, but a creamy tan, and satin smooth.

"Hello, everybody!" She swung out of the saddle while we crowded through the door. She hugged Mother, kissed me and Marjorie, and threw her arms about Father. "Gee, it's grand to see you all. You haven't changed a bit. Of course Marjorie's bigger and Opal's taller—but honest, it's so good to find you folks haven't changed."

Mother laughed. "You have—but only in looks. Goodness! How I've missed you. When you wrote us you were homesick and might come home, I kind of half-hoped you would."

"And if you had," Father said, "she'd have given you a verbal spanking and sent you back."

"I reckon that's why I stayed," Sammy said. "I didn't want you-all to think I was a quitter." She plopped herself down on the bed. "Now tell me everything that's happened since I left."

Father and Mother took turns telling Sammy the events of the past nine months. But each of them avoided mentioning that Tom

Craddock had fallen hard for Rose Mahoney. Finally Sammy asked, "Has Tommy Craddock come home yet?"

Father answered. "He is supposed to come today. I don't know whether Brother Craddock drove to Big Spring to pick him up, or if he will ride out with the freighters."

"The freighters—" Sammy sprang to her feet. "Now don't anybody leave." She flew to the door and was on her horse and riding toward town while we sat and looked at each other.

"It does beat all," Mother said sadly, "what a girl will do. When Sammy gets an idea, she hangs on for dear life. Once she has pledged herself she never stops until the pledge is fulfilled. But she forgets that Tom made no pledge."

"You forget," Father said, "that Sammy's pledge was made with herself and not with Tommy."

This talk seemed sort of abstract to me, but it was concrete enough to irritate Mother and to stiffen Father's resistance. Mother worked off her pique in getting a super-excellent dinner. Sammy came back on the dot of noon. As we sat down she looked over the loaded table, touched the linen cloth and the bone-handled knives and forks.

"Honestly, you'd think I was company."

Father smiled. "We just killed the fatted rooster to welcome home the prodigal daughter after her riotous season in the city."

Half-way through the meal Sammy said, "I saw Tommy Craddock when I was down at the wagon yard."

"I've been anxious to see him myself," Father said. "I must look him up this afternoon."

Sammy laughed a little, harsh laugh. "Then you'd better look for him at Brother Betz's store—or somewhere close to Rose Mahoney."

"I shouldn't be surprised." Father's voice was as even as though all this were small talk. "At Christmas I noticed that he had taken quite a shine to Rose. But of course it could have been temporary."

"Not if I know anything about men folks," Sammy said, "and I think I know a lot more about them than I did last fall."

"Has Tommy changed a great deal?" Mother asked.

"In looks?" Sammy's gaze glanced off Mother, came to rest at the window. "His clothes fit better and he's more polite. But Tommy was always good-looking and polite. He has changed, though. He acts more like he knows what he wants and nobody's going to stop him from getting it. That's all to the good—" Sammy's words faded away as though she were somehow bewildered.

Father's tone was tempered to her thoughts. "But with all those things in his favor, you didn't get the exhilaration from seeing him again that you had thought you would."

"That's it. But how did you know?"

Father smiled. "That's easy. Just by knowing you."

"You mean I've changed?"

"Not essentially."

"Tell me," Sammy demanded. "I got to know."

"Well, Tommy had a gentle manner, a little more polish than anyone you had ever known. But now that you have known many men more polished—"

"Yeah, that's it. When you find it's something anybody can get, it don't mean so much."

"I think that's the answer," Father said.

"Spunk and go-get-'em, that's what a man's got to have. I'd just naturally lord it over him if he didn't have that."

"And be unhappy in the doing," Father told her.

Sammy's hands came down flat on the table. "You know what? I found out one thing this past year. When I get married I'm going to marry a real man. Not a city dude and not a swaggering cowpuncher. If a man is a real, honest-to-God man, he's the same in the city or on a ranch."

"You're right," Father said. "And how is Ford?"

"Fine. He's at the ranch. The folks will all come out soon."

"Did he marry the chorus girl?" Mother asked. "The one that kicked up her legs in public?" Mother was smiling.

Sammy blushed. "I sure was dumb, but I finally doped it out that it was my leg he was pulling instead of hers."

Father laughed more heartily than he had for a long time.

"You probably had that all figured out," Sammy said to him. "I ought to thumb my nose at you for not putting me wise."

We all heard a wagon drawing up to the house. Mother got up and looked out the window. "It must be another mission box, but nobody wrote us about it." She went in the front room and opened the door. Sammy and I were behind Father. There was a huge box in the freighter's wagon, tall and narrow, and on it in big black letters, "Bush and Gerts."

"It isn't ours," I said. "It belongs to Bush and Gert."

"Shhh—" Sammy whispered. "The men know what they're doing."

The two freighters slid the box down the end-gate and into the door. With claw hammers they loosened the boards on one tall side. Father looked at Sammy and Sammy shook her head at him.

"What in the world—" Mother read a tag tacked to the box. Then she looked at Sammy. As the boards came loose I saw yellow varnished wood, but when the boards were off the freighters took hold of two handles and slid the thing out of the box. Its ends were red-brown mahogany, and then I saw the front—not so tall and plainer than any I had ever seen in the catalogues—a gorgeous brand new piano.

I must have shrieked. "Look Father—look Mother! Isn't it beautiful?"

Mother cleared a space and the freighters lifted the piano into place. They had to stop and admire it before they gathered up the excelsior and papers.

"Is it really ours?" I asked Father. "You didn't tell me—"

"He didn't know," Sammy said. "Remember, Opal, when I caused Prince to throw you? I promised I'd make it up to you someday? Well your father's letter asking me to price pianos gave me an idea. I told Ford and he wanted a part in it. He insisted we share on it. So here it is—from both of us."

"It's wonderful," I gasped, "just wonderful."

"The darn thing's no good if it won't play," Sammy said.

Father whirled the spool up so that my foot barely touched the pedal. My hands trembled and my eyes blurred. I didn't even have presence of mind enough to make the coy apology of every amateur pianist—"I'm really so out of practice." In my case it would have been true. I simply plunged in, and fumbled and bungled through the worst rendition of *The Black Hawk Waltz* that was ever perpetrated upon four innocent and loving people.

Chapter Twenty-three

E<small>VERY</small> land, regardless of its harshness, its tortures and cruelties to those who would temper it, its bitter animosities and ironic retaliations, has its moments of sheer beauty. It was so of the Llano Estacado on a June night. The wind sank with the sun, to give the still tender vegetation a double rest. The new moon appeared like a red-hot horseshoe and the sky was filled with the sparks of its forging and fashioning.

All this I saw as I stood outside the privy door, waiting for Sammy. An unwritten law of the prairie was that no female guest should ever leave the sanctuary of a home unaccompanied after dark.

Sammy came out and fastened the door with its leather hasp. She turned her face to the stars that looked so friendly and flippant.

"Gosh," the word was a prayer and a paen, "do I love it—and am I glad to get back. I'll never leave it for so long again—so help me God!"

We went in to supper, and afterward, like a magnet, the piano drew us back to the front room. At Father's request Sammy played and sang for us. With but nine months of study she played exceptionally well, and through training her voice had developed its natural musical quality. It was full, round, and no longer nasal.

Dutifully she sang *My Mother Bids Me Bind My Hair*, with nice interpretation.

"That was lovely," Mother told her.

"I'd never get any place with that sort of thing," Sammy said. "This is my kind of song." She moved both hands down the keyboard, struck a few harmonic chords, then sang,

> *"Remember, my dogie, wherever you come from,*
> *Wyomin's as wild as the sagebrush that blows,*

The grass is as thick as the hides that you carry,
The sod underneath it will stick to your toes.

You'll grow up as fast as the sandburs and jimson,
Dependin' on how much your bellies can hold,
So pull up the weeds by the roots that they spring from,
Don't wait for the snow when the grasses turn cold.

Oh, take some advice from a man with experience,
A minute that's wasted you cannot recall,
So sniff the alfalfa and chew up the clover,
And git along dogies, 'til after the fall.

Sammy swung herself about on the piano stool. "You know," she said, "I'm a dogie. Dogies have to learn a lot of things for themselves. And those things you learn most awful well."

I began to see why Father had always had such faith in Sammy. There was something about her that was wonderfully rare and fine.

Mother made tea and set out a tray of tea cakes. Marjorie was sleepy, and while we ate Mother made her a bed on the box couch and tucked her in, with a chair backed up to the couch to prevent her falling off.

Sammy no longer used her saucer to cool her tea, but sipped from the cup.

"You know," (her gaze was on Father) "I'm worried about Pa. Slim Breedlove's threatened to get him."

"What has your father done to Slim?"

"Nothing so far. But Slim rode in yesterday and told Pa he'd heard Pa'd turned him in to the government men. That they were already somewhere around. Pa called him a liar and drawed his gun. Pa had the drop on Slim and ordered him off the place. But one of these days they'll tangle again, and it will be either Pa or Slim. Or Slim may lay for Pa and shoot him in the back."

Father's face had a haunted look. "Slim threatened to burn my house. I suppose he's been too busy lately to attend to it."

"Is he still griped because Brother Betz wouldn't start another saloon?" Sammy asked.

"More recently because Dr. Bachellor's bootleg whiskey and

gambling activities were attacked from my pulpit. I wonder if Slim is conducting a one-man campaign against law and order?"

"He—heck no," Sammy said. "He's got a gang of cutthroats with itchy trigger fingers. He's picked up every bad hombre in this part of the country. But I ain't even sure that he's the ringleader. I can't feature old Slim getting so all-fired brave and tough all of a sudden."

"Why did he think your father had reported him?"

"Some of his gang spotted a government man in Big Spring several days running. Those fellows know every sheriff and deputy and vigilante north of the Pecos and have been chased by them at some time or other."

Father studied the table cloth. "Does your father know who reported Slim?"

"If he does, he ain't tellin'. That's Pa. Keeps his mouth as tight shut as a yearling with the lockjaw."

"Sammy," Father said, "would you come in next Friday and stay over the week-end? It's my Sunday in Seminole, and I dislike to leave Mrs. Berryman and the two children alone."

"Sure as shootin'," Sammy said, "I'll be here."

Now that I had a piano on which to practice, Father said I might arrange with Sister Bachellor to resume my music lessons. I started for her house with skirts and pig-tails flying, but put on the brake when I thought of the dogs. It was a fight to get to the house with them jumping on you and swabbing your face with their dripping tongues.

The dogs discovered me before I discovered them. From inside the house came a terrific barking and I could see their two spotted heads bumping the window pane. But something was peculiar. There were no curtains tied back with ruffles and bows. I circled the house and heard the scampering of toenails on bare floors. I ran all the way home and told Father. He took our skeleton key from its nail by the back door and together we went back to the Bachellor house.

As we let ourselves in, the dogs almost knocked us down in their dash outside. Father threw open doors and windows, for the stench was unbearable. In the three vacant rooms not a stick of furniture remained. Several bottles, some of them broken, littered the place, and two empty pans sat on the kitchen floor. That and the dogs were all that was left of the Bachellors.

"What do you suppose happened to them?" I asked Father.

"It's evident they didn't die. So they must have pulled out under their own steam. I can only surmise the reason."

"What was it?" I prodded, curious as a cat.

"Someone probably tipped off Dr. Bachellor that there were federal men in the area. Possibly he had more to fear than the felony of selling liquor without a license and operating an illegal gambling house. But that's only a supposition based on rumor. What he would have had to answer for here was enough to cause him to skip the country."

"Good riddance of bad rubbish," I chirped, as smugly as Brother Dissey might have. "He won't bother us anymore."

Father's look made my ears burn. "Now he's free to operate in some other town and demoralize their youth. Is a young man less valuable because he happens to live in another county or state?"

"Well," I hedged. "He wouldn't be our young man."

"So you aren't concerned about what you can't see? Like the good deacon who prayed, 'Oh Lord, bless me and my wife, my son John and his wife, us four and no more,' and was content to let the devil take those who hadn't sense enough to pray for themselves? When every man is as concerned about the welfare of his fellowman across the world as he is about his own family, then and then only will we have a Christian world."

At the kennel Father found an old stub of a broom. He pumped water into the dogs' pans and cleaned the floors as best he could. He sent me for rope with which to leash the dogs and we took them home and cleaned out our supply of bread and milk in order to feed them.

"Whatever will you do with them?" Mother wanted to know.

"Brother Falloon is coming in today," Father said. "I think it likely he will have some solution."

"Is Sister Falloon coming too?" Mother asked.

"I think not." Father looked from Mother to me. "I must ask both of you not to mention a word of this. We will have other guests also. Ford Hamilton, Brother Severn, and Brother Kelso— and several men who will be strangers to you. They will come on foot after it is dark. Draw all the shades and put the chairs in the front room. Then the three of you remain in here."

"I don't like this," Mother protested, "not a little bit."

"I don't either," Father said, "but I like far less the cause that necessitates it."

Ford Hamilton was the first to come. Father brought him to the kitchen. "I think Opal has something to say to you," he said.

And then I remembered. The beautiful piano, rich in color as the cape of a prince of Burgundy, was Ford's gift as well as Sammy's. Ford was so tall and fair he might well have been a prince, standing there smiling, his big white hat in his hand.

"Thank you so very much, Mr. Hamilton—"

"Ford," he said. "All my girls call me Ford."

I was as fussed as a big girl. "Ford—the piano is just beautiful and I thank you a million times."

"You're plumb welcome. But I guess we were too late. Your father told me this afternoon that now you've lost your teacher."

Father spoke up. "A fine, growing town like this will have another teacher shortly. We even have one in Seminole."

"Sammy should have kept it," I said. "She plays and sings so beautifully."

"Sammy's good at everything," Ford said, "except making up her mind. And one of these days I hope she'll do that."

"Be patient," Father said. "Sammy's wise to be absolutely sure before making a decision."

"It's got me on needles and pins," Ford said. "But just in case, I'm building a ranch house. An architect in Fort Worth drew up the plans, then we revised them to suit our needs out here." He glanced at me. "There'll be a piano in it."

"Building close to your father's home?" Father asked.

"No. Dad and I thought it best to build at the farthest section of the ranch. It's right close to the Colorado road, just below the cap rock. There are natural springs there and the cap rock makes a windbreak. There's trees—lots of vegetation—"

"I know where it is," I exploded. "Remember, Father? We stopped there to eat our lunch—and there was a mud turtle in the pool—and up on the cap rock I looked down—" I ran out of breath.

Father smiled. "I remember very well. We could hardly drag Opal away. Perhaps you'd better revise your plans again and in-

234

clude a lean-to for her. She longed to live in that particular spot."

"I'll do that," Ford promised, "and make it big enough for a music teacher-chaperon. If I should have to live there all alone, it'll be pretty damned lonesome."

There was a tapping on the door and Father and Ford went back in the front room.

Mother and I sat on the bed, straining to catch sounds. There was another knock, short and muffled, and we recognized Brother Falloon's big voice. After that Father opened the door several times, but the conversation was pitched so low that we could not understand a word. Mother entertained Marjorie with stories of Red Riding Hood and Goldilocks, and after she fell asleep Mother and I played Tit-Tat-Toe on the kitchen table, she from the low level of the sewing rocker and me from the height of a dry-goods box.

Finally they left, one at a time, and the door to the front room opened. Father came in and snapped open the lid of his watch.

"It isn't so late but that we've time for Evening Devotion."

We helped Father replace the chairs, then seated ourselves while he took his place by the lamp. He opened his Bible and read a short psalm. We knelt while Father prayed for the success of an undertaking, the precise nature of which we were not aware. I went to bed knowing that I must not ask, for had Father wanted us to know, he would have told us.

In the east the next morning the sun rose unusually brilliant. By mid-morning this contrary land had whipped up a great dun wall in the west, hurled it at the sun, and the whole area stood the brunt of the senseless battle.

During the night the wind subsided, and with the house to clean Mother decided to eradicate the bedbugs. Father set to work with his can of kerosene while I examined the sunning feather beds and pillows and disposed of the occasional occupants of each crease. Our constant warfare was showing results and fewer and fewer came to plague us after each drive.

Bright and early Friday morning Father left for Seminole, and before the end of the day Sammy rode in to spend the week-end with us. She brought with her a pair of black silk stockings for Mother, a bangle bracelet for me, and a little ring with a tiny topaz birthstone for Marjorie (which Mother tied on Marjorie's fat finger with a silk thread cord). Mother modeled the black silk stockings. I was amazed at the lovely contour of her legs, which so seldom showed beneath her long skirts.

Some lovelorn fellow in Fort Worth had sent Sammy the bangle bracelet. By all the laws of etiquette she should have sent it right back; but tempted by the pleasure she knew I would derive from it, she had kept it. As she put it, "The money was already spent. Somebody ought to get some good out of it. If I sent it back, I wouldn't and he wouldn't and you wouldn't. What's the good of that?" So I had the lovely bangle bracelet with its gold chain, its pendant padlock, and the tiny, exquisite key that unlocked it.

In mid-afternoon on that Saturday, Sammy and I were picking chickens for Sunday dinner when Sammy straightened up and laid her hand above her eyes. Squinting, she looked across the prairie far to the east, out the road to old Chicago. I could see nothing, but Sammy had eyes and ears conditioned to the heat waves and dimming haze. She saw through it as Dr. Mesropian's new X-ray machine saw through the flesh of your hand.

"Something's happened—something bad. I've got to find out." She threw the checked gingham apron inside the door and headed for town on a dead run. Listening intently, I could distinguish the faint, far pounding of a horse's hoofs; and then I saw him, a rider bent low over the saddle horn, coming toward town with the speed of a racer. Mother was standing in the door, her features sharp in her white face.

"May I go?" I asked. "Please—I'll stay with Sammy."

Mother nodded. "Find out—it might be your father—"

I ran in the direction Sammy had taken, toward Mahoney's boarding house and wagon yard. People were coming from up and down the street, Brother Slade and Brother Hipplehite and Brother Craddock. Children, too. Even Brother Hinkins was on the steps of his bank. The rider stopped short before Sister Mahoney's, threw the reins over his horse's head, and flung himself from the saddle. Brother Betz and Dr. Mesropian came from the drug store on the run. Sammy had the cowpuncher by the arm.

"What's happened?"

236

"All I know, ma'am, is there's been a shootin' at Joyner's Well. They're bringin' in one dead man and two all shot up."

"But who—" Sammy choked. "Who are they?"

"I don't know, ma'am. A rider come to our place for a wagon and told me to git to town pronto and have two beds and a doctor ready. Now leggo me—" He gave his arm a tug and looked around. "Which one of you hombres is a doc? And which one owns this here hotel?"

Dr. Mesropian stepped forward. "I'm a doctor," he said.

"Then whet up your knives. One of 'em's pretty bad."

Sister Mahoney spoke up. "I own the boarding house. I'll clear two rooms on that side—those first two—"

"I'll need plenty of boiling water, Mrs. Mahoney," Dr. Mesropian was saying. He turned to Brother Betz. "Bring over a can of ether, some whiskey, bandages, iodine, an extra syringe, dressings, cotton—"

Sister Mahoney spoke to Rose. "Come and help me." They disappeared into the house. Now Sammy was talking to the rider.

"How long before they'll be here?"

"Not long. I stopped at Waterbury's and told 'em to have a fresh team and wagon waitin' on the road to bring 'em on in. A half hour maybe."

I turned and ran for home in order to tell Mother the news and be back before the wounded—and the dead—arrived.

"Thank God," Mother said when she heard my story, "it's not your father. But I'd better get down there. I might have to send for him. If it should be Brother Falloon, he'd want his priest."

Mother was tying on Marjorie's sunbonnet when I saw the wagon and riders coming. I called to her.

"Poor Sammy," Mother said, "not knowing whether it is her father or brothers—killed or wounded. We must get there."

We got there just before the riders and wagon did. The whole town had gathered. Brother Slade and Brother Craddock had to keep the people pushed back from Sister Mahoney's front porch. Sammy was at the front, her fingers rammed into her hair, her eyes straining. We worked in beside her, next to the Pothasts and Mrs. Tuttle.

Brother Kelso was driving the wagon, and beside him sat Sheriff

Lubeck. The sheriff jumped to the ground and helped direct Brother Kelso in getting the back of the wagon to the steps. "Where is he—" Sammy whispered, but she was talking to herself. They were lifting a man from the wagon and they were being very careful.

Dr. Mesropian stepped up. "Is he the worst one?"

"We ain't sure," one of the men said. Dr. Mesropian directed them to lay their burden on the table in his office. Four men carried him in on a wagon-sheet. For a fleeting second I saw his face, no longer red, but now only a kind of grayish green under the thatch of red hair. It was Brother Falloon.

Three more men and Brother Kelso had the second man half out of the wagon when Sammy cried, "Ford! Oh my God—"

"Stand back, Miss," a man commanded. "He can't hear you."

"Stand back, everybody," someone shouted, and we all pressed back. Sammy had her fists clamped against her mouth.

"On the cot here beside the table," Dr. Mesropian called. "Another pail of boiling water, please, Mrs. Mahoney."

Tom Craddock passed the door, a white cloth tied over his face just below his eyes. Sammy's palms covered her face. "Please, God—don't let him die—please, God—" It was like a chant. Then her hands fell, she took a deep breath, and walked over to the door of Dr. Mesropian's office.

"Tommy," she said, "tell me, please, the minute you know."

Tom paused and his eyebrows made two arches. "Sure, Sammy. Sure, I'll tell you."

By now everyone had turned to the second wagon drawn up by the wagon yard. Sister Mahoney's head appeared in the doorway.

"Use the third room back. It's a little room with one cot in it. It's big enough."

Men lifted a form shrouded in a wagon-sheet. Brother Kelso was passing directly in front of us.

Brother Slade spoke to him. "Who is it, Emmett?"

"Slim Breedlove," Brother Kelso told him.

My personal relief registered like a sigh on my ear drums. Mother and I looked for Sammy. She had stopped Brother Kelso and was talking to him. When their conversation ended, she joined us.

"Could you learn anything about what happened?" Mother asked.

"Brother Kelso says they spent days watching this gang at work. They'd even seen them rebranding whitefaces. About daylight this morning they jumped the guy on guard with the cattle and cut out all the whitefaces and rebranded stock. He and Falloon and Ford had driven them back as far as Joyner's Well and stopped there for water. Slim got wind of things and a half-dozen of the gang ambushed them at Joyner's Well."

"Caught them off guard," Mother said.

"Not exactly. Slim hit Ford right off, but his shot was a little wild; and before he could pump more lead into Ford, Pat Falloon had whipped out both guns, plugged Slim deader'n a door nail, and had put daylight through every man in the gang. Boy, can that guy shoot! With six-to-one odds, he got everyone of them before one got him. Brother Kelso was back of the herd, and with a bum arm his shots went wild. The gang got away, a couple of them draped over their saddle horns and bleedin' like stuck hogs. But they hadn't got a mile before at least those two were nothin' but buzzard meat. Sheriff Lubeck met them as they were ridin' back."

Sammy had caught sight of someone being carried from Dr. Mesropian's office. Sister Betz hovered at the head of the cot. She nodded to Kate and John Ellis, who followed them around to the wagon yard. The men came back with the empty cot and Mother went to John, standing outside the door of the first room.

"How is Brother Falloon?" she asked.

"It's pretty hard to tell, Sister Berryman," John replied.

"Should I try to get word to Mr. Berryman?"

John shook his head. "Dr. Mesropian says it will be a few days before we'll know and Brother Berryman will be back by that time."

"I'll keep in close touch with you," Mother promised.

The cot was carried through the gate, this time bearing Ford Hamilton. Rose stood at its head and Sammy was close by. Rose stooped to tuck the loosened sheet. Sammy looked for a moment as though she might strike away Rose's hand.

"What does Dr. Mesropian say?" Mother asked. "Or can he tell as yet?"

"Ford's wound is in his shoulder—just missed his heart. He's lost a lot of blood. I'm going to stay with him," Sammy said firmly.

"I think you should," Mother agreed. "But I must go home. Will you keep me informed about both Ford and Brother Falloon?"

"Sure, I will. I'll be back at supper time. If I don't show up before, you'll know everything's all right so far."

Reluctantly I turned and went with Mother. The atmosphere of uneasiness that pervaded the town was almost a tangible thing. People still stood about in tight little groups as though afraid to re-enter their homes and businesses, lest the earth shake again with tragedy. As we passed the bank, where Brother Hinkins was talking with Judge and Mrs. Pothast and Mrs. Tuttle, I heard him say, "When this section becomes important enough for the government to send men out to keep law and order, it's about time we got busy and got a railroad."

"How perfectly lovely," Mrs. Tuttle exclaimed. "Then we could run down to Big Spring each week to do our shopping."

Chapter Twenty-four

WE stopped by the store and Brother Clevanger put some groceries in the wagon with Marjorie. Otho handed me two letters and a paper from the mail window.

"No love letters for Miss Opal Berryman today," he announced sweetly, smirking at me through the bars.

Having no gift of repartee, I stared at him disdainfully.

"Go on away," he ordered. "You can bank on what I tell you."

"Like about who was going to perform the double wedding ceremony?" I asked in a honeyed voice, then turned and fled for fear I'd not be able to clear the door before I got a swift kick in the pants.

Mother and I spent the afternoon inventing excuses to go outside where we could look toward town, expecting and fearing to see Sammy coming on the run. Finally Mother remembered the two letters, which were still unread. One was from the Board and the other from Aunt Tennie. Mother spread Aunt Tennie's letter on the table and read:

"Dearest Sister: I hadn't the heart to write you before. Johnnie has done it again—traded our ranch here for one close to a wide place in the road called Hobbs, New Mexico. Our ranch there is much larger and we will also homestead two adjoining sections. Johnnie insists that if we can just live and prove up on our land, someday we will be rich from the oil that lies under the shale. You know Johnnie—every new venture will eventually make us rich. I'm glad that disposition doesn't run in his family or you'd be in for it too.

"Our closest town is Seminole, across the state line in Gaines County. We'll probably go in once a month for groceries and between times never see a living soul. If Johnnie and I should die in that godforsaken spot, no one will know it for months. Honestly, if I didn't love him so much I'd never pick up and move to another desolate place. You really are lucky not having that to contend with.

"Your loving sister, Tennie."

"Poor Tennie," Mother sighed. "She has a difficult lot."

This Jeremiad had me almost in tears over Aunt Tennie's sad fate. I couldn't trust myself to comment on Uncle Johnnie's horrible habits.

"What's the other letter?" I asked.

"Probably your father's check. We'll let him open it himself."

I went out to ride herd on Henny-Penny and her brood, and incidentally to watch for Sammy. The moment I saw her I got my charges into the shadow of the shed and ran for the house.

By the time I got there Sammy had sagged into a chair. Mother was setting the table.

Finally Mother said, "Can't you tell me, Sammy?"

Sammy's head jerked up. "It's that damned Rose Mahoney. She's got Tommy Craddock. That's O.K. by me. But now she wants Ford, and there's just one way she'll get him—over my dead body!"

"What has Rose been doing?" Mother asked.

"What ain't she been doin'? Everything—every last little turn.

241

Won't let me lift my finger. I've stood all of it I'm going to, I tell you."

"You don't understand, dear. Rose is going to be a nurse."

"Well, she's not nursin' my man. Some of the things she wants to do, nobody but me's goin' to do. She can keep her hands off him."

"Sammy," Mother said firmly, "do you really love Ford?"

"Of course I love him." Sammy dropped her head on her arms and cried out all the grief and anxiety and fear that packed her heart. "I just didn't know it before. I love him so much I could cut myself to bits if it would help. I'd gladly lie there in place of him. If he dies—"

"There, there." Mother touched her shoulder. "Dr. Mesropian is an excellent doctor. I don't think Ford will die. He's young and strong. Now wash your face and tidy up. Some good, hot food will help you."

Sammy dipped water from the bucket into the wash pan and bathed her face. From behind the towel she peered at Mother. "I guess I'll never learn to be a lady. I'm an awful fool."

"We're all fools about those we love," Mother admitted, "but be more tolerant of Rose. Put yourself in her position. She's trying to conquer her natural modesty—seeking to impress Dr. Mesropian so that he'll recommend her to take training in a good hospital. And she's endeavoring to prove her efficiency to Tommy. Why don't you cooperate with her? She'll let you assume duties you wish to handle."

Suddenly Sammy came to life. "Maybe you're right."

"Rose wants Ford to recover too," Mother went on, "but for a different reason. Suppose you tell her you love Ford. Then notice the difference."

Sammy smiled. "I'll tell the world I love Ford. I'm telling him as soon as he's awake."

"Try showing him," Mother advised, "and let him tell you."

So while Sammy bolted her supper she explained that Dr. Mesropian had said that Brother Falloon was holding his own. Sister Betz was watching him constantly. The moment she finished eating, Sammy was gone.

She came home about midnight and slipped quietly into bed.

"Are you awake, Opal?" she asked.

I nodded.

"Ford's conscious. He knew me. Dr. Mesropian said he was going to be all right. Oh God—I forgot—" She rolled out of bed, knelt beside it, and I could hear her whispering her thanks into the covers.

Late Sunday evening Father drove in. Mother and I met him.

"What's wrong?" Mother asked. "You didn't stay for the service tonight."

"I had a feeling that things might break before I got home," Father answered. "Since I'd gone a day early and made my pastoral calls, I dispensed with the evening service and drove back by way of Brother Severn's."

"Then you know what has happened?" Mother asked.

"Most of it. How are Ford and Brother Falloon?"

"Ford is recovering. Brother Falloon is holding his own. Come in as soon as you can. There is so much to talk over."

There was indeed much to talk over while Father ate a supper of cold fried chicken, okra, and custard pie. When Mother tried to pass the green onions and radishes to him, he said, "I'll have to pass them up. I had better sit with Brother Falloon tonight and let Sister Betz get some rest."

Brother Severn had told Father that the wounded members of the rustling gang seemed to have disappeared, but that government men were after them—possibly over in Borden County—and were sure to get them finally. The ranchers had identified and reclaimed their own cattle.

It was well that Father did sit with Brother Falloon that night, for the latter regained consciousness and was much relieved to have his priest by his side. He began to improve immediately.

Between the hours that Father and Sammy spent with their patients, Mother was always fixing quick meals. Father read his letters the next morning at breakfast. The one from Aunt Tennie he laid aside; the one from the Board he put in his pocket. He pushed back his chair and reached for his hat.

"If you need me, I'll be with Brother Falloon or with Ford."

"But you've had no sleep at all," Mother protested.

"Tonight Sister Betz will be back on the job."

When he had gone I said, "What was the letter from the Board about? It didn't have any check in it."

"It likely wasn't important. He has so much on his mind now. He'll probably mention it later."

But it was much later when we really did discuss the letters. First there was the ordeal of Slim Breedlove's funeral. And once the crisis for Brother Falloon had passed, the only way to keep him in bed was for Father to get the men started digging the basement for the new church building. Brother Falloon was determined that the first unit should be usably complete, with altar installed, before the fall roundups began.

The Hamiltons came to be with Ford, and all agreed on a wedding at the Hamilton ranch as soon as Ford was up. Mother and Sammy were beside themselves, planning and starting the necessary sewing. I was in a dither because we were to be house guests of the Hamiltons during the week of the wedding.

Finally life resumed its normal routine. Father once again took Marjorie after Mother had prepared her for bed, and rocked and sang her to sleep. He began by rocking strongly with great undulations of the chair, for nothing less satisfied Marjorie. As he moderated the pace of the rocker he went into one of the old, familiar spirituals. I sat and listened, but Mother took the pen, the bottle of ink, and the slick-paper tablet to the kitchen table to compose a reply to Aunt Tennie's letter.

As the rocker slowed, Father's voice became low and mellow:

> "De pig squeal loud in de middle ob de night,
>   One mo' ribber to cross,
> Dey make de haar fly in a warmin' up fight,
>   One mo' ribber to cross.
> Hit's a wide ribber, de ribber over Jordan,
> Hit's a wide ribber. One mo' ribber to cross.
>
>
> De mule am stiff an' de sheep am lame,
>   One mo' ribber to cross,
> De gray colt's back am bent lak a hame,
>   One mo' ribber to cross.

Hit's a wide ribber, de ribber over Jordan,
Hit's a wide ribber. One mo' ribber to cross.

Rake out de taters, Tillie, wipe 'em on de towel,
One mo' ribber to cross,
De ash cake's done, so am de guinea fowl,
One mo' ribber to cross.
Hit's a wide ribber, de ribber over Jordan,
Hit's a wide ribber. One mo' ribber to cross.

When Marjorie was asleep Father rose slowly, carried her into the kitchen, and tucked her into bed. I followed him in and stood by Mother's chair. She looked up from the paper that as yet said only, "Dear Tennie."

"Words seem so inadequate. All I can do is condole with Tennie, which might sound very smug and superior."

"Couldn't you point out the hardships you have borne, and make her feel fortunate by comparison?" Father suggested.

"I doubt if I could make it ring true," she replied, "since from now on our life here will be comparatively easy."

Father drew out the chair opposite Mother and sat down.

"It is my belief," he said, "that a man who chooses the life of a missionary pastor shouldn't search for ease primarily or be influenced by it unduly. Would you be willing to pioneer another church in another field?"

Mother gazed at him for a long moment. Her hands dropped into her lap. "What did you have in mind?" she asked.

"For some time now the members of the church at Seminole have been urging me to move there. They are beset with many problems and need constant leadership if they are to survive. They have taken up the matter with the Board and have received promise of sufficient aid to make a resident pastor possible. I might even get to teach the school for the first year—"

"So you want to move to Seminole," (Mother's voice was hollow) "leaving our church building only started and Brother Falloon laid up."

Father smiled. "I'm not quite that impetuous. We would not move until fall. In the meantime, the building would be completed and a new pastor called and ready to assume his duties. This would give us time to have a house built in Seminole, ready to move into by fall."

"Full of bedbugs, no doubt," Mother said.

"No doubt," Father agreed, "but we know from previous experience that two years is sufficient to eradicate them. About the same length of time required to eradicate other things that plague us."

"Well," Mother snapped, "it seems that you and the Seminole people have things all figured out. Had you by chance considered the Board and what they might think of your leaving here?"

Father nodded. "I had. I feared to approach them on the matter, but I needn't have." He drew from his pocket the letter from the Board. "Here they take up the problems the Seminole people have presented, and suggest that when I feel that I can safely leave this work in other hands that I heed their call to 'Come over into Macedonia and help us.'" Father passed the letter across the table to Mother. "They have enclosed a contract for my signature."

With elbows on the table, her forehead resting against her palms, Mother read the letter. Then on top of it she spread the contract with its ornate heading.

Father spoke. "The verbiage is the result of poor collaboration between financial and evangelical departments, I think. But the meaning is clear."

Mother lifted her face, and her gaze wandered vaguely to the corner of the room, where from the edge of the window the coffee-grinder smeared a grotesque black shadow. But she was seeing another shadow far more appalling—the shadow of days ridden with anxiety, nights haunted by fear, of rampant lawlessness, of menacing disease unattended, of long, hard months devoted to injecting the spirit of brotherly love into people whose very existence depended upon self-love and the invulnerability of the shell in which they could encase themselves. Then she spread her hands on the table.

They were young hands, finely moulded and delicate of contour, but already becoming large of knuckle and coarser in texture than when we came to this stern land. Father looked at them too. and his eyes sought the red pattern in the oilcloth.

Mother picked up her pen and dipped it into the ink. The smile

Board of Directors
Baptist General Convention
of Texas
==

This Contract, entered into between the Board of Directors of the Baptist General Convention of Texas party of the first part, and *Rev S Carroll Berryman*

party of the second part.

Witnesseth, That in consideration of labor to be rendered by the party of the second part as ....

missionary supply at Seminole, and Shafter Lake in Texas and Monument, and Knowles in New Mexico all in El Paso Baptist Association from Decr 1, 1907 to Oct 31, 1908.

Salary Nov. 1st — 60

The said Board of Directors Agree to pay the said *Rev S Carroll Berryman*

$25 .... per month, payments to be made quarterly; but in no case will any payment be due till a report of work done for the quarter shall be duly made according to a blank furnished by the said Board for that purpose.

This Board commends you to God and the word of His grace, also to the faithful servants of Jesus Christ, wherever you may go, as the Messenger of Salvation to lost souls.

By order of Board of Directors of the Baptist General Convention of Texas.

J B Gambrell

Cor. Sec'y and Gen'l Supt. of Missions.

Dallas Tx Decr 3 1907

Please Keep. G. Carroll Berryman.

that touched her lips did not lighten the somberness of her eyes.

"At least it will ease Tennie's lot to know that she is not alone in her trials. The pursuit of Daphne is after all a family characteristic." Mother's laugh was a bit tremulous and wistful. "I wonder if on Judgment Day the starry crown will interest you as little as has the laurel wreath."

Mother's smiled deepened, and now it included her whole face. Even I could see that she was not unhappy. Father laid his hand over hers.

"All the jewels I have ever craved are within these walls," he said. "I am glad that it is well with you."

Something of Father's zest for fields new and untried communicated itself to Mother. The quick movement of her head was a challenge.

"As though you didn't know it would be."

Father's eyes were on me, questioning. "And you, Opal?"

Poignant in my memory were those first days in a new land, when every face was strange. Dear were the ties of friendship and the security of well-known paths. But before me was Father's eager face, and beside me was Mother, whose unselfish gallantry I could not hope to match. What shallow resources I possessed were gathered into a supreme effort to be casual, lest Father suspect how weak and no-good I really was.

"At least I'll get rid of Otho Clevanger," I said.

Father did not laugh as I had expected. Instead he put his arm about my skinny shoulders and drew me to him. Just as his hand upon Mother's had made things right for her, so also did I know that wherever Father was, there only would be home for me.

Date Due

NOV 8 '60			
OCT 31 '61			
NOV 13 '61			
	PRINTED	IN U. S. A.	